*Opportunities and Options in*

# Classroom Management

# *Opportunities and Options in*

# Classroom Management

Supportive Techniques

Corrective Strategies

Preventive Strategies

Effective Teaching

**Patricia B. Kyle**
*University of Idaho*

**Lawrence R. Rogien**
*Boise State University*

PEARSON

*and*

Boston  New York  San Francisco
Mexico City  Montreal  Toronto  London  Madrid  Munich  Paris
Hong Kong  Singapore  Tokyo  Cape Town  Sydney

**Senior Editor:** Arnis Burvikovs
**Series Editorial Assistant:** Christine Lyons
**Marketing Manager:** Tara Whorf
**Editorial Production Administrator and Designer:** Karen Mason
**Composition and Prepress Buyer:** Linda Cox
**Manufacturing Manager:** Andrew Turso
**Cover Administrator:** Linda Knowles
**Editorial-Production Service:** Susan McNally
**Electronic Composition:** Galley Graphics

For related titles and support materials, visit our online catalog at www.ablongman.com

**Library of Congress Cataloging-in-Publication Data**

Kyle, Patricia,
    Opportunities and options in classroom management : comprehensive classroom management / Patricia Kyle, Lawrence Rogien.— 1st ed.
        p. cm.
    Includes bibliographical references and index.
    ISBN 0-205-32413-4
    1. Classroom management.   2. Teacher effectiveness.   I. Rogien, Lawrence.   II. Title.

LB3013.K95 2004
371.102'4—dc21

                                                                2003052434

Printed in the United States of America

10  9  8  7  6  5  4  3  2  1    08  07  06  05  04  03

# Contents

Supportive Techniques

Corrective Strategies

Preventive Strategies

Effective Teaching

Supportive Techniques

Corrective Strategies

Preventive Strategies

Effective Teaching

# Section Three
## Preventive Component                          79

Comprehensive
Classroom
Management

Supportive
Techniques

Corrective
Strategies

Preventive
Strategies

Effective
Teaching

P  A
C  E

Using PACE for Prevention

# Section Four
## Corrective Component                                    *119*

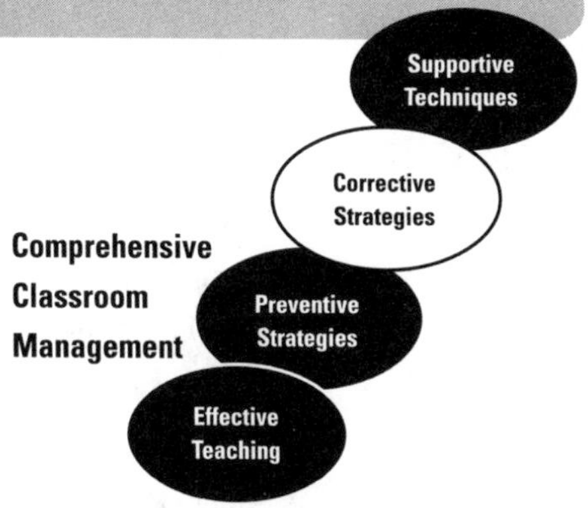

Supportive
Techniques

Corrective
Strategies

Comprehensive
Classroom
Management

Preventive
Strategies

Effective
Teaching

**⑫ "<u>B</u>" Options for Controlling Behaviors** . . . . . . . **164**

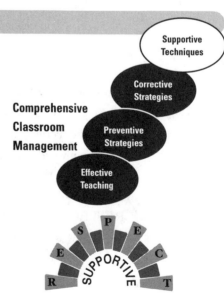

# *Appendix* *281*

Comprehensive Classroom Management

Supportive Techniques

Corrective Strategies

Preventive Strategies

Effective Teaching

# Preface

## Unique Organization of the Book

*Opportunities and Options in Classroom Management* is uniquely organized around four major components that emphasize the integration of effective teaching, proactive preventive strategies, practical corrective strategies, and positive supportive techniques. An expanded view of effective teaching as a viable prevention tool in classroom management permeates the book. Proven discipline approaches are woven together rather than presented as discrete entities. Based on research and focused on practical application, this book includes:

- ✔ Unique icons running through each chapter linked to chapter content to visually and cognitively focus the reader on the topic at hand
- ✔ Mnemonic devices and cognitive maps to aid student retention and instructional organization
- ✔ Clear examples and scenarios to facilitate implementation
- ✔ Open formatting with ample white space for recording ideas, reflections, and examples from personal experience
- ✔ Notes and quotes in boxes with unique shadings to make connections to relevant research, instructional techniques, illustrative quotes, and definitions of critical terms.
- ✔ Strategies tested across cultural, ability, and learning style differences
- ✔ Reflection questions to check thorough understanding of the concepts

From the learners' perspective, this book offers:

- ✔ A structure and process for developing classroom management plans

✔ First day/first week strategies that prevent future discipline problems

✔ Practical intervention tools geared to various levels of seriousness of misbehaviors

# Purpose of the Book

*Opportunities and Options in Classroom Management* helps teachers create learning environments that motivate their students through active involvement in the learning and discipline processes with the goals of acquiring learning skills, self-management skills, and a repertoire of responsible behaviors.

Given that even the best-laid plans of teachers can be thwarted by free-thinking students, teachers must still be prepared for behavior interventions when the teaching and learning environment is disrupted. At this point, a teacher needs alternatives—a selection of tools for dealing with diverse students. Dealing with a student who is angry requires different tactics than dealing with a student who is bored. Communicating with a student whose family is experiencing divorce would suggest different strategies than responding to a student who is apathetic.

No single discipline program will prevent or solve all classroom management challenges. Many independent, stand-alone programs are effective for a certain population or cultural group, but fail miserably with another population or cultural group. Teachers need to have an array of options, a variety of approaches for a variety of students and situations, to be applied in concert with effective teaching and careful monitoring.

This book is about opportunities:

✔ Teachers have opportunities to prevent management maladies through thoughtful planning, effective teaching, and preventive classroom management techniques.

✔ Teachers have opportunities to help students learn about themselves by modeling expected, responsible behaviors and by developing mutual respect for each other and the learning process itself.

✔ Students (P–12) have opportunities to develop and share in a unique learning environment, as each class has its own corporate personality.

✔ Instructors using this book as a text have opportunities to help pre- and in-service teachers make connections between the tools presented in the book and the applications that vary from classroom to classroom, from community to community, and from student to student.

# Memory and Implementation Aids in the Book

Opportunities and options are not enough, though. So often, when teachers find themselves in the position where they have to make a management decision, survival mode takes over, and they revert back to what they remember their teachers did in a similar situation—whether it was effective or not—and imitate those mental images in their own situations. How many times do teachers reflect back on how they handled that situation and muse, "If I had only remembered to use that discipline strategy I learned during the in-service . . ." or the class or from the book I read last summer. If teachers have a way to remember what works, they are more likely to implement effective strategies when under pressure. Our strategies and techniques are presented with mnemonic devices, cognitive maps, case studies, and scenarios specifically designed to aid memory retention. If our assumption holds true, then retention should, in turn, aid implementation, and the task of classroom management will be less daunting. Our purpose is to present readers with a variety of approaches, each with a mnemonic device, to make planning, remembering, and implementing classroom management techniques easier.

# The Book at a Glance

The book is organized into four main components essential for effective classroom teaching, management, and discipline:

✔ Effective Teaching Component
✔ Preventive Component
✔ Corrective Component
✔ Supportive Component

The beginning chapters in this book are about effective teaching. Teachers who have strong instructional skills have students with higher interest and attention levels, and fewer classroom management problems. We will review the most pertinent principles of effective teaching and principles of learner centered classrooms. The CLEAR Model is presented as a model for making professional decisions about most effectively matching your teaching with the learners in your classroom and the content you are teaching. We follow the instruction chapters with the section on prevention and establish an effective learning environment that encourages responsible behavior. Next we will present correctives—practical strategies for dealing with misbehaviors—in order of level of seriousness. What will emerge is a hierarchy of behavioral maladies and an accompanying set of intervention strategies. When order has been restored, ongoing support is needed to maintain the behavior and the classroom atmosphere, so strategies to build support systems are presented.

# Features of the Book

- ✔ Formatting and mnemonics specifically designed to aid retention of the material
- ✔ Section snapshots at the beginning of each section
- ✔ Chapter snapshots
- ✔ Chapter objectives
- ✔ Unique icons running through each chapter linked to chapter content
- ✔ Research boxes
- ✔ Quotes
- ✔ Instructional boxes
- ✔ Term/definition boxes
- ✔ Main point boxes
- ✔ Model synopsis boxes
- ✔ Tables
- ✔ Graphics and illustrations
- ✔ Enlightening tips
- ✔ Bullet point lists
- ✔ Summaries

✔ Reflection questions
✔ Classroom management scenarios and case studies
✔ Reference lists at the end of each chapter and at the end of the book
✔ Glossary
✔ Index

# Resources for the Instructor

Resources for the instructor are available electronically as downloadable material. To access these resources, please contact your Allyn & Bacon representative. If you need help locating the rep in your area, visit www.abacon.com/replocator.

✔ PowerPoint presentation of key points from throughout the book with a list of transparencies and handouts available for each chapter
✔ Chapter objectives
✔ Teaching outlines for each chapter
✔ Chapter snapshots and maps
✔ Reflection questions answers
✔ Scenarios and case studies analyses
✔ Undergraduate and graduate student application exercises
✔ Key terms and definitions for each chapter
✔ Management plan and discipline form handouts
✔ And more!

# Intended Audience

We make several assumptions about our readers. Based on our collective experiences, we believe that many effective teaching strategies and comprehensive management techniques work across cultures. We assume that you are enrolled in a teacher education program or are currently teaching. We assume you have taken some course work in child development, serving children with exceptional needs, multicultural differences, psychology, or educational psychology. We further assume that you have a desire to expand your knowledge and skills in the area of classroom management, and that

you believe that this knowledge and these skills can contribute to your success as a teacher. We believe that we can build on your knowledge and give you a basis for skills development. Your instructor should be able to facilitate skill development through class discussions, case study review, responding to scenarios included in the book, and connecting with field-work if that is a part of your course.

The focus is on learning: planning for learning, teaching, establishing and maintaining a learning environment. Our goal for your students is life-long learning that helps develop productive members of society. Join us as we explore opportunities and options to facilitate learning for you and for your students.

# Acknowledgments

We would like to acknowledge the spice of our lives, Gene and Fran, for having to take vacations without us, and supporting us throughout the planning and writing process. We could not have accomplished this under-taking without their ongoing encouragement and help.

Our reviewers provided us with insightful critiques, which we have incorporated into the book. We especially want to thank Mr. Daniel Koop-man, Principal, Boise Public Schools, and Dr. Thomas V. Trotter, Professor of Counseling and School Psychology, University of Idaho.

The editorial staff at Allyn and Bacon has been most helpful from prospectus to printing. We appreciate Arnis E. Burvikovs, editor; Christine Lyons, editorial assistant; Karen Mason, designer; Susan McNally, editorial-production; and all of the other staff from Allyn and Bacon for their patience and understanding.

Finally, we thank our many students—who are classroom teachers and administrators—for providing the case studies, scenarios, stories, examples, and field-testing of the strategies that are an integral part of the book. Classroom teachers, administrators, school counselors, and school psy-chologists very generously shared many of the forms in the appendix. We appreciate their generosity in supplying practical resources for you.

*Section One*

# Four Components of Management

**Comprehensive**

**Classroom**

**Management**

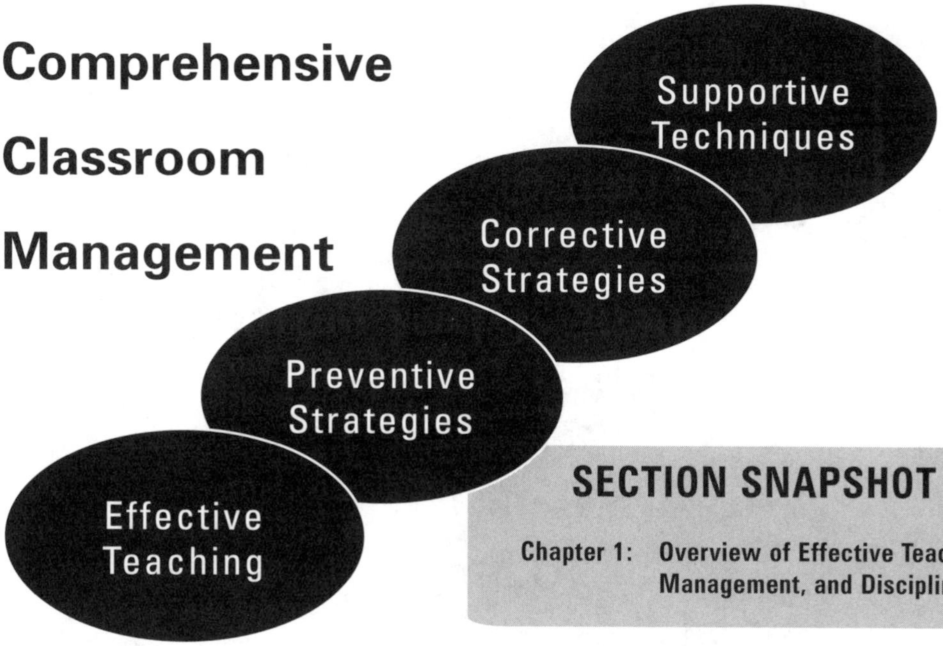
Supportive Techniques
Corrective Strategies
Preventive Strategies
Effective Teaching

## SECTION SNAPSHOT

**Chapter 1:** **Overview of Effective Teaching, Management, and Discipline**

# Overview of Effective Teaching, Management, and Discipline

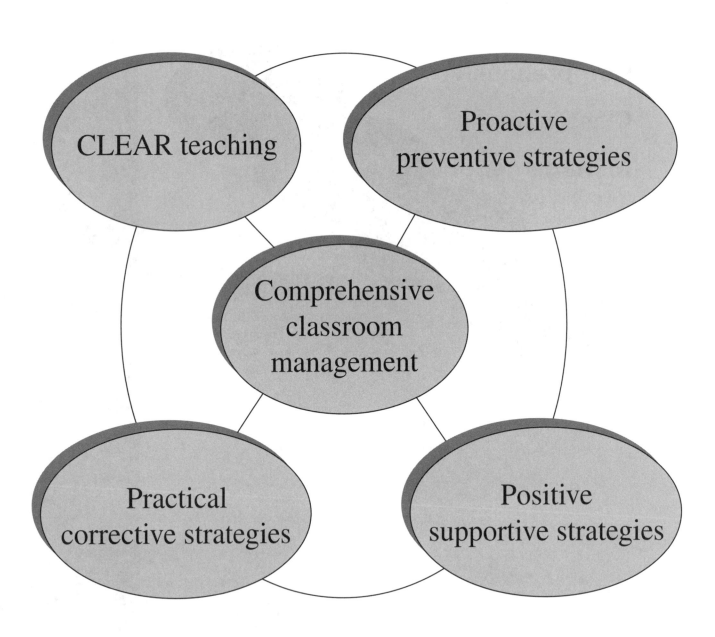

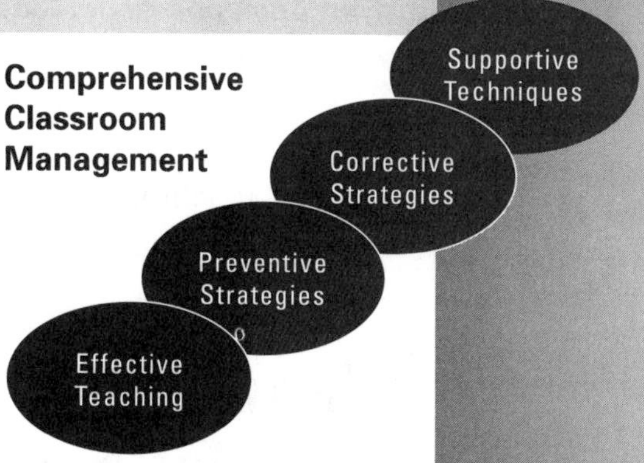

Supportive
Techniques

Corrective
Strategies

Preventive
Strategies

Effective
Teaching

Effective classroom management exists when excellent teaching combines with well-thought-out preventive strategies, practical corrective strategies, and a supportive classroom environment. A comprehensive approach to classroom management gives educators the tools they need to create positive environments conducive to learning, helps them to identify opportunities for positive character development in their students, and offers practical options for strategies when student misbehaviors indicate a need for intervention. Comprehensive classroom management incorporates four inter-related components:

- ➤ CLEAR Teaching Component
- ➤ Preventive Component
- ➤ Corrective Component
- ➤ Supportive Component

When these four components are implemented together in your classroom, effective teaching, management, and discipline are woven together into a tapestry that facilitates learning.

# Many Options Provide Opportunities for Solutions

Integrating ideas from many sources provides the breadth of strategies necessary to be prepared to teach today's students. Incorporating a variety of strategies into your Effective Teaching Component, your Preventive Component, your Corrective Component, and your Supportive Component contributes to a comprehensive teaching and management approach that gives you the confidence to be successful in today's classrooms. *Opportunities and Options in Classroom Management*, therefore, draws from many different effective teaching principles, and recognized management and discipline approaches to give you a framework for creating an effective learning environment for all students. *Opportunities and Options* presents various management and discipline approaches as working together within those four components rather than as separate models.

# Effective Teaching Component

Tapping into the motivation within students is critical. Classroom management does not operate in isolation from the teaching decisions that are made. They are intertwined and complement one another. For classroom management to be comprehensive, it is essential to incorporate teaching opportunities and options into the on-going management process. Having a rich, relevant curriculum that is implemented through a wide variety of teaching strategies combined with activities that involve students in their own learning is an essential ingredient of successful classroom management.

The CLEAR Model is new way to view all teaching strategies, not a new teaching strategy in and of itself. It helps teachers to make good decisions about implementation of a wide variety of teaching strategies in a clear, effective manner. Clear teaching includes clear **C**ommunication, accommodation for **L**earner differences, effective lesson **E**xecutions, as well as accurate **A**ssessments, and careful **R**eflection about your teaching. Effective teaching impacts management and discipline exponentially. Using the CLEAR model helps you increase the effectiveness of your teaching.

The effective teaching principles included in the CLEAR Model come from extensive research investigating student perspectives on effective teaching. The CLEAR teaching principles focus on what teachers did to help students learn most effectively. Literally thousands of students from elementary through university level were asked about their best teachers and what those teachers did to help them learn. The recurrent themes of those student comments are captured in the CLEAR Model. This model focuses on learning and the decisions teachers make to facilitate learning.

Utilizing a CLEAR approach to lesson delivery enhances management as well as teaching. Integrating different content areas, teaching and connecting concepts, and teaching to multiple intelligences are examples of teaching tactics that can enrich the learning environment and prevent many discipline problems.

**THE CLEAR MODEL**

➤ **C**lear communication
➤ **L**earner differences—making accommodations
➤ **E**xecution of the lesson
➤ **A**ssessment of learning
➤ **R**eflection for improvement of instruction

# Preventive Component

Long-term prevention strategies are the glue that holds the classroom management plan together. Setting the **PACE** is the focus of this component of comprehensive management. Planning and designing the class ahead of time to eliminate problems is the first step to long-term success. Focusing on implementing management strategies in the first week of school comes next. Active involvement of the students in the process is critical. Continually maintaining and re-evaluating your management approach is also needed. When the appropriate **PACE** is set in your classroom, you prevent problems through having **P**roactive options, **A**ccountability options, **C**hoices, and **E**nvironment options.

**PREVENTIVE COMPONENT**

➤ **P**roactive Options
➤ **A**ccountability Options
➤ **C**hoices
➤ **E**nvironmental Options

Preventing problems before they occur is important to a comprehensive approach. As important as corrective strategies for the moment of misbehavior are, they are short-term solutions only. Without prevention strategies, you are caught in an endless cycle of short-term solutions for the immediate situation. Establishing classroom rules, procedures, and accountability are the initial steps toward establishing the **PACE** in your classroom. The Prevention Component is essential to having long lasting results.

# Corrective Component

Excellent teaching and proactive prevention keep a lot of classroom problems from developing, but reality indicates that these two components will not eliminate all problems. Being prepared with practical strategies to deal with the moment of misbehavior is also vital to a comprehensive approach. Recognizing the type of misbehavior is necessary so that a corrective intervention strategy that fits the situation can be utilized. Students may act out to seek attention, power, or revenge, or to avoid someone or something. They may act impulsively or in an unmotivated manner. Different irresponsible behaviors need different strategies to effectively deal with the misbehavior. Having a process for implementing corrective strategies is necessary. We present the following options for dealing with different levels of misbehaviors: **A** Options for Distracting behaviors; **B** Options for Controlling behaviors; and **C** Options for Angry or Violent behaviors.

## **A OPTIONS FOR DISTRACTING BEHAVIORS**

➤ **A**ctive Body Language
➤ **A**ttention Focusing Strategies

## **B OPTIONS FOR CONTROLLING BEHAVIORS**

➤ **B**utton Pusher Exits
➤ **B**rief Choices
➤ **B**usiness-like Consequences

## **C OPTIONS FOR ANGRY AND VIOLENT BEHAVIORS: KEEPING ABOVE THE "C" LEVEL**

➤ **C**hill Out Time
➤ **C**onsequences
➤ **C**hat Time with Students
➤ **C**ontracts
➤ **C**urbing Violence

# Supportive Component

Helping students to learn **RESPECT** for themselves, for other people in their communities, and for property becomes a pivotal feature of this comprehensive management approach. Giving students the support they need to choose appropriate behavior is vital to have a comprehensive approach. Teaching **R**esponsible behavior, **E**stablishing classroom harmony, and actively involving **St**udents in the discipline process are keys to going beyond the immediate situation, resulting in newly learned prosocial behaviors. Eliciting **P**arent cooperation is an essential element to support students in choosing alternative behaviors to disruption. Infusing **E**ncouragement strategies throughout all aspects of the classroom is an on-going need. Helping students feel **C**apable of performing classroom tasks supports learning. Positive **T**eacher/student relationships form the foundation for classroom **RESPECT.**

# Interconnectedness of the Four Components

The four essential components of comprehensive classroom management (Effective Teaching, Preventive, Corrective, Supportive Components) are explored in depth throughout the book as discrete entities. It is crucial to remember that in actuality they act in concert with each other. It is the integration of the four components that results in classrooms where learning can take place. Even though we must look at each of them separately, you need to envision them as integral to each other.

When your teaching choices are effective, students are engaged in the learning and misbehave less. When you organize and design the class to prevent problems from occurring, expectations are clear and down time that can breed disruptions is lessened. When you have a wide variety of strategies that you use with the inappropriate behaviors, then misbehavior is handled with little disruption of the learning process. When students are supported in making responsible behavior choices, then you create a classroom where everyone wants to be and can learn. The four components working together help you manage your class and deal with discipline problems as they arise. Your teaching and your classroom climate encourage responsible behavior.

> **SUPPORTIVE COMPONENT**
>
> ➤ **R**esponsible behaviors intentionally taught
> ➤ **E**stablishing classroom harmony
> ➤ **S**tudent involvement
> ➤ **P**arent and staff involvement
> ➤ **E**ncouragement and effective praise
> ➤ **C**apable strategies
> ➤ **T**eacher/student relationship

# Management Styles

Each one of you is a unique individual who has your own unique teaching style. You also have your own management style. It is important, though, that you make a conscious choice about what your management style will be like. Without a conscious choice, you will tend to recreate whatever you experienced in your life. You want to make sure that you create a management style that reflects who you are and what kind of teacher you want to be. Don't just fall into a particular style by default. Sometimes teachers think that there are only three management styles:

> ➤ Collaborative or Democratic
> ➤ Authoritarian
> ➤ Permissive

Actually there are many management styles. Think of management styles as falling on a continuum rather than as three points. On one extreme end is the Authoritarian—"my way or the highway" approach. On the other extreme end is the Permissive—"whatever happens, happens," approach. Neither extreme works very well. In the middle of the continuum is a middle ground where teacher and students work collaboratively.

There is a range in the middle where a variety of management styles work just fine. Some teachers will be a little closer to the authoritarian side because it fits their style or they are working with students who need more direction from the teacher. Some will be closer to the permissive side because it matches their style or they have very self-motivated students. Finding where you fit on the Management Styles Continuum is an important choice for you to make as you make sure that strategies you choose for your management plan are right for you and will help you to accomplish your goals in your classroom.

# Management Styles Continuum

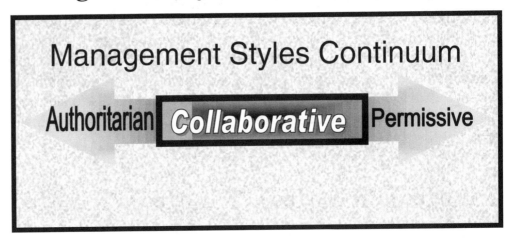

Where are you on the Management Styles Continuum? Where do you want to be? Make a conscious choice about your discipline style. Anywhere in the middle range will work. It is the extreme ends—being "very" authoritarian or "very" permissive—that do not work. With the former you have a tense class that does not foster creative thinking. With the latter you have a chaotic class that does not foster responsibility.

## Authoritarian Management Style

At the extreme left end of the Management Style Continuum you find the Authoritarian, or sometimes called Autocratic style. This is a teacher-in-charge approach or what Curwin and Mendler (1988) of Discipline with Dignity describe as an "Obedience Model." The teacher makes sure that the students obey. In the extreme form the teacher rules by fear, with threats and intimidation as major weapons. The students have little choice in this classroom.

This is the traditional management style that some teachers, administrators, and parents are still longing to go back to. They have this rosy picture in their minds of students sitting politely in desks with their hands folded saying, "You are my teacher. Of course, I will do whatever you say." Unfortunately, even though the authoritarian style has an outward appearance of working, there are some decided drawbacks to getting too far over on the authoritarian end of the continuum.

> **FROM RESEARCH**
> A positive discipline approach brings about a positive atmosphere in the classroom.
> —*Nicholson, Stephens, Elder, and Leavit (1985)*

**Authoritarian Style Drawbacks**
➢ Discipline disappears when the teacher is not there
➢ Lack of self-discipline
➢ Fearful and intimidated students
➢ Rebellious students
➢ Withdrawn students
➢ Stifles critical thinking
➢ Poor model of the democratic process
➢ Tense classroom atmosphere

## *When the authoritarian style is needed*

If your management style is a little towards the authoritarian side, it will work, but avoid getting too near the extremes where negative side-effects are found and teacher/ student relationships are top-down and strained. Some classes have a lot of students with poorly developed responsibility skills. Moving on the Management Styles Continuum towards the authoritarian side is necessary then. A class that is particularly difficult to manage would require moving closer to the authoritarian side of the continuum.

## *Self-discipline is lacking*

The extreme authoritarian style is ineffective with today's students because what they see all around them is adults questioning authority—no longer do adults just accept authority as they did back in the days when the authoritarian style was prevalent in classroom. Students have picked up on the "I have my rights" tenor of the times. Unfortunately, they have not correspondingly adhered to "of course, I have responsibilities to go along with those rights." Since many adults in society miss that point as well, is it any wonder that the students are questioning authority with little sense of personal responsibility?

There is hope, though, that those same questioning behaviors of today's students that are often annoying can be channeled into effective decision-making skills in a classroom that teaches responsible behavior.

One of the major weaknesses of the authoritarian approach is highlighted by the following question: What if you, the teacher in charge of making sure that students are obeying, are not there? Yes, the system tends to break down because the students have not developed any internal control. The authoritarian approach does not promote the development of self-discipline.

# Permissive Management Style

Back in the sixties and seventies, we decided in education that the authoritarian style was not working so well and we did what we often do in education—we overreacted and went to the opposite end of the Management Styles Continuum. We went to the extreme Permissive—"whatever happens, happens"—end of the continuum. Unfortunately, instead of students making wise choices in a field of unlimited choice and openness, a breeding ground for chaos and anarchy ensued. In permissive classrooms there are too many choices. Students often do not have the maturity level to make wise choices with little or no direction from the teacher. The permissive style has its own drawbacks:

> **Permissive Style Drawbacks**
> ➤ Little teacher guidance
> ➤ Students uncomfortable from the lack of boundaries
> ➤ Chaotic, unpredictable atmosphere
> ➤ Lack of follow-through from unmotivated students
> ➤ Frustrated teachers
> ➤ Indecisiveness from too many choices
> ➤ Less learning taking place

## *When the permissive style is appropriate*

Being too far over towards the permissive end of the Management Style Continuum usually does not work. Movement towards the permissive end is appropriate when you have a class that is mature and self-motivated.

# Collaborative Management Style

The middle range on the Management Styles Continuum represents the Collaborative, or sometimes called the Democratic style. This style exemplifies teacher and students working together toward self-discipline and responsible behavior choices. Active involvement of students in the discipline process is viewed as central to having long-lasting results. Student follow-through is often lacking when discipline solutions are imposed on students. Co-creating discipline solutions contributes to ownership for the students—a catalyst for long term responsible behavior (Kyle, 1991).

The collaborative style is based on the concept that students need to have their "say," but not necessarily their "way." When students have legitimate avenues for power in the class they don't have to battle the teacher for power in inappropriate ways. "Voice and choice" are keys to students feeling ownership of the classroom and cooperating in creating a positive learning environment. Students are held responsible for irresponsible behavior choices using one of the many corrective strategies, but in a way that makes it more likely that they will choose responsible behavior in the future. Curwin and Mendler (1988), authors of *Discipline with Dignity,* described the collaborative or democratic style as a "Responsibility Model."

Even though the collaborative style is also called democratic, this doesn't mean that everyone in the class gets a vote. Some teachers misperceive that this means we have one teacher vote and around twenty-five student votes, so the needs of the teacher are drowned out. Rather it refers to students having the opportunity to be heard and to give their input into the operation of the class. You need to be the ultimate authority guiding students through the process of class participation, accepting their input when they are participating responsibly, pulling back when they are not, and using student participation in the classroom as an opportunity to teach responsible behavior. You have a responsibility as their teacher to create an environment conducive to learning. You invite students to be an integral part of helping to create a positive learning atmosphere, but when they make poor choices, holding them responsible is essential.

You structure choices for students so that they can learn to make developmentally wise choices over a period of time. They are making choices within given limits that you establish. You are guiding them through the process of being effective decision-makers by giving them an opportunity to not only make choices, but to learn from their mistakes. You are helping them prepare to be productive citizens in a democratic society through the strategies you use.

That's what the democratic or collaborative style is all about. How can we expect young people at eighteen to be ready to contribute to democracy if we have done all their thinking for them and were in charge of making sure that they behave, instead of instilling self-discipline in them? Your classroom can be a

> **FROM RESEARCH**
> Students need to experience full participation in their classrooms, then they can learn about the democratic process through experiencing it.
> —*Fleming (1996)*

> **FROM RESEARCH**
> Experiencing democracy is the only way to teach it to students. As science courses need lab assignments, democracy needs to be hands-on in order for the students to learn it.
> —*Gerzon (1998)*

laboratory for democratic participation through the strategies you use to ready your students for a responsible role in the future. The collaborative style has benefits.

**Collaborative Style Benefits**
➤ Actively involves the students in the discipline process
➤ Students develop effective decision-making skills
➤ Students experience the democratic process
➤ Students have more ownership of the class
➤ Warm, supportive, encouraging classroom environment
➤ Students are motivated to choose responsible behavior

# Teaching Responsible Behavior

Comprehensive Classroom Management — Supportive Techniques, Corrective Strategies, Preventive Strategies, Effective Teaching

Teaching responsible behavior is equally as important as the content you teach. Sometimes we hear teachers say, "I am not going to teach discipline. I am here to teach math, science, or English." The content that you teach is, of course, of utmost importance, but in the immediate sense, misbehaviors in the class can impede the process of students learning your content. In the long-term sense students need to have a combination of knowledge and responsibility skills to be a democratic citizen.

It is not the premise of this book that you stop teaching your content and teach responsible behavior instead, but rather that students learn responsible behavior as an integral part of your effective teaching, management, and discipline program. They learn responsible behavior from:

➤ What you model when you interact with students
➤ The strategies you use
➤ The way you involve students in the discipline process

**FROM RESEARCH**
Incorporating democratic practices into the discipline strategies works effectively even with young children.

—*Greenberg (1992)*

There are times when there is a need to directly teach an aspect of responsible behavior, but most of the time the students are learning it through what you do and how you treat them on an on-going basis in your teaching, management, and discipline program and, of course, what management style you use. This book will give you the tools to accomplish that.

# Creating Your Own Management Plan

The main goal of this book is to supply you with lots of options, so you can:

> ➢ Execute effective teaching that will positively impact the behavior choices that students make
> ➢ Plan and organize your class ahead of time to prevent problems from happening
> ➢ Deal with misbehavior effectively while it is occurring
> ➢ Support and encourage responsible behavior
> ➢ Connect effectively with the parents and/or guardians of students in your class
> ➢ Feel confident that you are well prepared to orchestrate management and discipline in your class
> ➢ Create opportunities for students to learn responsible behavior from the strategies you use
> ➢ Craft your own management plan uniquely designed for your management style

We encourage you to use this opportunity for practical application. Choose strategies that will work for your:

> ➢ Effective Teaching Component
> ➢ Preventive Component
> ➢ Corrective Component
> ➢ Supportive Component

Read the book with the purpose of creating your own management plan. Make your choices and create an enjoyable classroom for yourself and your students.

**FROM RESEARCH**
Discipline that emphasizes positive interaction and affirmation of students promotes learner self-concept and student responsibility.

*—Shandler (1996)*

# Summary

Effective Teaching, Management, and Discipline consists of four integral components: the *CLEAR Teaching Component*; the *Preventive Component*; the *Corrective Component*; and the *Supportive Component*. These four components are very *interconnected*. None of them is as effective without the other three.

You need to make a choice about your *management style.* It is recommended that you choose a management style somewhere in the middle range of the styles continuum, where the style is *Collaborative.* Getting too far over toward either the *Authoritarian* or *Permissive* style is ineffective because either fear or chaos is created. *Teaching responsible behavior* to your students helps to have long-lasting results. When you have all four components in place, your students can learn responsible behavior from what you "do" in your class. The main purpose of this book is to give you the tools *to create your own management plan.* You incorporate strategies from each of the components that will work for you. Here are *options* for you to turn into *opportunities*!

# Reflection Questions

1. Explain each of the four major components of the text:
   Effective Teaching Component
   Preventive Component
   Corrective Component
   Supportive Component
2. How are each of the components related?
3. Explain the management styles continuum. Give characteristics of each of the three styles.
4. How is the outcome of responsible behavior for the students in your classroom achieved?
5. How can you use this text for creating your own management plan?

# References

Curwin, R. L., & Mendler, A. N. (1988). *Discipline with dignity.* Alexandria, VA: Association for Supervision and Curriculum Development.

Fleming, D. (1996). Preamble to a more perfect classroom. *Educational Leadership* 54 (1): 73–76.

Gerzon, M. (1997). Teaching Democracy by doing it! *Educational Leadership* 54 (5): 6–11.

Greenberg, P. (1992). Ideas that work with young children: How to institute some simple democratic practices pertaining to respect, rights, responsibilities, and roots in any classroom (without losing your leadership position). *Young Children* 47 (5): 10–17.

Kyle, P. (1991). *The effects of positive discipline strategies and active student involvement in the discipline process upon selected elements of classroom climate.* Doctoral dissertation. University of Idaho.

Nicholson, G., Stephens, R., Elder, R., & Leavitt, V. (1985). Safe schools: You can't do it alone. *Phi Delta Kappan* 66 (7): 491–496.

Shandler, S. (1996). Just rewards: Positive discipline can teach students self-respect and empathy. *Teaching Tolerance* 5 (1): 37–41.

Comprehensive
Classroom
Management

Supportive
Techniques

Corrective
Strategies

Preventive
Strategies

Effective
Teaching

# CLEAR Teaching: Effective Teaching Component

**Comprehensive**

**Classroom**

**Management**

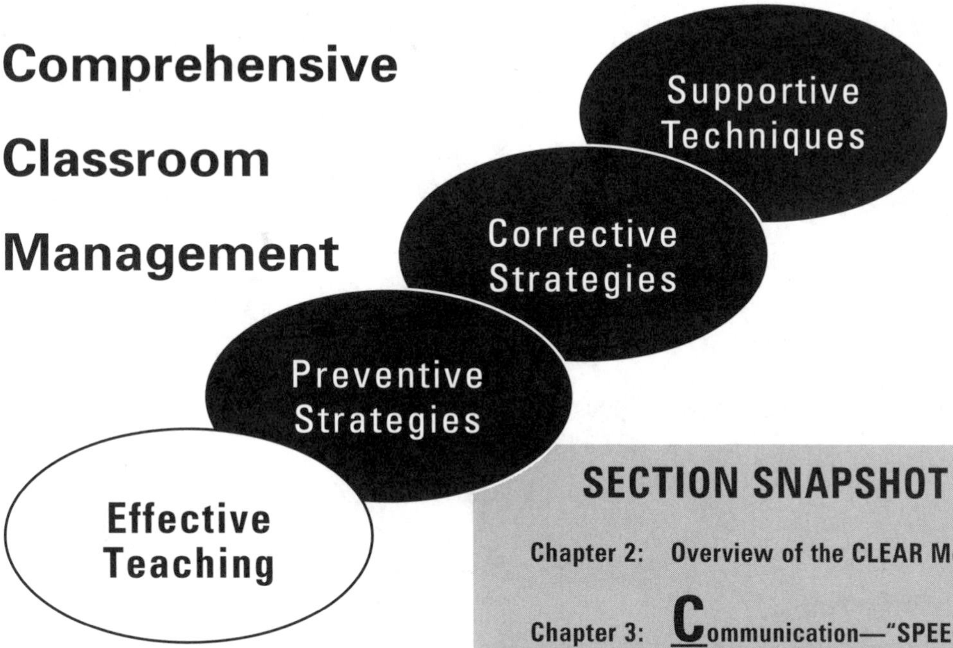

Supportive
Techniques

Corrective
Strategies

Preventive
Strategies

Effective
Teaching

## SECTION SNAPSHOT

Chapter 2: Overview of the CLEAR Model

Chapter 3: **C**ommunication—"SPEECH"

Chapter 4: **L**earners—"PEOPLE"

Chapter 5: **E**xecution of the Lesson—"MODELS"

Chapter 6: **A**ssessment—All "A's"

Chapter 7 **R**eflection—"MIRROR"

# The CLEAR Model

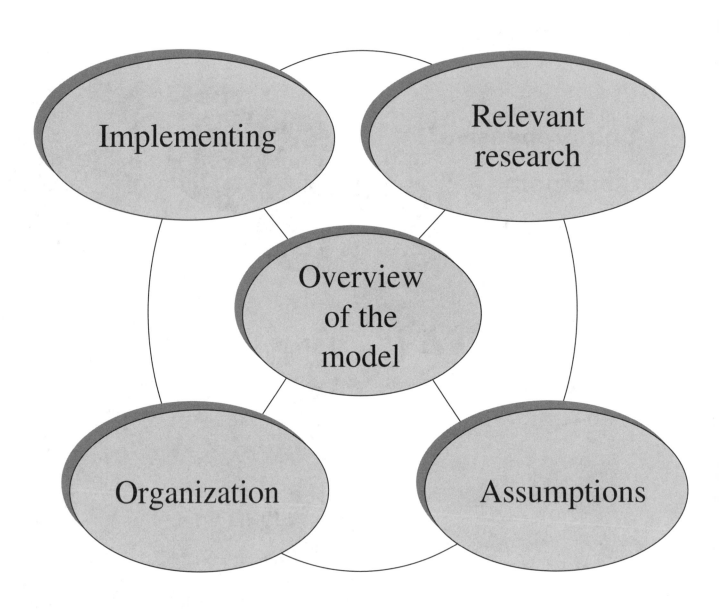

## OBJECTIVE

Learners will be able to explain the background, purpose, underlying assumptions, and organization of the CLEAR Model, as well as how to implement the CLEAR Model.

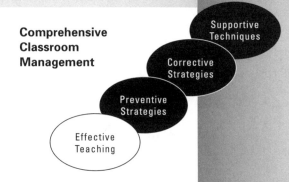

Comprehensive
Classroom
Management

Supportive Techniques

Corrective Strategies

Preventive Strategies

Effective Teaching

## CHAPTER SNAPSHOT

- Relevant Research
- Assumptions
- Organization of the CLEAR Model
- Implementing the CLEAR Model

How many times have you experienced a sentiment similar to the quote on the right? I will forever remember sitting through an inservice during the previous millennium that qualified for an evaluation like this. At that time I had no aspirations for becoming an inservice provider, university professor, or anything beyond a classroom teacher. However, I made a vow to myself then and there that, if I were ever in a position to provide an inservice presentation to teachers, I would give teachers something that they could really use in a classroom. I prided myself in being a successful and effective practitioner and was quick to evaluate the worth of information being disseminated by some ivory tower Ph.D. I knew very well that those initials stood for Piled Higher and Deeper, and followed degrees in B.S. (politically correctly known as Bovine Secretions) and M.S. (More of the Same). I had neither an understanding of nor any appreciation for educational research, which I perceived was so far removed from my real world classroom as to be an irrelevant and irresponsible waste of taxpayer money. Fortunately, for my own sense of integrity, I did not say I would never do one of those inservice presentations or buy boots big enough to wade through the necessary evils toward that irrelevant Ph.D. degree. Alas, here I sit with the paper hanging on my wall that says I did the necessary

> **❝** I hope I die during an inservice, because the transition from life to death would be so subtle. **❞**

> *" He knows enough who knows how to learn. "*
> —Henry Adams

wading. However, the vow remains fresh in my mind. Now, as opportunities arise to provide inservice presentations, I have waded through the irrelevance and found some practical information that fellow practitioners, who don't have the time to do the tall boot wading through reams of research reports and published studies, can use.

# Relevant Research

**FROM RESEARCH**
Effective teaching behaviors have been identified through extensive research.
—*Cruickshank and others (1979); Hines (1981)*

What I found was research done on real students in real schools. These students were asked who their best teachers were, and what those teachers did that helped them learn. At first, researchers focused on junior high age students, but quickly expanded their pool of subjects to include elementary through university-aged students. As research data came in and was analyzed, patterns of answers and principles for effective teaching began to emerge (Cruickshank, Meyers, and Moenjak, 1975; Cruickshank and others, 1979; Cruickshank and Kennedy, 1986; Metcalf, 1992a). This is the same body of research that was used to develop state and national standards for teaching effectiveness (National Board for Professional Teaching Standards) and teacher competencies for Colleges of Teacher Education (see Table 2.1). The CLEAR Model (Table 2.2) comes directly from these student answers and principles, adds principles of educational psychology for organization of the principles into themes, and employs mnemonic devices (acronyms) to help teachers remember the principles of effective teaching.

You will find the same principles in your coursework and textbooks in educational psychology, cognitive psychology, constructivism, behaviorism,

---

**LEGEND FOR TABLE 2.1** (*Researchers*)

BKC = Bush, Kennedy, & Cruickshank, 1977
C = Cruickshank & others, 1979
CMM = Cruishank, Myers, & Moenjak, 1978
CTP = Metcalf (1992b) Clarity Training Program
H = Hines, 1981
HS = Hatton & Smith, 1994
K = Kennedy, Cruickshank, Bush, & Myers, 1978
L = Land, 1987
M = Metcalf, 1992a
P = Pugach, 1990
RF = Rosenshine & Furst, 1971

S = Smith, 1978
SC = Smith & Cotten, 1980
SL = Smith & Land, 1981
S-LC = Sparks-Langer & Colton, 1993
Sn = Snyder & others, 1993
T = Trindade, 1972
W = White, 1979
WB = Whitson & Bodycott, 1992

For a complete review of the research literature that contributed to the CLEAR Model, see Rogien, 1998.

**TABLE 2.1** **Research on the CLEAR MODEL**

| CATEGORY | BEHAVIOR (Mnemonics Not Shown) | RESEARCHERS OF STUDIES (See Legend) |
|---|---|---|
| **COMMUNICATION** | Clear / simple / understandable: Explanation / presentation / directions | BKC; C; CMM; H RF; CTP; K |
| | Clear examples | BKC; CMM; H; K; M; S; W; CTP |
| | Stress difficult points / key ideas | BKC; H; K; S; Sn; CTP |
| | Organized / structured / logical | BKC; H; K; M; RF; S; T; CT |
| | Step by step presentation | C; CMM; H; K; S; CTP |
| | Repeat / review / synthesize / summarize | BKC; C; CTP; CMM; H; K; M; W |
| | Avoid vagueness | L; SC; SL |
| | Explains what to do and how to do assigned work | BKC; H; K |
| | Gives specific details when teaching | H; K |
| | Verbal fluency | BKC |
| **LEARNERS** | Pace appropriate for learners | BKC; H; K |
| | Pauses / takes time / gives learners opportunity to learn / think / practice | BKC; C; CMM; K; RF; W; CTP |
| | Individual help for learners | BKC |
| | Provides standards / rules / expectations | C; CMM |
| | Adjusts teaching to the learners | C; CMM; RF |
| | Makes lesson meaningful / relevant / motivating | BKC; C; CMM |
| **EXECUTION** | Variety in teaching | BKC; CMM; RF |
| | Match model of teaching to the learners | CMM |
| | Prepares / orients students / states objectives | C; CMM; H; RF; S; CTP |
| | Answers learners' questions | BKC; H; K; RF; S |
| | Maintains task orientation / business-like / takes initiative | BKC; RF |
| | Enthusiasm / interest in the subject | RF |
| | Points out differences / similarities | CTP; H; K |
| | Stays with the topic until learners understand | K; H |
| | Suggests mnemonic aids | W; K |
| | Demonstrates / writes out examples / goes over difficult assignments | C; CMM; CTP; H; K |
| **REFLECTION** | Self-evaluation: Journal writing / reviews videotapes of lessons / writes reflective comments about videotaped lessons | S-LC; WB; HS |
| | Seeks student evaluation and feedback | S-LC; WB |
| | Seeks peer evaluation and feedback | S-LC; WB; P |
| | Seeks experienced teachers' evaluation and feedback | S-LC; WB; P |
| | Engages in problem solving toward improving instruction | S-LC; HS |

**TABLE 2.2** **The CLEAR Model**

| CATEGORY | BEHAVIOR |
|---|---|
| C O M M U N I C A T E | *Speak* fluently / avoid vagueness / adjust for learners' level |
| | *Point out* key ideas / difficult points |
| | *Explain clearly:* Step by step / logical / understandable / make connections |
| | *Examples*: Clear, relevant / specific details |
| | *Check modalities*: AVK, global/detailed |
| | *Highlights*: Repeat / review / synthesize / summarize / draw closure |
| L E A R N E R S | *Pace*: Match with learners' abilities |
| | *Expectations*: Provide standards / rules / expected outcomes |
| | *One-on-one*: Provide individual help for learners |
| | *Pause*: Give learners time to learn / think / practice |
| | *Link* lessons to student interests / meaningful / relevant / motivating |
| | *Engage* students according to ability / learning style / cognitive style |
| E X E C U T E | *Match* model of teaching to the learners and content / use variety in teaching |
| | *Objectives*: Prepare / orient students / state objectives |
| | *Demonstrate:* Work examples / point out similarities and differences |
| | *Enthusiasm:* Interest in the subject / business-like / stay on-task |
| | *Link* learning with previous knowledge / suggest mnemonic aids |
| | *Stay* with the topic until learners understand / answer learners' questions |
| A S S E S S | *Assess* student learning: body language, facial expressions, eye contact |
| | *Ask* questions to check for understanding |
| | *Allow:* Encourage learner questions / go over difficult assignments |
| | *Assign* a variety of activities / vary your assessments / appropriate |
| | *Ample* feedback / reasons for errors |
| R E F L E C T | *My time*: Self-evaluation: journal writing / review videotapes of lessons / write reflective comments about videotaped lessons |
| | *Invite* student evaluation and feedback |
| | *Read* supervisor's observations and suggestions |
| | *Reframe:* Restructure / resolve problems: use reflection for problem solving |
| | *Other teachers*: Ask for a peer review |
| | *Resolve problems:* Improve instruction |

*Source:* Copyright © L. Rogien 1999.

child development, teaching methods, classroom management, communications, and other courses. Each of these perspectives shares research, and when viewed as a whole, presents many common principles. Unfortunately, the principles are all too often taught in isolation and we rarely get to see the big picture of effective teaching. Further, education students tend to take courses over the period of several years. What was learned a year or two ago may have been forgotten when the time finally arrives to apply that learning in real classrooms. What we need is a way to remember the important principles so we have them ready for use when we need them.

The CLEAR Model is a synthesis of the research put in practitioners' terms so that research can become relevant for teachers and their students. The mnemonics within the model place the principles in an order with cues to aid recall when you are ready to prepare, present, and/or reflect on your teaching. Everything in the model is based on solid research, demonstrated in hundreds of classrooms with thousands of students. The references are included both in Table 2 and at the end of the book if there are certain principles about which you would like to learn more. A complete review of the literature behind the CLEAR Model can be found in Rogien, 1998.

# Assumptions

As you read through the principles in the CLEAR Model, it will probably occur to you that there is nothing new contained in the principles that effective teachers don't already do. You are exactly right! The point of the CLEAR Model is not that these principles are new, but that even expert teachers get so busy and focused on the content of the lessons we teach that we may overlook the process of learning the content from the learner's point of view. Even more so, beginning teachers just completing their teacher education classes have very likely covered the principles of effective teaching in their professional education classes. However, when they stand in front of a class for the first time as interns or student teachers, they forget what they were taught about good teaching. They go into a survival mode and again focus on the content rather than on the learners. The purpose of the CLEAR Model is to offer a set of reminders to help us remember those aspects of the teaching and learning process that are more likely to help make learning happen for the learners. This notion of using a reminder to promote more effective teaching was the focus for several years of research on both preservice and inservice teachers. The results indicate that use of the CLEAR Model was effective for helping teachers to incorporate the principles of effective teaching into their daily lessons (Rogien, 1995a, 1995b, 1998). You will very likely be

> **"** The one exclusive sign of thorough knowledge is the power of teaching. **"**
>
> *—Aristotle*

able to remember a teacher or college professor that could have benefited from these principles. The distinguishing characteristics are lectures filled with accurate content and sophisticated illustrations, but no variety of presentation, no relevant examples, no attempt to put the material in the language of the student, and no honest attempt to find out if the students were really understanding the information. It was obvious that the instructor knew the material, but just didn't know how to teach effectively. Or could it be that, if you know only the material, and not how to teach it, you really don't know the material thoroughly? Aristotle captures that thought in his quote on the previous page. The CLEAR Model is a research-based strategy to put power into your teaching.

# Organization of the CLEAR Model

The CLEAR Model organizes the principles of effective teaching as viewed by students into four major categories:

> **C**ommunication
> **L**earner accommodations
> **E**xecution of the lesson, and
> **A**ssessment of learning. The fifth category,

**R**eflection, is to help teachers with strategies for identification of areas in their teaching that need improvement, target a CLEAR Teaching Principle that would improve the area of weakness, and implement that principle into their daily teaching. Each category of principles contains a set of related principles unified by another mnemonic device. For example, the first category, **C**ommunication, contains six principles of effective teaching:

> **S**peak fluently
> **P**oint out key ideas
> **E**xplain clearly
> **E**xamples relevant to the students
> **C**heck for modalities (audio, visual, kinesthetic)
> **H**ighlight: repeat, review, summarize

The mnemonic "SPEECH" emerges from the set of principles that fall under the area of Communication, and the concepts of Speech and Communication are closely related so as to be more easily remembered. Each of the areas has a nested mnemonic to help you remember the associated principles of effective teaching. Each of the areas and each principle under each area will be covered in upcoming chapters. Clear explanations with relevant examples are provided for each principle so that you can see the CLEAR Model implemented at least in text format and can more easily envision what CLEAR teaching will look like in your classroom.

The CLEAR Model has been validated across grade levels K-16 and across content areas. It is most effective when teachers using the model are interested in their students understanding and applying concepts, not just memorizing and regurgitating information. It has also been validated that teachers who teach more effectively have fewer management and discipline problems in their classrooms. The major benefits of this model, then, are learning outcomes at the higher levels of Bloom's Cognitive Taxonomy (see chapter 5 for more information on Bloom's Taxonomy), and reduced classroom management and discipline challenges. Further, in applying the concept of CLEAR Teaching to classroom discipline, each discipline situation becomes an opportunity to teach a principle of self-management and personal responsibility with multiple options (student choices) for success in both learning and appropriate classroom behaviors that contribute to an effective learning environment.

> **FROM RESEARCH**
> Vagueness in teacher's explanations is linked with lower measures of student achievement and satisfaction.
>
> —*Land (1987); Smith (1984); Smith & Cotton (1980); Snyder & others (1993)*

# Implementing the CLEAR Model

Remember the movie *What About Bob?* Richard Dreyfus plays a psychiatrist who works with his patients in small steps toward personal improvement—baby steps. The same approach applies to using the CLEAR Model for improving teaching. Use the principles under each area to help you assess both your strengths and weaknesses in teaching. Celebrate your strengths first. Then choose one of the principles that you believe will help improve the effectiveness of your teaching the most. Focus on improving that one identified area. Write a reminder in your plan book. Write a symbol on your board to remind yourself to implement that principle. Put a sticky note on the back wall, door, or window—wherever you tend to look during a lesson—so that you will have a visual reminder to implement that identified effective teaching principle. After several lessons, if you have demonstrated to yourself (your students, your supervisor) that you are consistently implementing your identified effective teaching principle, then celebrate your success, and identify one more principle to implement, along with the appropriate physical and visual reminders. Just remember to take baby steps. Teaching is complex enough without having to remember all the steps of the CLEAR Model. Take one principle at a time. Plan to implement it, practice it, and assess your effectiveness. Take

> **❝** What I have done is due to patient thought. **❞**
> —*Sir Isaac Newton*

baby steps. This will take time and effort, but the benefits are well worth the investment.

We will cover implementation of the CLEAR Model in more detail after we have covered each individual area and principle of the model.

# Reflection Questions

1. What kind of research was used as the background to the CLEAR Model?
2. What is the purpose of the CLEAR Model?
3. The CLEAR Model includes assumptions about previous knowledge for those who would implement the Model. What are those assumptions?
4. How is the CLEAR Model organized?

# References

Bush, A. J., & Cruickshank, D. R. (1977). An empirical investigation of teacher clarity. *Journal of Teacher Education* 28 (2): 53–58.

Cruickshank, D. R., & Kennedy, J. J. (1986). Teacher clarity. *Teaching & Teacher Education* 2 (1): 43–67.

Cruickshank, D. R., & others. (1979). Clear teaching: What is it? *British Journal of Teacher Education* 5 (1): 27–33.

Cruickshank, D., Meyers, B., and Moenjak, T. (1975). *Statements of clear teaching behaviors provided by 1009 students in grades 6-9.* Unpublished manuscript, The Ohio State University, Columbus, Ohio.

Hatton, N., & Smith, D. (1994). Facilitating reflection: Issues and research. Paper presented at the Conference of Australian Teacher Education Association (24th, Brisbane, Queensland, Australia, July 3–6, 1994).

Hines, C. V. (1981). *A further investigation of teacher clarity: The observation of teacher clarity and the relationship between clarity and student achievement and satisfaction.* Unpublished doctoral dissertation. The Ohio State University.

Kennedy, J. J., Cruickshank, D. R., Bush, A. J., & Myers, B. (1978). Additional investigations into the nature of teacher clarity. *Journal of Educational Research* 72: 3–10.

Land, M. L. (1987). Vagueness and clarity. In M. Dunkin (Ed.) *The international encyclopedia of teaching and teacher education.* New York: Pergamon, pp. 392–397.

Metcalf, K. K. (1992a). *Instructional clarity: A review of research.* Unpublished manuscript, Indiana University, Bloomington, Indiana.

—— . (1992b). The effects of a guided training experience on the instructional clarity of preservice teachers. *Teacher and Teacher Education* 8 (3): 275–286.

Pugach, M. C. (1990). Self-study: The Genesis of reflection in novice teachers? Paper presented at the Annual Meeting of the American Educational Research Association (Boston, MA, April 17–20, 1990).

Rogien, L. (1998). *The effects of cognitive strategy training in clarity of instruction on lesson planning and instruction for pre-service teachers.* Doctoral dissertation. Ann Arbor, MI: UMI Dissertation Services (Microfilm).

Rogien, L. (1995). *Effect of training in cognitive awareness of student knowledge on lesson planning and micro teaching for secondary preservice teachers.* Unpublished manuscript, Indiana University, Bloomington, IN.

Rosenshine, B., & Furst, N. (1971). Research on teacher performance criteria. In B. Smith (Ed.) *Research in Teacher Education* (pp. 37–72). Englewood Cliffs, NJ: Prentice Hall.

Smith, L. R., & Cotten, M. L. (1980). Effect of vagueness and discontinuity on student achievement and attitudes. *Journal of Educational Psychology* 72 (5): 670–675.

Smith, L. R., & Land, M. L. (1981). Low-inference verbal behaviors related to teacher clarity. *Journal of Classroom Interaction* 17:37–42.

Smith, S. (1978). The identification of teaching behaviors descriptive of the construct: Clarity of presentation. *Dissertation Abstracts International* 39 (06): 3529A (University Microfilms No. 78-23, 593).

Smith, L. R. (1984). Effect of teacher vagueness and use of lecture notes on student performance. *Journal of Educational Research* 78 (2): 69–74.

Snyder, S. J., & Others (1993). *Instructional clarity: The role of linking and focusing moves on student achievement, motivation, and satisfaction.* Paper presented at the Annual Meeting of the American Educational Research Association (Atlanta, GA, April 12–16, 1993).

Sparks-Langer, G. M., & Colton, A. B. (1993). Synthesis of research on teachers' reflective thinking. In A. Woolfolk (Ed.), *Readings & Cases in Educational Psychology.* Boston: Allyn & Bacon.

Trindale, A. L. (1972). Structures in teaching and learning outcomes. *Journal of Research in Science Teaching* 9 (1): 65–74.

White, J. (1979). Clarity and student opportunity to learn: An investigation of two components of instructional communication as assessed by situational testing of pre-service teachers. Doctoral dissertation, University of Maryland. College Park, Maryland. (Dissertation Abstracts International, 40, 5319A.)

Whitson, G., & Bodycott, P. (1992). Using feedback and reflection as tools in bridging the theory-practice link in language teacher training at the primary level ERIC #: ED369282.

# CLEAR Communication

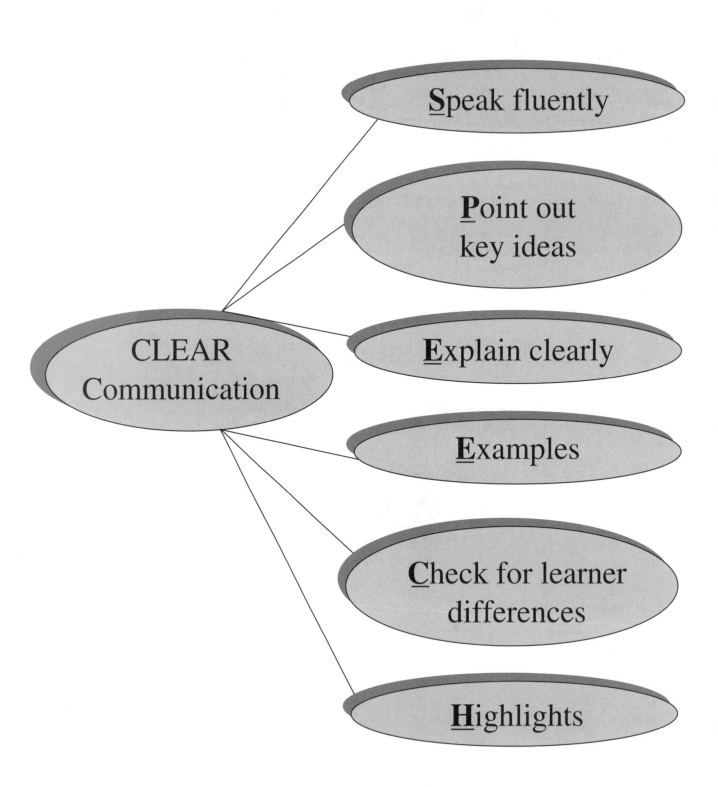

## OBJECTIVES

Readers will be able to make decisions toward effective communication concerning:

- Speaking fluently, avoiding vagueness, and adjusting for learners' level
- Pointing out key ideas and difficult points
- Explaining clearly
- Including good examples
- Checking for learning differences during the lesson
- Including highlights of the lesson

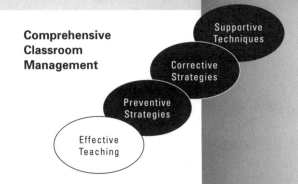

Comprehensive Classroom Management

Supportive Techniques

Corrective Strategies

Preventive Strategies

Effective Teaching

## CHAPTER SNAPSHOT

- **Speak Fluently**
- **Point Out Key Ideas and Difficult Points**
- **Explain Clearly**
- **Examples**
- **Check for Learning Differences**
- **Highlights of the Lesson**

It was Friday afternoon, and a junior high school teacher was running out of time in the 47-minute period as she tried to finish her lesson. As the bell rang, she announced, ". . . and your assignment for tomorrow is to do the chapter review questions on page 237." Students were scrambling for backpacks, papers, books, and pencils, some were heading for the door, and a few were even writing down the assignment.

When was the assignment due? To a junior high school student in this class, how do you interpret "tomorrow"—the due date for the assignment? Did the teacher mean Monday, the next day of classes? Several will draw that conclusion. Or, does that mean Saturday, the day after Friday, and there is no school? Are they expected to drop off the assignment at school or at the teacher's home? Or, a more popular conclusion, since there is no school on Saturdays, then there is no assignment due at all! How many times have your teachers been vague, unwittingly communicated the wrong information, or failed to communicate at all?

This chapter addresses the importance of communication between teachers and students. It covers not only spoken communication, but also visual and non-verbal communications. The perspective is that of the students. That means the operant questions are: What is effective communication from the perspective of students? How should teachers communicate so that students can learn most effectively?

The principles of clear communication that follow are synthesized from thousands of student comments in response to questions about their most effective teachers. *SPEECH* is the mnemonic to help remember the key points of communication. For a more in-depth study, the research supporting these principles is listed in Table 2.1 in chapter 2.

# <u>S</u>peak Fluently

Speaking fluently seems easy enough. But students were very annoyed by teachers who gave directions or deadlines for assignments with vague vocabulary. Last week while observing a student teacher in a math class, the student teacher compared the day's assignment to an assignment from a month ago: "It's kinda like the assignment we did with imaginary numbers." That is like saying you are "kinda pregnant." Which part of "kinda" are we talking about? The factoring part? The FOIL process? The point is that the teacher's communication about what was similar ("kinda like") was vague. Students want to know exactly how this assignment is like a previous assignment, or they may not see the connection at all.

A common expression of vagueness is the length of writing assignments:

"How long should our reports be?"
"Oh, about 3 or 4 pages, longer if you need the space."

> **FROM RESEARCH**
> Vagueness in teachers' explanations is linked with lower measures of student achievement and satisfaction.
>
> —*Land (1987); Smith (1984); Smith and Cotton (1980); Snyder and others (1993)*

Does that mean full pages? What is the font size? Do scanned pictures count? Does the bibliography count as a page? How about the title page? The point is for teachers to be precise.

It is the concrete sequential learners (see the section on LEARNERS in chapter 4 for more information on learning styles) that suffer the most with ambiguity. They need clear directions, definite due dates, and distinct points made in the lesson. A teacher who is vague raises the level of anxiety for many students, but the anxiety is raised to the point of stress for those who are highly concrete sequential in their thinking. Similarly, a teacher or presenter who uses technical language, unfamiliar terms, or vocabulary above the ability level of the learners is limiting communication effectiveness.

The key points for speaking fluently are:

➢ Avoid vagueness in spoken and written communication.
➢ Use language that the learners understand.
➢ Be precise.

# <u>P</u>oint Out Key Ideas and Difficult Points

In a tenth grade history class, a teacher was presenting a lesson on America in the 1920s. She had been telling stories about speakeasies, flappers, swing dancing, mob activities, and prohibition. There were references to many names, places, and dates. Near the end of the period, a boy on one side of the room raised his hand and asked, "How much of this do we need to know?" The teacher stopped, looked a bit bewildered, hesitated, and then said, "All of it." Not satisfied, the boy probed further. "Let me put it this way: How much of this stuff will be on the test?"

The teacher had a very blank look on her face now. She glanced at her notes, back at the boy, back behind her podium at the board, and back to the boy.

"I don't know," she finally admitted. Not once in 45 minutes had she pointed out any key ideas or concepts. She had not drawn the students' attention to important terms, vocabulary, concepts, or conflicts. There had been no reference to confusing or difficult concepts that might need close attention while studying. Nor had there been any reference to any kind of assessment. The boy with the question was asking, indirectly, for the key points of the lesson.

Students want to know what is important. Cues like "This is an important point," "Write this down," "Make sure you know this table top to bottom," and even "You will need to know this for the test" are ways of letting the learners know that the point you are making is important. Writing points on the board, overhead projector, or using presentation software to allow students to view the key points on a television or digital projector and screen help communicate important information for visual learners.

The key point for this section is for teachers to draw attention to the key points they want students to learn.

# <u>E</u>xplain Clearly

Have you ever tried to get directions to a point of interest from a person who could not get the order of turns or the major landmarks correct? Frustration builds quickly as you try to piece together the logic of the directions. If you are not familiar with the surrounding area, it becomes even more difficult to make sense of jumbled directions. And yet, how many times have you been asked to follow directions in a class that had conflicting steps or were unclear in describing the final product or project?

Research on clarity of explanations points to three key components. Students preferred explanations that:

➤ Were *step by step*
➤ Included logical *connections*
➤ Were clear from the *learners' perspective*

The first two are self-explanatory. It is the third point that is the most frequent cause for misinterpretation of explanations. People who are in the business of teaching or training often become so good at what they do that they forget how long it takes to process the information they are presenting for a new learner. Or they become experts at their skill, and have difficulty in explaining to others what they do and how they do it. While this is more common at the college level, we have observed new teachers give presentations that seemed perfectly clear to them, but their students were lost and confused by the presentation. The lesson here is that the clarity of an explanation must be gauged by the learners. If the presentation is understandable to the majority the third graders you are teaching, then you are explaining clearly. What is clear to eighth graders for a lesson on impressionism in an art class may not be at all appropriate for introducing impressionism to fourth graders. A good starting point is what my students know as "Rogien's Rule": Know your students. Before designing your lessons, crafting your directions, and explaining your key points, consider the perspectives of your learners, their reading level, their cognitive abilities, their life experiences.

To draw closure to this section on explanations, the three main points to remember are that good explanations:

➤ Cover information *step by step*
➤ Include *logical connections*
➤ Consider the *learners' perspective*

# <u>E</u>xamples

There is nothing uncommon about giving examples in a presentation to help the learners understand the concept being presented. Where the breakdown in communication occurs is in the relevance of the example. What may be a perfectly clear example for the presenter may not be understood at all by the listener. For example, a first grade teacher presenting the concept of fractions may refer to a pizza as an example of a whole being cut into equal parts. Pizzas are a great example for kids who experience mainstream American lifestyle. But what about Bosnian or Afghani refugees? If these students have never had a pizza before, how well will they understand the concept of fractions when given pieces of a pizza as an example? As with explanations above, examples must be relevant to the experiences of the learners.

Equally as important as relevance, a good example is specific. For a teacher to say that an example of a persuasive essay is the editorials in the newspaper is not specific. While some editorials are indeed persuasive, others are pejorative, some are informative, and some are just whiny. To be a good example, the teacher must bring in copies of *persuasive* editorials to read to the students, or give them access to the copies to read. Highlighting key points that demonstrate how the editorials are persuasive makes the example even more potent for instilling learning. The purpose of a good example is to demonstrate the key points of the concept you are teaching.

Three components of a good example are:

➢ *Relevant* to the learners
➢ *Clear* to the learners
➢ *Specific*

# <u>C</u>heck for Learning Differences

The clarity of an explanation depends on the perspective of the listener. Learning and cognitive styles, learning preferences, multiple intelligences, personality differences are all critical components to consider for any person giving a presentation. But how can a teacher keep all of these learner differences in mind while keeping track of the content and the clock? For this discussion, we will deal only with the communication aspect. For the basic presentation there are two major points to consider with respect to learner differences. Following the basic presentation, more attention can be paid to students with special needs or learning styles. We will cover that more com-

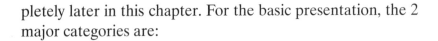

**AVK LEARNERS**

➤ Audio—learn best by hearing
➤ Visual—learn best by seeing
➤ Kinesthetic—learn best by doing
➤ Tactile—learn by touching

Most learners are a combination with strengths in one or two areas.

pletely later in this chapter. For the basic presentation, the 2 major categories are:

➤ Auditory, visual, kinesthetic, and tactile (AVK)
➤ Global versus detailed

What does this mean for the teacher? For every presentation, say it, let them see it, and let them do something to reinforce it. The auditory learners need to hear clear explanations of presentations, directions, assignments, and due dates. If they don't hear it, they have a more difficult time processing the information.

The visual learners need to see the key points written on the board, on a handout, projected on a screen, on a web site, or any other style of visual presentation. If they can't see the information, they have a more difficult time processing it. The graphics and insets in this book are an attempt to meet the needs of the visual readers.

Finally, the kinesthetic learners need to get their bodies moving to be able to get their brains working. Requiring kinesthetic learners to "SIT STILL!" is akin to turning off the switch to their synapses. Sitting on the floor while coloring, standing up while taking notes, hands-on activities, role-playing, or acting out the phases of cellular reproduction will help kinesthetic learners process and remember information. Also, tactile means touch and kinesthetic means whole body movement. While simply moving a pencil or pen during note taking works for some students, this is only a tactile activity. Some students need more whole-body, physical movement to get their whole brains to work.

The point of the AVK discussion is that it is not difficult to incorporate all three into every presentation. While making key points in a lesson, always write them somewhere—on the board, overhead, or on a PowerPoint™ slide. Then ask your kinesthetic learners to demonstrate key points as appropriate, or respond to questions in pairs at their places in the classroom, gymnasium, field, riser, or wherever they may be. For some kinesthetic learners, simply visualizing a good example from a clear explanation can help make a whole-body connection if the example is something observable that happens in real life.

The global vs. detailed aspect of **C**hecking for learner differences refers to checking to see if you have presented the big picture for the global thinkers so they know how this lesson fits in with previous lessons or previously learned concepts. Each chapter in this book begins with a global overview so that global readers can get an idea of the big picture before they begin reading the chapter. The detailed aspect means that you give sufficient details during explanations to meet the needs of your detailed thinkers. They enjoy thinking about the details in a story, the fine points of a movie, and they don't like shortcuts or assumptions about any steps in a procedure. Detailed learners are bothered by gaps in information, and can get hung up by focusing on a step that the teacher assumed, but they didn't see or hear. But, when you come to the end of the lesson, to wrap the lesson up, a summary of the key points is very helpful for the global thinkers, while some questions about specific points are helpful for the detailed thinkers. For two examples of the CLEAR Model adapted for global learners, see the end of this chapter.

**GLOBAL LEARNERS:**
- See the forest of trees and can pick out patterns
- Need to know the big picture—where does a concept fit?
- Are often more social
- May have trouble with remembering details

**DETAILED LEARNERS:**
- See the individual trees and notice fine discriminations
- Need to know the details of a concept
- May prefer to work alone
- May have trouble seeing patterns

The point of this section is that you, as the teacher, should always be thinking about your learners as you present information. *AVK* and *global vs. detailed* are two good guidelines to keep in mind as you make presentations to a diverse group of learners. Attention to the other kinds of learning styles will be covered in the Learners section of the CLEAR Model.

# Highlights of the Lesson

When someone asks you about a movie you recently watched or a book you read, what do you tell him or her? Don't you repeat the important one-liners, review the main plot, shorten but summarize the main scenes, and tell how it ended? That recap is an excellent metaphor for the end of a lesson.

Not only is this an excellent teaching strategy for the global thinkers in your class, it serves as a review of the key points for all the learners. When you are nearing the end of a lecture period in a secondary classroom, or just prior to the reinforcement activity in an elementary classroom, cover the highlights of your presentation as a way of bringing closure to the cognitive processing portion of the lesson. That is not to imply that what comes next is

not going to be cognitive. It is to say that closing off the presentation part of a lesson with highlights is a good way to help the key points be remembered. Strategies that can be used to bring out the highlights of the information just presented are:

➢ *Repeat* and *review*
➢ *Synthesize* and *summarize*
➢ *Closure*

For the sake of clarification, closure does NOT mean asking the famous, generic, end-of-lesson question "Are there any questions?" while looking down at your notes. Nor does it mean giving the assignment. Closure does mean restating the objective that was just presented or learned through discovery or through a cooperative group activity. It can be stated by the teacher or solicited from the learners with questions. Closure can often be completed in less than one minute, but can contribute to learning that can last a lifetime.

The main point of **H**ighlights is that you make one last purposeful effort at helping your learners see the main point of the lesson.

# Summary

Clear communication, from a learner's perspective, means that the teacher *speaks with fluency, points out key points, explains clearly,* gives relevant *examples,* checks to see whether he or she is *communicating to diverse learners,* and hits the *highlights* at the end of the lesson. And, this is an example of closure that took less than a minute to read!

# CLEAR Model

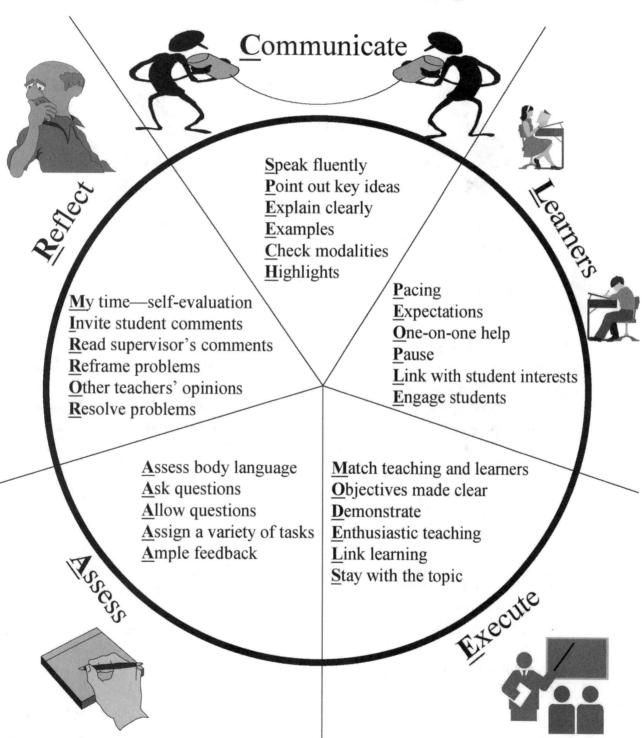

**Communicate**

**Speak** fluently
**Point** out key ideas
**Explain** clearly
**Examples**
**Check** modalities
**Highlights**

**Reflect**

**My** time—self-evaluation
**Invite** student comments
**Read** supervisor's comments
**Reframe** problems
**Other** teachers' opinions
**Resolve** problems

**Learners**

**Pacing**
**Expectations**
**One**-on-one help
**Pause**
**Link** with student interests
**Engage** students

**Assess**

**Assess** body language
**Ask** questions
**Allow** questions
**Assign** a variety of tasks
**Ample** feedback

**Execute**

**Match** teaching and learners
**Objectives** made clear
**Demonstrate**
**Enthusiastic** teaching
**Link** learning
**Stay** with the topic

# CLEAR Model

## Communicate

<u>S</u>peak fluently
<u>P</u>oint out key ideas
<u>E</u>xplain clearly
<u>E</u>xamples
<u>C</u>heck modalities
<u>H</u>ighlights

## Reflect

<u>M</u>y time—self-evaluation
<u>I</u>nvite student comments
<u>R</u>ead supervisors' comments
<u>R</u>eframe problems
<u>O</u>ther teachers' opinions
<u>R</u>esolve problems

## Learners

<u>P</u>acing
<u>E</u>xpectations
<u>O</u>ne-on-one help
<u>P</u>ause
<u>L</u>ink with student interests
<u>E</u>ngage students

## Assess

<u>A</u>ssess body language
<u>A</u>sk questions
<u>A</u>llow questions
<u>A</u>ssign a variety of tasks
<u>A</u>mple feedback

## Execute

<u>M</u>atch teaching & learners
<u>O</u>bjectives made clear
<u>D</u>emonstrate
<u>E</u>nthusiastic teaching
<u>L</u>ink learning
<u>S</u>tay with the topic

# Reflection Questions

1.  When presenting a lesson or directions to learners, what factors should influence your choice of vocabulary?
2.  Give examples of speaking fluently, avoiding vagueness, and adjusting for learners' level for each of the following:
    a.  An early elementary class
    b.  A middle school class
    c.  A high school class
    d.  A class of adults
3.  To practice the concepts of pointing out key ideas and difficult points, name the key points in this chapter, and point out any points that you found difficult to understand at first reading.
4.  Practice with a partner. Give directions to a local landmark. Focus on explaining your directions clearly.
5.  Recall presentations you have attended in the past. See if you can identify good examples. Why were these examples memorable? What makes an example memorable for your learners?
6.  What are learning differences? How can you accommodate for learner differences during the lesson?
7.  Recall a movie you saw recently, a book you read, or a presentation you attended. What were the highlights of the movie, book, or presentation? What would you include as highlights of this chapter? What should be included in the highlights of a lesson?

# References

Land, M. L. (1987). Vagueness and clarity. In M. Dunkin (Ed.) *The international encyclopedia of teaching and teacher education.* New York: Pergamon, pp. 392–397.

Smith, L. R. (1984). Effect of teacher vagueness and use of lecture notes on student performance. *Journal of Educational Research* 78 (2): 69–74.

Smith, L. R., & Cotten, M. L. (1980). Effect of vagueness and discontinuity on student achievement and attitudes. *Journal of Educational Psychology* 72 (5): 670–675.

Snyder, S. J., & Others (1993). *Instructional clarity: The role of linking and focusing moves on student achievement, motivation, and satisfaction.* Paper presented at the Annual Meeting of the American Educational Research Association (Atlanta, GA, April 12–16, 1993).

# CLEAR Model: Learners—"PEOPLE"

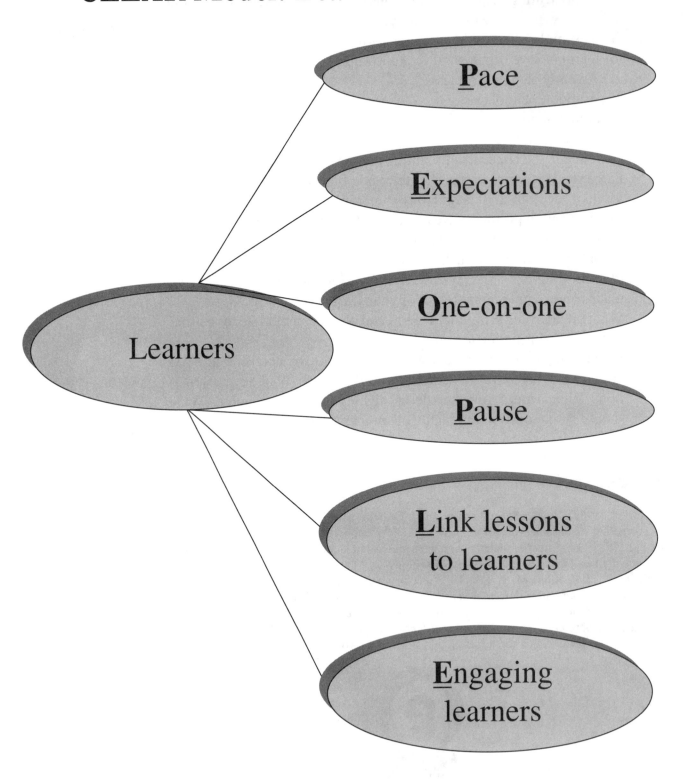

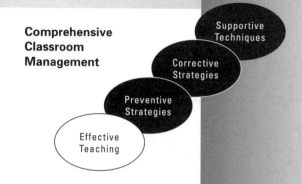

Comprehensive
Classroom
Management

Supportive
Techniques

Corrective
Strategies

Preventive
Strategies

Effective
Teaching

## OBJECTIVES

Learners will be able to make decisions toward effective teaching concerning:

- Appropriate pacing for your learners
- Setting appropriate expectations for your learners
- Offering one-on-one scaffolding for your learners
- Using pauses for reflection and connection
- Linking lessons to learners' personal experiences
- Engaging learners according to ability levels, learning styles, and cognitive styles

## CHAPTER SNAPSHOT

- **Pace**
- **Expectations**
  - ➤ Behavior expectations
  - ➤ Academic expectations
  - ➤ Rules, procedures, and standards
- **One-on-One Scaffolding**
- **Pause for Reflection and Connection**
- **Link Lessons to Learners**
- **Engaging Learners**

Recall a class, most likely in your college experience, in which the instructor was in love with the content of the course, but the students in the class almost seemed to be a bother. Frequently a lecture format, the instructor often spoke so fast that taking notes was a nightmare. Seldom were there clear expectations for what was coming on the exam. To ask a question in class or to go to the professor for help outside of class was too often a denigrating experience. Students were there to absorb the material, make connections with the real world, and accommodate the presentation style of the instructor. This type of class often produces memories, but seldom fond, and recall of the information covered in that class is often limited.

> **❝** They won't care how much you know until they know how much you care. **❞**

> **" What sculpture is to a block of marble, education is to a human soul. "**
> —*Joseph Addison*

Teaching cannot occur without learners. And effective teaching implies that learners are learning. Learners responding to the survey questions (See CLEAR Overview) noted that the teachers that really helped them learn paid attention to them as *people*—as human beings with needs and differences. PEOPLE is also the mnemonic for this part of the CLEAR Model, which focuses on some of those learner needs and differences. This section will illustrate how critical Rogien's Rule (know your students) is for effective teaching. The principles and terms in the following sections should all be familiar to you from course work you have taken in your teacher education program. If some terms or concepts are unfamiliar to you, refer to textbooks in educational psychology and child development for a refresher.

# <u>P</u>ace

Because people learn at different rates, effective teachers need to match the pace of the lesson with the abilities and learning styles of the learners. Learners with a learning disability often need to go slower, while high ability learners are sometimes capable of proceeding even faster than the teacher. The slower learners are often frustrated with a pace that is too fast, while the high-speed learners are bored with the pace of that same lesson. It is the teacher's challenge to get to know the learners in the class, and then match the pace of instruction to the needs and abilities of the learners. A class of learners with a wide range of abilities and learning differences may require significant differentiation in pacing, teaching approaches, and assignments to reach the same standard-based outcomes.

# <u>E</u>xpectations

> **" Students will rise to the level of expectation. "**
> —*Jamie Escalanté*

In the now classic movie *Stand and Deliver,* Jaime Escalanté is a math teacher in Garfield High School in East Los Angeles. His class is predominantly Hispanics, and most are low achievers. In one scene, Mr. Escalanté is requesting to teach an Algebra class for his students. The response from the other faculty is that these students are not able to do basic math, let alone the rigors of Algebra. Mr. Escalanté responds, "Students will rise to the level of expectation."

Students will rise (or sink) to the level of expectation set by their teachers. That is the same as the conclusion of the Pygmalion research studies (Rosenthal and Jacobson, 1968) and the focus of the TESA (Teacher Expectations and Student Achievement) teacher training of the 1970s and '80s. Whether you talk about self-fulfilling prophecies, sustaining expectations (student improvements are not recognized because of a history of poor performances), or raising the bar, the message is the same: Teachers tend to get what they expect from their students.

But what about pacing, and matching the pace to student abilities? If the expectations are too high, the pace too fast, won't that frustrate students and precipitate their giving up?

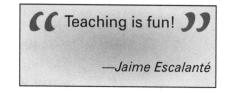

*( (* Teaching is fun! *) )*

—*Jaime Escalanté*

True. So how do we set high expectations without frustrating our students? Know your students. Find out who the fast and slow learners are. Find out the leader and follower personalities. Look for signs that indicate when your learners are approaching frustration and intervene before frustration sets in. Piaget's disequilibrium, Vygotsky's Zone of Proximal Development, Humanistic motivation theory, goal setting research, and self-help books all point toward setting goals slightly ahead of your current ability level, and then striving to reach that goal. You, as a teacher, act as the scaffolding to help your students reach this new level of expectation without doing it for them. You are the coach for your learners, modeling how to learn, how to stretch, how do deal with disequilibrium, how to solve difficult problems, all as you work toward higher levels of expectations.

What kinds of expectations can teachers hold for their learners? Read on.

# Behavior Expectations

If your classroom is disrupted with undesirable behaviors, disrespectful comments, or a disorganized room arrangement, then learning is impeded if not prevented from occurring at all. Your first responsibility as a teacher is to establish the behavioral expectations for your students. Section III of this book is dedicated to helping teachers establish behavioral expectations during the first days, hours, even minutes of a new classroom experience.

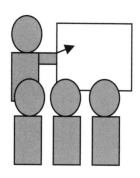

## Academic Expectations

> **❝** I expect my students to be winners. I expect my students to be the best. **❞**
>
> —*Jaime Escalanté*

The previous discussion about Jaime Escalanté focused predominantly on academic expectations. However, it soon becomes apparent that it is impossible to separate behavioral expectations from academic expectations. If your classroom atmosphere tolerates any kind of misbehavior with no consequences, learning is compromised. If there are no high expectations for academic performance, learners become bored and often engage in "creative behaviors" (interpreted: "undesired behaviors"). As a teacher establishing a learning environment, you are obliged to establish expectations for both classroom behaviors and academic performances. That includes the rules, procedures, and standards for work in your classroom.

## Rules, Procedures, and Standards

Section III deals with this topic in detail. For now, let's link rules, procedures, and standards with the previous two sections on behavioral and academic expectations. When you establish rules (do's and don'ts), procedures (how to do routine tasks), and standards (how well something has to be done) for your classroom, you must be clear that you are stating your expectations for behavior and academic work in your classroom. To rise to the level of expectations will result in a positive learning environment and lifelong learning for your students. To deviate from the established rules, procedures, and standards will incur consequences. Concurrently, you are the guide, coach, and scaffolding to help your students meet your expectations. Your rules, procedures, and standards are tools and guidelines to facilitate learning in your (you and your learners') classroom. Your rules, procedures, and standards should be descriptors of an effective learning environment. It is your learners' efforts and your expertise as a coach of learners that combine to create an effective learning environment that will lead to successful outcomes for <u>all</u> the learners in your classroom—including you.

## <u>O</u>ne-on-One Scaffolding

How can you make your learners feel like they are people that are important to you? When they were climbing the learning curve and needed help, learners indicated that teachers who met with them individually to get through the disequilibrium contributed to effective learning. After a lesson presentation there are usually a few students who didn't understand the concepts, missed a step in the procedures, or just plain weren't paying attention, and they needed some support. Peer support is one way to resolve the gaps in understanding. However, learners indicated that they gained a sense of acceptance when their teachers offered individual assistance. That one-on-one help may occur at their desks following a presentation, in working groups during an activity, or before or after class when a student comes to you for extra input. If your tone of voice or body language gives the message that the learner is inconveniencing you with the request for aid, your whole classroom of learners will quickly deduce that you are not willing to give one-on-one help. On the other hand, your modeling of genuinely offering and giving individual attention could spread to the learners in your classroom, contributing to a community of learners that scaffold each other as the learning situations warrant.

> **❝** Teaching means helping the child realize his potential. **❞**
> —Eric Fromm

# Pause for Reflection and Connection

Do you remember giving a presentation to the class in high school or college and coming to the end of a section with a pause in your delivery? That pause may have felt like an eternity—no sound, no movement, all eyes on you. Or can you remember a presenter giving a lecture at a fast pace, and you were wishing that there was a pause so you could catch up with your notes? There are two sides to the pause issue. Many new teachers want to keep the class moving, just like the experience of giving a presentation in high school or college. In that case a pause seems deadly, like an indication that you don't know what to say or do next. But the other side of the issue is that learners who are engaged in a learning process need time to mentally process what they are learning. They need to be convinced in their own minds that they are understanding the incoming information, and can make links to previously learned concepts. Or, if they are taking notes, a pause is a welcomed opportunity to catch up taking notes.

Here is the point: Pauses are good. Pauses are opportunities for the learners to process the incoming information. Pauses are also an opportunity for you as a teacher to assess your students—to check for those question marks on their foreheads that indicate confusion or at least disequilibrium. Pauses are an opportunity for you as a teacher to check the current status of the lesson: Have you been **C**ommunicating clearly? Have you been accommodating your **L**earners' differences? The pause gives you a few seconds to assess the effectiveness of your teaching as well as the understanding of your learners. We will address this aspect of an effective pause in more detail in the section on **A**ssessment.

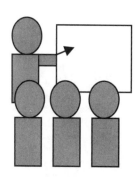

# <u>L</u>ink Lessons to Learners

Several years ago I was driving to a resort town a couple of hours north of where I live. I remember passing through a small community that had a small automotive repair shop. There was a chain link fence around the back of the building that was corralling a number of vehicles. The particular car that caught my eye was a 1973 Volkswagen Bug. I know it was a '73 because of the style of taillights, and the type of exhaust emerging from the back of the car. I can remember the name of that small town because of this memory of the '73 Bug in the corral behind the repair shop. The name of the little town is Lake Fork. I drove through once, but the name of the community, the position of the repair shop in the town, and the picture of the '73 Bug are all in long-term memory. So what's the point? *Interest. Meaning. Relevance.* When you find something that is personally interesting, meaningful, or relevant, the probability for storage in long-term memory increases significantly. My first car was a Bug. I have owned numerous VW's over the years, and still drive a '73 Bug to work every day. The Bug behind the repair shop held personal meaning for me, so the location and name of the town were immediately stored in long-term memory.

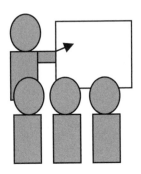

So what? What do Volkswagens have to do with your learners? Read on.

Do you want your learners motivated to learn what you want them to learn? Then tie your lessons to their interests. Use examples that are personally relevant. Demonstrate the meaningfulness in each and every lesson.

But what about chemical bonds? Algebra and graphing? Fractions and long division? The Pilgrims? Phonics? I watched a master chemistry teacher demonstrate chemical bonds—electrons, protons, attraction, repulsion—using for his advance organizer the known couples in the school. Everyone in the class knew who was going with whom, so to show positive attractions and positively repulsive relationships was easy. "It works the same way in chemistry," he said. And he had their attention for the entire period. He had linked their personal interests with the concepts in the lesson. Chemistry now had taken on a new meaning, a new relevance, and would much more likely be remembered in the future. Similar connections can be made for learners of all ages, all abilities, and across all content areas. Once you get to know your students, you will be able to link learning to the learners. Teaching with relevant links will also force you to get to know your content better.

# Engage Learners

The last letter in the mnemonic PEOPLE stands for **E**ngaging your learners. Busy learners are better behaved. We are not talking about busy work. There are not many more effective ways to frustrate your high ability learners than to give them mindless assignments, busy work, or irrelevant tasks to keep them out of mischief. When students perceive that the activities you have planned are designed to fill up class time rather than to engage them in thinking, learning, and stretching, you will shortly have an increase in behavior management problems. On the other hand, when students perceive that your planned learning activities are intended to engage them, challenge them, and that you have high expectations for their success, your learners are much more likely to engage in the learning activities and much less likely to engage in "creative behaviors."

> **"** The mind is not a bucket to be filled, but a fire to be ignited and continually kindled. **"**
> —*Plutarch*

If you don't remember much about learning differences consult a good educational psychology textbook. Look under learning styles, learning preferences, multiple intelligences, mind styles, or cognitive styles.

This concept of engagement ties all the other concepts in this category together. For a lesson or activity to be engaging, it can't be too fast or too slow. You as the teacher are expecting participation and engagement. You are supportive in a one-on-one role as needed. You pause when you see that the learners need time to process. You link lessons and activities with experiences that are interesting, relevant, and meaningful to your learners. You accommodate the learners' differences by being sensitive to their differing ability levels, learning styles, and cognitive styles, and adjusting instruction and learning activities accordingly. Refer to the insets for more information on learning differences. With this level of engagement in learning, the learners will have little interest in non-learning behaviors (disruptions), and you have prevented a lot of classroom management challenges with effective planning and teaching. This level of engagement is sometimes called "academic learning time" and tends to produce successful, long-term learning. The key point is to engage your students in learning that they perceive is worthwhile.

# Summary

Learners are people—not robots, not indentured servants, not conforming clones. When we focus on our learners and worthwhile learning activities, everyone has the potential to be successful in your classroom. Keep close tabs on the *pace.* Keep your *expectations* high but achievable. Offer *one-on-one* help as needed. *Pause* for potent processing. *Link* learning with the learners' real world experiences. *Engage* your learners in worthwhile learning. Above all, have fun—learning IS fun!

# Reflection Questions

1. What is appropriate pacing for your learners? How do you determine what is an appropriate pace?
2. Why should teachers set expectations for their learners? What are the outcomes of setting appropriate expectations? What kinds of expectations can be set for learners? Give specific examples.
3. What is scaffolding? What effect does offering one-on-one scaffolding have on your learners? What does one-on-one scaffolding look like in a classroom?
4. How can teachers use pauses effectively to help students make connections? How can teachers use pauses effectively for professional reflection?
5. What does linking mean in this context? What kinds of links should you help your learners make? What is the difference between relevant and personal links? What makes a lesson interesting from a learner's perspective?
6. Give examples of how you would engage learners according to:
   a. Ability levels
   b. Learning styles
   c. Cognitive styles

# References

Dunn, K., & Dunn, R. (1978). *Teaching students through their individual learning styles*. Reston, VA: National Council of Principals.

Gardner, H. (1983). *Frames of mind: The theory of multiple intelligences.* New York: Basic Books.

Gardner, H. (1989). Multiple intelligences go to school. *Educational researcher* 18 (8): 4–10.

——— . (1993). *Multiple intelligences: The theory into practice.* New York: Basic Books.

Goleman, D. (1997) *Emotional intelligence.* New York: Bantam Books.

Gregorc, A. F. (1982). *Gregorc style delineator: Development, technical, and administrative manual.* Maynard, MA: Gabriel Systems.

Hines, C. V. (1981). *A further investigation of teacher clarity: The observation of teacher clarity and the relationship between clarity and student achievement and satisfaction.* Unpublished doctoral dissertation. The Ohio State University.

Kagan, S., & Kagan, M. (1998). *Multiple intelligences.* San Clemente, CA: Kagan Publishing.

Snyder, S. J., and Others (1993). *Instructional clarity: The role of linking and focusing moves on student achievement, motivation, and satisfaction.* Paper presented at the Annual Meeting of the American Educational Research Association (Atlanta, GA, April 12–16, 1993).

Witkin, H. A., Moore, C. A., Goodenough, D. R., & Cox, R. W. (1977). Field-dependent and field-independent cognitive styles and their educational implications. *Review of Educational Research* 47: 1–64.

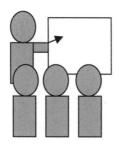

# CLEAR Model:
# Execution of the Lesson—"MODELS"

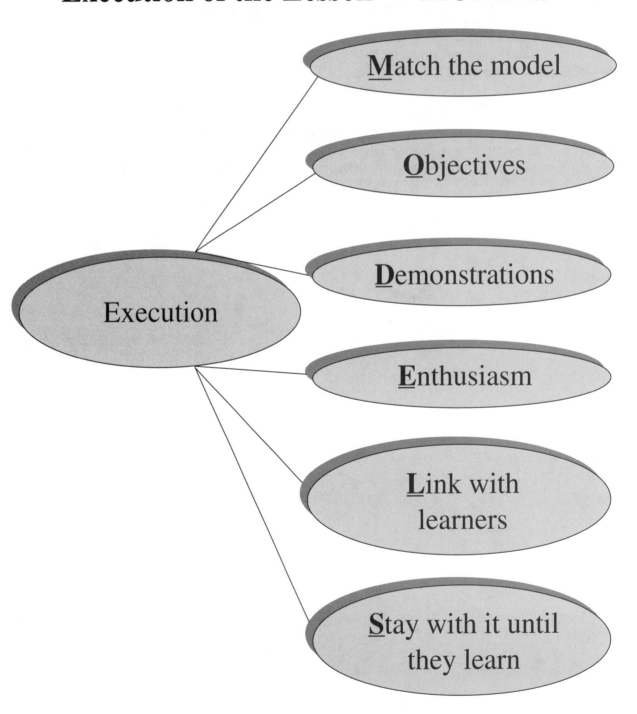

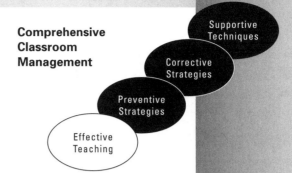

Comprehensive
Classroom
Management

Supportive
Techniques

Corrective
Strategies

Preventive
Strategies

Effective
Teaching

## OBJECTIVES

Learners will be able to make decisions toward effective teaching concerning:

- Selecting appropriate *models* of teaching
- Making *objectives* of the lesson obvious
- Appropriate *demonstrations* for the lesson
- Awareness of your level of *enthusiasm* for the lesson
- *Linking* the current lesson with previous learning
- *Staying with the topic* long enough so learners really learn the concept

## CHAPTER SNAPSHOT

- <u>M</u>atching the Model of Teaching to the Lesson
- <u>M</u>odels of Teaching
- <u>O</u>bjectives
- <u>D</u>emonstrations
- <u>E</u>nthusiasm
- <u>L</u>inking Learning to Learning
- <u>S</u>tay With It!

When an architect presents an idea for a new mall to a potential developer, she will very likely bring a model of the mall along with the blueprints, cost predictions, and schedule for construction and completion. The model is particularly critical, because it is the method the architect uses to help the developer visualize what the final product will look like, and often what the infrastructure and internal components look like. Finally, the model guides the construction of the actual building, along with the blueprints, so that the foundations are the appropriate depth and size, the supporting walls are in the right places, and the roof structures will help hold everything together. The model is a mental picture of the real building. Metaphorically, an architectural blueprint creates a

> **❝ What the teacher is is more important than what she or he teaches. ❞**

"mental picture" of the real building. In the same way the CLEAR Model creates an organizing framework for visualizing and making decisions about effective teaching. The sub-section **E**xecution uses the word "MODELS" as an organizing mnemonic. This section is about choosing the best models of teaching to match your learners, your content, and your own teaching strengths. Every teacher should know at least five different models of teaching in order to offer learners a variety of teaching and learning approaches, so that all learners can have their learning preferences met at least part of the time. The little icon throughout the chapter is intended to remind you of this big idea as you read about the supporting concepts.

# <u>M</u>atching the Model of Teaching to the Lesson

Matching the model of teaching to the lesson implies several assumptions about you as a teacher:

> ➤ You know several different models of teaching
> ➤ You know your learners (Rogien's Rule)
> ➤ You know the structure of your content
> ➤ You know your own strengths and weaknesses as a teacher

## Models of Teaching

> **❝ America must provide educational challenges for her bright people or else tomorrow we will be led by the mediocre, and on the day after, by the incompetent. ❞**
>
> —Harrington, J., Harrington, C., and Karns, E. (1991)

You should be familiar with several models of teaching from previous coursework in educational psychology or a methods of teaching class. Examples of different models include direct instruction (Hunter and Russell, 1981; Rosenshine, 1985), discovery learning (Bruner, 1966), inquiry (Taba, 1966), concept learning (Ausubel, 1963; Tennyson and Cocchiarella, 1986), problem based learning (a constructivist model), and cooperative learning (Johnson and Johnson, 1994). Each of these models has several variations. It is not necessary to know every variation of every model to be an effective teacher. However, every teacher should be familiar and comfortable using at least five of the models for the sake of meeting the needs of diverse learners. Brief reviews of the common models are included in the Highlights boxes.

Some models of teaching do not work well with some content. For example, learning times tables by discovery can be very inefficient and frustrating for your learners. Similarly, direct instruction for learning the concept of democracy may not produce the long-term application level of learning you may want your students to demonstrate. A cooperative learning or problem-based simulation may be much more effective. The point is that you match the model of teaching to the content, as well as to your learners.

> **❝ A problem is a chance for you to do your best. ❞**
> —*Duke Ellington*

Finally, with respect to the various models of teaching, you will find some you really like, some with which you are comfortable, and others that just don't seem to work well for you. These opinions about the various models are indications of your teaching style. For your learners' sakes, you need to have a variety of teaching models in your repertoire. However, you need a variety that *works for you.* As you continue to gain experience and confidence in the classroom, you may choose to add new models of teaching to your repertoire for the purpose of professional development, and to add to your own personal satisfaction from teaching well.

# <u>O</u>bjectives

You don't always have to write objectives. Many teachers' editions of textbooks provide objectives for each lesson. Also, many states now have published standards that include many objectives by content area and grade level that teachers are required to use and that students are required to master.

Instructional objectives are clear statements of what you intend your learners to learn by the end of the lesson. When learners know what intended outcome(s) you have in mind, it helps them to focus on the key points of the lesson. It also helps you in preparing, presenting, and assessing the effectiveness of your lesson. When your objectives are clear, the main points of the lesson should be easier to identify. After identifying your objectives, you should check to see whether your learners have the appropriate background knowledge to assimilate this new objective, or whether they have the prerequisite cognitive skills to accommodate new skills or knowledge. If you plan to use a test or quiz as an assessment, refer back to your objectives to make preparing the assessment instrument much easier. This is where

> **❝ The most important educational goal is learning to learn. ❞**
> —*Luis Alberto Machado*

**TABLE 5.1   Highlights for Models of Teaching**

| MODEL | BENEFITS | LIMITS |
|---|---|---|
| **Direct Instruction: Hunter Model**<br>■ Get students <u>**set**</u> to learn<br> • Create anticipatory set—gain student attention<br>■ State the lesson objectives<br>■ <u>**Present**</u> information effectively<br>■ <u>**Check**</u> for understanding and give guided practice<br>■ Allow for independent <u>**practice**</u> | ■ Increases achievement scores<br>■ Structured for concrete sequential learners<br>■ Works well with lower and mid-level ability learners | ■ Tends to limit critical and creative thinking<br>■ Discourages self-directed learning<br>■ Frequently not challenging for highly able learners |
| **Lecture**<br>■ Teacher presents information verbally<br>■ Typical format is:<br> • introduction<br> • body of the presentation<br> • closure<br>■ Visuals often used to illustrate points<br>■ Examples are often included to clarify points | ■ Efficient way to cover a large volume of content<br>■ Relatively short period of time required to present<br>■ Works well with large groups of students<br>■ Relatively easy to prepare<br>■ "Low overhead"—no equipment required | ■ Easy to overload learners with information<br>■ Slow note takers may be at a disadvantage<br>■ Motivation tends to be low<br>■ Relevance or interest may be overlooked<br>■ No guarantee of application of information |
| **Expository Teaching: David Ausubel Model**<br>■ Advance organizer to begin the lesson<br>■ Concepts are presented by the teacher<br>■ Examples and non-examples to clarify the concept<br>■ Teacher refers back to advance organizer to link the organizer with the concept in the lesson<br><br>This model emphasizes deductive reasoning. | ■ Good for presenting concepts, especially abstract<br>■ Focus is on comparison and contrast thinking<br>■ Higher level yet teacher directed | ■ Requires teacher skills for linking advanced organizer with targeted concept(s), pointing out similarities and differences<br>■ Some abstract concepts may be too challenging for concrete thinkers |
| **Cooperative Learning Principles: Johnson and Johnson, 1994**<br>■ Positive interdependence<br>■ Face-to-face interaction<br>■ Individual accountability<br>■ Social skills<br>■ Group processing<br><br>This model emphasizes academic and social objectives. | ■ Increases achievement scores<br>■ Easy to integrate multiple intelligence or learning style theory<br>■ Works well with any content | ■ Requires careful monitoring<br>■ Takes time to plan various activities and distinct job descriptions for group members<br>■ May not work as well with gifted students |
| **Inquiry and Problem-Based Learning**<br>■ Teacher presents a puzzling event<br>■ Learners formulate hypotheses<br>■ Collect and analyze data<br>■ Draw conclusions<br>■ Reflect on original problem<br>■ Reflect on the thinking process | ■ Authentic tasks are highly motivating for learners<br>■ Application of problem solving skills<br>■ Uses steps of the scientific method | ■ Little or no positive effect on achievement scores—in some cases may even decrease standardized achievement scores<br>■ This model takes time for the process to be completed |

**TABLE 5.1** **Highlights for Models of Teaching** *(continued)*

| MODEL | BENEFITS | LIMITS |
|---|---|---|
| **Concept Attainment**<br>■ The teacher explains the rules of the game<br>■ Teacher gives "Yes" and "No" examples<br>■ Learners look for similarities and differences<br>■ Learners propose hypotheses<br>■ The class tests each hypothesis with more teacher-supplied examples<br>■ The object is to discover the rule (concept)<br>■ When the hypothesis seems correct, students generate examples for the teacher to check<br>■ Teacher transitions into a lesson or an assignment | ■ Focus is on deep understanding of a concept<br>■ High learner motivation and involvement<br>■ Can be adapted for simple to very sophisticated concepts<br>■ Encourages clarification of concepts and similarities and differences between concepts | ■ May be too challenging for convergent thinkers<br>■ Takes more time to prepare this type of lesson—particularly identifying good examples and non-examples of the concept |
| **Discovery Learning**<br>■ Discovery focuses on questioning<br>■ Inductive reasoning<br>■ Intuitive thinking<br>■ Can be guided or unguided<br>■ Begin with examples<br>■ Teacher asks questions to lead students to discover the big ideas | ■ Increases learner interest and motivation<br>■ Stimulates creative and critical thinking | ■ Little or no positive effect on achievement scores—in some cases may even decrease standardized achievement scores<br>■ May be too challenging for lower ability and highly concrete sequential learners |
| **Socratic Questioning**<br>■ Teacher does not present material<br>■ Teacher uses questioning techniques to lead students to analyze, critique, evaluate their own thinking and beliefs<br>■ Types of Socratic questions:<br>  · History of their thinking<br>  · Implications and results<br>  · Perspectives<br>  · Evidence and support | ■ Stimulates careful observation<br>■ Stimulates skill development<br>■ Encourages communication skills | ■ Little or no positive effect on achievement scores—in some cases may even decrease standardized achievement scores<br>■ Appeals to higher level thinkers—may intimidate lower ability learners<br>■ Requires high level of teacher skill |
| **Cognitive Behavior Model**<br>■ Overt self-guidance<br>■ Faded self-guidance<br>■ Covert self-guidance<br><br>(I do it, we do it, you do it) | ■ Stimulates critical and reflective thinking<br>■ Stimulates concept development<br>■ Encourages independent learning | ■ May not emphasize concepts/ big picture<br>■ Requires accurate teacher demonstrations |

Bloom's Taxonomies can help teachers in preparing objectives. The taxonomies can help you match objectives, questions, and assessments to the level of your learners.

The key point for objectives is that when you make the objectives obvious for your learners, you are preparing them for the coming lesson. They are more

**BLOOM'S COGNITIVE TAXONOMY**
➢ Knowledge (lowest level of difficulty)
➢ Comprehension
➢ Application
➢ Analysis
➢ Synthesis
➢ Evaluation (highest level of difficulty)

For a recent revision of Bloom's Taxonomy, see Anderson and Krathwohl (Eds.), *A Taxonomy of Teaching and Learning: A Revision of Bloom's Taxonomy of Educational Objectives.* New York: Addison Wesley Longman. Copyright 2000 by Addison Wesley Longman.

likely to be focused on the importance of the lesson, more likely to remember key points, and more likely to do better on assessments of achievement.

# **D**emonstrations

My dad was terrible at explaining things, but he was a master at showing people what he wanted. He was a general contractor with an uncanny ability to show his employees exactly what he wanted done on a building project. One of his common phrases was "I can't explain it. Just watch me."

While this may seem to be a model of teaching for visual learners, demonstrations are not limited to visuals. A math teacher can explain out loud how he mentally works through an algorithm. A science teacher can use a working model of a volcano as she demonstrates how and why the lava emerges.

The point is that many learners need demonstrations of the knowledge or skills to be learned in order to completely process the new knowledge or construct an effective model of the skill in their brains. The following are different ways to demonstrate a concept:

> ❝ Setting a good example for your students is twice as good as giving them good advice. ❞

➢ Working examples
➢ Modeling skills
➢ Modeling cognitive processes
➢ Pointing out similarities and differences

The last point is critical for teaching concepts. Learners must be able to tell concepts apart from similar concepts in order to apply the knowledge to new situations. For example, the concepts "inductive" and "deductive" are frequently confused. The words look and sound similar except for the prefix. The significant difference is how the prefix changes the meaning of the words. Inductive is a process that begins with individual examples and looks for a pattern or general rule to describe the individual cases (inspection of *specific* cases *to* discover a *general* rule or patter). The "in" in both inductive and individual may help learners make a connection to help them remember the meaning of inductive. Deductive is the opposite. Deductive is a process in which you are done developing rules or patterns, and are now applying the names of the patterns or rules to individual cases (*general* rule applied *to* a *specific* case). Many learners learned the definitions of inductive and deductive as "specific to general" and "general to specific" respectively, but never had the concepts demonstrated, or never learned the similarities and differences so that they could apply them in future problems.

The main point about demonstrations is for teachers to show learners—not just tell them—the inherent logic in a concept, or the critical components in a skill.

# <u>E</u>nthusiasm

At first glance, enthusiasm seems to be more of a personality trait than an effective teaching component. Enthusiasm describes the vivacity with which something is done. Most of us have attended a lecture, church service, or participated in a tour in which the speaker was less than enthusiastic about the presentation. How much do you remember from presentations by unenthusiastic presenters? Or, vice versa, do you remember going to a presentation that you were not excited about, but once there, the speaker's enthusiasm for the subject rubbed off on you, and you actually enjoyed—and usually remembered—the presentation?

The movie *Dead Poets Society,* starring Robin Williams, is based on a true story.

<blockquote>❝ Honest enthusiasm is contagious. ❞</blockquote>

Enthusiasm affects your learners' attitudes. When you are genuinely interested in the content you are teaching, when you see the relevance for your students, when you are enjoying what you are teaching, your attitudes will often captivate your learners as well. In the now classic movie, *Dead Poets Society,* Mr. Keating is assigned to teach poetry to a class of high school students at an all male college preparatory school. The boys are initially less than interested in poetry, as evidenced by their groans in class. However, Mr. Keating soon has most of the boys engaged and interested because of his exuberant enthusiasm. His passion for poetry captivates their

<blockquote>❝ Knowledge is power, but enthusiasm pulls the switch. ❞
—*Ivern Ball*</blockquote>

**TOP Teachers**

➢ Thinking
➢ Observant
➢ Passionate

personal interests, and soon they are learning about poetry with their own enthusiasm.

What is enthusiasm not? Enthusiasm is not entertainment. Enthusiasm is not artificial excitement. Enthusiasm is not an act. Genuine enthusiasm is a natural passion for your learners, your subject, and teaching. Genuine enthusiasm keeps you on track, business-like, focused.

What is the point for this section? Let your natural and genuine enthusiasm for teaching and your content be visible to your learners.

# <u>L</u>ink Learning to Learning

This is the second time the concept of linking appears in the CLEAR Model. There are significant differences between the two types of links as dictated by their contexts. The first concept link appears under the category of Learners. With respect to learners, the links you want to make as a teacher are between the learners' interests and the lesson. The key points are relevance, meaningfulness, and interest from the perspective of the learners—not necessarily from the perspective of the teacher or the textbook. The current concept "link" falls under the category of Execution of the lesson. This link is an academic link, rather than a personal link for the learners. Both are critical to aid long-term retention. While the first type of link is personal, this link focuses on tying together important concepts within the lesson, between the current lesson and previous lessons, and between the current lesson and other previously learned knowledge regardless of the context. The similarity between the two types of links is that *they are both connections with previous learning or experiences.* The difference is that the first is a *personal connection,* and the second is a *content connection.*

One type of content connection to aid in recall is mnemonics. A mnemonic is anything that helps you remember something. Acronyms, rhymes, songs, silly sentences, cognitive maps, tables, color coded diagrams are all examples of things that can help a learner remember information.

For example, the word "CLEAR" in the CLEAR Model is an acronym to help teachers remember the components of effective teaching. Each category of the CLEAR model has its own mnemonic (SPEECH, PEOPLE, MODELS, AAAAA, and MIRROR) to remember important points for each of the sections. Other examples include "FOIL" as an aid to remembering how to expand equations in algebra, "Never Eat Sour Watermelon" to remember the points of the compass, and "ROY G. BIV" to remember the colors of the spectrum. Non-verbal examples include visuals like the periodic table, anatomy diagrams and coloring books, color charts in art, and pictures of orchestra instruments for teaching elementary music.

The point here is to help your learners make connections (links) between the important concepts in your content area, and give them methods to help them remember (mnemonics). As you practice demonstrating connections for your learners, don't forget to transfer the responsibility for making connections to them so they learn how to learn on their own.

# <u>S</u>tay With It!

Covering the curriculum in preparation for end-of-course or end-of-year achievement tests has long been a driving force for teachers. And yet finishing the book or covering the standards during the course is no guarantee that the learners have really learned the knowledge and skills that you covered. As long as we live in a society that is driven by grade levels and graduation requirements, teachers will always face the dilemma of whether to cover the curriculum, or teach for thorough understanding before moving on. With such a range of diversity in our classrooms, to do both successfully is a rare occurrence. So, what would learners prefer? In the research studies behind the CLEAR Model, learners preferred that their teachers stayed with the topic before moving on. They felt better about school, themselves, and their teachers when time spent on a topic or skill was sufficient for them to grasp it. Teachers who taught with a focus on understanding, who checked for understanding during the lesson, and required demonstrations of understanding through questions, written work, or authentic performances were rated as effective teachers by learners.

Although the preferences of learners will probably not change current legislation on inclusion, English Language Learners, state and national standards, and achievement testing, the notion of teaching for understanding is worthy of consideration. If we cover the material as teachers, but the learners cannot pass the required achievement tests, what have we accomplished? If we are really interested in learning as an outcome, perhaps considering the comments of thousands of learners with their observation that staying with the topic helps them learn and can help direct how we spend our time in our classrooms. Do we need to make accommodations for differing rates of learning, language differences, and special needs students? Of course. That is why we have accommodations like in-class teaching assistants, computers for simulations and practice, resource rooms, and special education for special accommodations beyond the scope of the regular classroom teacher.

Learning takes time. Give your learners time to learn. Stay with the topic until they get it. That is the point of this section.

# Summary

"Execution" in the CLEAR Model is the core of teaching. But to make good decisions about the *models of teaching*, clear and appropriate *objectives*, and effective *demonstrations*, you first need to know your students and be an effective communicator. Honest *enthusiasm* contributes to learner motivation and personal teacher satisfaction. *Linking* learning in the current lesson with previous learning, giving learners tools to help them remember important points (mnemonics) and *staying with the concept* until your learners understand completes the package of an effective lesson execution.

# Reflection Questions

1. Name at least five different *models* of teaching. Include the benefits and limits of each.
2. When would you use each of your chosen models of teaching?
3. How does a teacher make the *objectives* of the lesson obvious? Is it the same process in a discovery or inquiry lesson as it is for a direct instruction or expository lesson?
4. What are appropriate *demonstrations* for a lesson? Give examples.
5. How do you know if your level of *enthusiasm* for the lesson is enough? Too much?
6. This is the second time the concept "linking" appears in the CLEAR Model. How is this concept of linking similar to that in the Learner's section? How is it different?
7. Respondents to survey research on effective teaching said that teachers who *stayed with the topic* helped them learn. Explain why.

# References

Ausubel, D. (1963). *The psychology of meaningful verbal learning.* New York: Grune and Stratton.
Bloom, B. S., Engelhart, M. D., Frost, E. J., Hill, W. H., & Krathwohl, D. R. (1956). *Taxonomy of educational objectives. Handbook I: Cognitive domain.* New York: David McKay.
Bruner, J. (1966). *Toward a theory of instruction.* New York: Norton.

Harrington, J., Harrington, C., & Karns, E. (1991). The Marland report: Twenty years later. *Journal for the Education of the Gifted* 15: 31–43.

Hunter, M., & Russell, D. (1981). *Increasing your teaching effectiveness.* Palo Alto, CA: Learning Institute.

Johnson, D. W., & Johnson, R. T. (1994). *Learning together and alone: Cooperative, competitive, and individualistic learning,* Fourth Edition. Boston: Allyn & Bacon.

Joyce, B., Weil, M., & Calhoun, E. (2000). *Models of teaching.* Sixth edition. Boston: Allyn & Bacon.

Rosenshine, B. (1985). Direct instruction. *International encyclopedia of education* (T. Husen and T. N. Postlethwaite, Eds.) Vol. 3, pp. 1395–1400. Oxford: Pergamon Press.

Taba, H. (1966). *Teaching strategies and cognitive functioning in elementary school children.* (Cooperative Research Project 2404.) San Francisco: San Francisco State College.

Tennyson, R. D., & Cocchiarella, M. (1986). An empirically based instructional design theory for teaching concepts. *Review of Educational Research* 56: 40–71.

Woolfolk, A. (2001). *Educational Psychology,* Eighth edition. Boston: Allyn & Bacon.

# CLEAR Model: Assessment

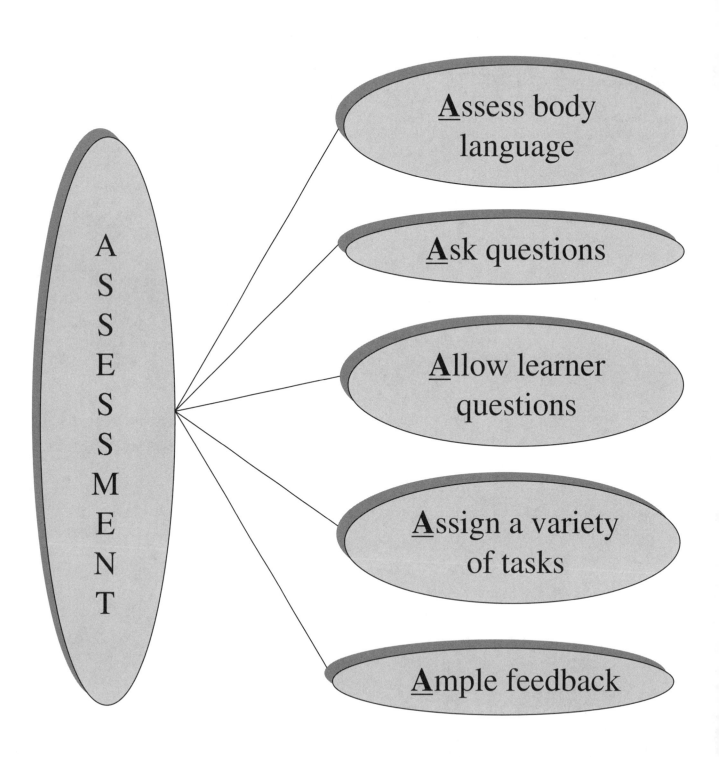

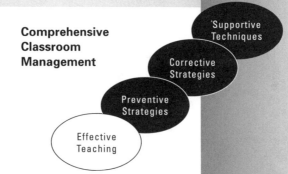

Comprehensive
Classroom
Management

'Supportive
Techniques

Corrective
Strategies

Preventive
Strategies

Effective
Teaching

## OBJECTIVES

Learners will be able to make decisions about effective assessment concerning:
- Assessing student learning through body language
- Asking questions
- Allowing learners to ask questions
- Assigning a variety of assessment tasks
- Providing ample feedback to students

## CHAPTER SNAPSHOT

- <u>A</u>ssess Learners' Understanding
- <u>A</u>sk Questions to Assess Understanding
- <u>A</u>llow and Encourage Learner Questions
- <u>A</u>ssign a Variety of Assessment Activities
- <u>A</u>mple Feedback

# <u>A</u>ssess Learners' Understanding

An important part of effective teaching is to assess whether the teaching really was effective. What we want to point out is that assessment is not an activity that happens just at the end of a unit or the end of the lesson. Assessment begins with the first words out of the teacher's mouth. As soon as you begin to communicate with the learners, you should be able to determine whether your learners are understanding your communication. Watch their body language. Observe their faces for clues as to whether your presentation is making sense to them or not. Learners who are understanding auditory and/or visual input should show signs of interest, listening, visually tracking the presenter, and engagement with the learning process. When communication breaks down, immediately signs appear in the learners that indicate a lack of understanding or even frustration. The wrinkled forehead, the questioning or squinting

**Assess:**
To observe; to purposefully consider.

eyes, cessation of note taking and looking up toward the presenter are indicators that understanding has stopped and disequilibrium has set in. An effective teacher uses these clues to determine if learning is taking place or if it is time to probe some of the learners who are displaying these signs and see where the breakdown in communication occurred. Often in methods classes, eye contact is stressed as a method to prevent discipline problems from arising and to see that learners are on task. Eye contact now serves another crucial role in the effective teaching package: assessing student learning.

An important distinction to make here is that these symptoms that indicate disequilibrium are a desired response when you are engaging your learners in discover or inquiry learning models. In these cases you want the students to experience discrepant events, apparently unexplained phenomena, or novel experiences for the sake of producing curiosity, which in turn you hope will produce learning. Scaffolding is critical in these situations, as is vigilant assessment of learners' body language, to make sure the student-centered learning experience is not pushing them beyond tolerable limits of disequilibrium and into frustration. Effective teachers are constantly monitoring and observing their learners.

# <u>A</u>sk Questions to Assess Understanding

> Questions are the creative acts of intelligence. "

Now that you are more aware of the first type of assessment, we will move into more traditional and overt techniques of assessment. Questioning has long been a mainstay for teachers to assess student learning. It is built into the most direct instruction models as a "check for understanding." One of the most common criticisms of teacher questioning is the level of difficulty of the questions. You will recall references to Bloom's cognitive taxonomy in chapter 5 with regard to instructional objectives. We stated there that Bloom's taxonomy was also useful for help in matching objectives, questions, and assessments to the level of your learners. Here we say again that Bloom's cognitive taxonomy is very useful to guide the level of questioning while assessing student learning when you are teaching a lesson. If the teacher only asks questions that elicit responses at the knowledge and comprehension levels, then the learners are unlikely to process the information at a higher level. Learners who are prompted to respond to questions at all levels of Bloom's taxonomy are more likely to understand concepts more completely and to see connections with other concepts. You can purposely ask questions that will help lead learners to make connections with personal experiences and previously learned concepts (personal and academic linking). Longer wait time, probing learner responses, specific feedback on both correct and incorrect responses (wrong answers) also contribute to the learning process and to your assessment of how well your learners are learning.

Bloom's taxonomy is not the only guide for asking good questions. Socrates was known for probing his students with incessant questions for the purpose of stimulating their thinking, and consequently high-level learning. Socratic questioning techniques include asking learners for clarification of a statement or response to a teacher initiated question, asking for examples, requesting evidence to support a point, and questioning assumptions. See the inset for a hierarchy of Socratic questions with examples. Asking good questions at a variety of levels of difficulty (using Bloom's cognitive taxonomy and Socratic questioning) is the main point of effective teaching for this section.

> *The teacher is like the candle which lights others while consuming itself.*

> *'Wrong' is a strong word to use, but sometimes it's the best word.*

---

### A HIERARCHY OF SOCRATIC QUESTIONING

- Teacher does not present material.
- Teacher uses questioning techniques to lead learners to analyze, critique, evaluate their own thinking and beliefs.

---

### CATEGORIES OF QUESTIONS

| | |
|---|---|
| ■ Clarification<br>—What do you mean by _____ ?<br>—What is your main point? | ■ Probing assumptions<br>—What are you assuming?<br>—Is that always the case? |
| ■ Reasons, Evidence, Causes<br>—What would be an example?<br>—Is there evidence for believing that? | ■ Perspectives<br>—What is an alternative?<br>—What would an opponent say? |
| ■ Implications and consequences<br>—What effect would that have?<br>—If this is the case, what else must be true? | ■ Questions about the question<br>—How can we find out?<br>—Do we all agree that this is the question? |

It is not only the question itself that is important when you are assessing your learners' knowledge with questions. Your tone of voice and body language can communicate whether or not you have confidence that the learners know the answer to your question. If you name a student before asking the question, only that student is likely to think about the answer, while the rest of the students wait for the chosen student to answer. Allowing time (wait time) for your learners to think about their response before you call on someone to answer contributes to reflective thinking on the part of your learners. Being careful not to focus on favorite students, or students you believe will have the correct answer, encourages all learners to participate. Conscientiously involving as many learners as you can in each lesson lets them know you are serious

about holding them accountable for learning. The way you give feedback will affect how your learners will participate in the future. If you embarrass or humiliate a learner for a poor response, you may be discouraging learners from trying their best in another discussion. Each of these factors affects how effective your questioning will be in assessing your learners' knowledge. Thinking about your questioning strategies and their effectiveness is an excellent topic for **R**eflection, the topic of chapter 6.

# **A**llow and Encourage Learner Questions

Indelibly etched in my memory is an exchange between a college student and a professor that will act as a counterexample for this section. During a lecture on the renal system in anatomy, a student asked the professor for a clarification on a process that had just been explained. The reply by the professor left no doubt that, in the professor's opinion, this particular student had an IQ the equivalent of his shoe size, and that if the student could not figure out simple questions like the one he had asked, he had no hope of passing the class. The entire auditorium was deathly silent after the professor's rebuke.

The next words out of the professor's mouth were "Are there any more questions?"

It would have taken a very brave person, or one who was totally oblivious to what had just taken place, to ask a question in the aftermath of the professor's rebuke. The professor had established an atmosphere that lasted the remainder of the semester. There were very few questions asked during the following weeks in that class.

If you have aroused your learners' curiosity for learning about the topic in the lesson, they will naturally want to ask questions. The nature of the questions they ask offers insight into the level of understanding of the concepts with which they are working. You can use Bloom's taxonomy or the hierarchy of Socratic questions to judge the sophistication of your learners' questions. If you are using constructivist approaches, allowing learners to ask questions is central to the method. Your learners need to ask questions of you and of each other in order to construct their understanding of the concepts at hand. It is your responsibility as a teacher to establish an atmosphere where your learners are comfortable asking and answering questions. In that question-friendly atmosphere, you can quickly assess understanding by the nature of your learners' questions and responses. The main point here is to *allow your learners to ask questions* by establishing a question-friendly atmosphere in your classroom.

# Assign a Variety of Assessment Activities

Questions are not the only way to assess learners' understanding. Quizzes, work sheets, tests, laboratory procedures, demonstrations, performances, role-playing, writing papers or reports, and creating a video or audiotape are among the various techniques for assessment of learning. A key point for the assessment process goes back to the section on Learners. Your learners will be much more motivated to engage in assessment activities when they perceive the tasks you ask them to do are valid indicators of their learning and are worthwhile from their perspective. The more authentic the tasks for assessing their knowledge or skills, the more likely the learners are to engage seriously in the assessment task. Similarly, not all learners have strengths in all of the various assessment methods. Some learners are very comfortable with multiple choice testing and hate essay tests, book reports, or anything that involves writing. Other learners can tell you the answer to any of the questions on a test in an interview but, because of test anxiety, will fail any kind of written test. Still others can perform flawlessly on the floor, field, or board, but cannot function on a piece of paper.

The point of this discussion is that learners are diverse, and so, too, should be our assessments of their learning. Your methods of assessment should match your learners, your content and objectives, and the models you choose to use for the learning experiences.

> ### AUTHENTIC ASSESSMENTS
>
> Real world applications of learned knowledge and skills. Examples include:
> - Piano recitals
> - Speeches
> - Sporting events
> - Science fairs
> - National history day
> - Building a model
> - Mentorship
> - Internships
> - School-to-work jobs
> - School newspaper
> - School annual
> - Closed circuit TV announcements
> - Art or photography exhibits

# Ample Feedback

Do you remember getting back a research paper with a less-than-perfect grade, but there was no explanation for why you had lost points? Do you remember the frustration, especially if there was another paper due in the same class? You had no way of knowing how to improve your performance on the next assignment. Feedback is more than just a grade or a number on an assignment. Ample feedback is enough information for the learner to improve on his or her next performance.

What is ample feedback? Ample means enough. Feedback is information so that the learners know how to improve on the next similar task. That implies that your comments—written or verbal—need to be specific as to strengths and weaknesses of the performance, why their answers or work products were wrong (if their work was not up to criteria), and specific suggestions on how to improve. Pointing out examples is helpful to learners so they have concrete evidence of how you arrived at your evaluation of their performance. Constructively critical feedback is especially appreciated by your highly able learners. They especially want to know why they were wrong on each and every incorrect response.

> **"** The object of teaching a child is to enable him to get along without his teacher. **"**
>
> —Elbert Hubbard

The principle of ample feedback is true for written work, dioramas, art exhibitions, music or dance performance, physical education and athletics, technical skills, or debate competitions. Ample feedback is the basis for learning new knowledge and skills.

The pertinent point here is to give your learners ample feedback—accurate information to help them learn on their own. Your objective should be to help your learners get along without their teacher—that means you!

# Summary

Assessment is another critical component of effective teaching. Without ongoing assessment, you do not know whether or not your teaching is effective. *Assessment begins with the first word out of your mouth—watching* your learners for clues of understanding or confusion. Next, *ask questions to check for understanding.* Third, establish a question-friendly atmosphere and *allow questions* so your students' natural curiosity will be encouraged. *Assign* a variety of assessment techniques. Do not rely solely on tests. Finally, give your learners *ample feedback* so they learn how to learn on their own.

# Reflection Questions

1. What are the first indicators of your students' understanding or lack of understanding during instruction?
2. Give examples of questions using each level of Bloom's taxonomy.
3. Give examples of Socratic questions from each level of the hierarchy (see table, page 63).
4. How can you foster an environment in which students feel safe to ask questions?

5. Describe a variety of assessments you could use with a single lesson within your content area.

6. What is ample feedback? What is the rationale behind giving students ample feedback?

# References

Geocanis, C. (1996–1997). Increasing student engagement: A mystery solved. *Educational Leadership* 54 (4): 72–75.

Hines, C. V. (1981). *A further investigation of teacher clarity: The observation of teacher clarity and the relationship between clarity and student achievement and satisfaction.* Unpublished doctoral dissertation. The Ohio State University, Columbus, Ohio.

Land, M. L. (1980). Teacher clarity and cognitive level of questioning: Effects on learning. *Journal of Experimental Education* 49 (1): 48–51.

Trindale, A. L. (1972). Structures in teaching and learning outcomes. *Journal of Research in Science Teaching* 9 (1): 65–74.

Woolfolk, A. (2001). *Educational psychology,* Eighth edition. Boston: Allyn & Bacon.

# CLEAR Model: Reflection—"MIRROR"

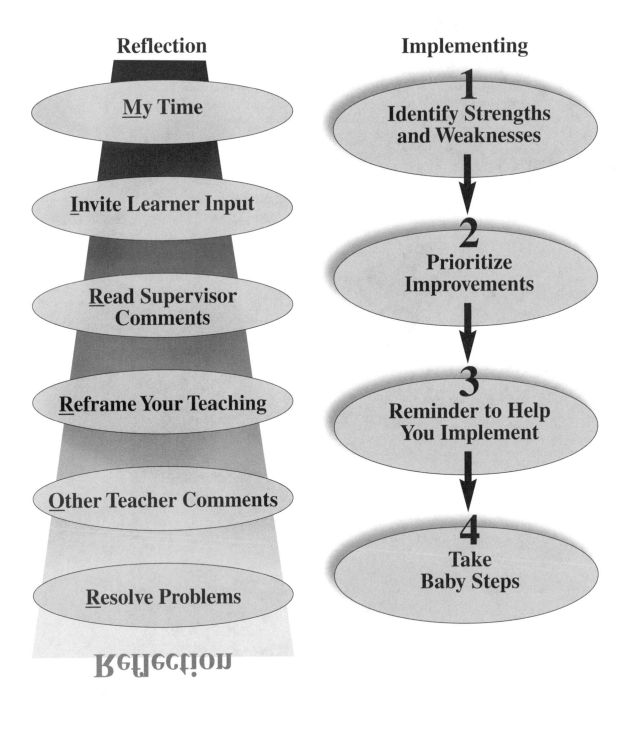

Reflection

**My Time**

**Invite Learner Input**

**Read Supervisor Comments**

**Reframe Your Teaching**

**Other Teacher Comments**

**Resolve Problems**

Reflection

Implementing

**1**
**Identify Strengths and Weaknesses**

**2**
**Prioritize Improvements**

**3**
**Reminder to Help You Implement**

**4**
**Take Baby Steps**

**OBJECTIVES**

Learners will be able to make decisions about effective teaching using reflection strategies.

Comprehensive Classroom Management

Supportive Techniques

Corrective Strategies

Preventive Strategies

Effective Teaching

Reflection. Reflectiveness. Reflexivity. These are terms that describe a cognitive process that effective teachers engage in for the purpose of improving their teaching. Typically it refers to thinking back on what has transpired during the course of a lesson—what went right, what went wrong, and how to improve the teaching performance for the next time. It is the process of improving your future teaching based on previous experiences. It is learning from your mistakes, making changes in your strategies, and celebrating your successes. It is a key component in professional development. Reflective teachers tend to be better problem solvers, better at recognizing why their learners are making mistakes, better at analyzing teaching situations for the purpose of improving instruction (Floden and Klinsing, 1990; Leinhardt, 1987).

So, how does one become reflective as a teacher? You don't have the previous experience with which to compare today's experience. But you do have the knowledge of what comprises effective teaching. That is what the CLEAR Model is all about. And you have experienced expert teaching as a student somewhere in your past. You have studied educational psychology, which focuses on teaching, learning, and how to improve both teaching and learning. So, while you may not have a broad

> **"** Experience is the name that everyone gives to his mistakes. **"**
> —*Oscar Wilde*

> **"** If you always do what you always did, you'll always get what you always got. **"**
> —*Verne Hill*

experiential base, you do have a knowledge base. That is what we are going to build on using the last component of the CLEAR Model—Reflection—and its mnemonic, MIRROR.

# <u>M</u>y Time: Self-Evaluation

Have you been in a classroom after the school day is over? There is a golden silence, an emotional letdown, and time. The bells, buzzers, and tones have all ceased, the students are gone, teaching is done. The experiences of the day are still fresh in the mind of the teacher as plans for the next day begin to formulate. I am not talking about lesson plans. Many teachers are planned for weeks in advance—at least the unit plan is in place, and the goals and objectives are laid out and tentatively scheduled. This is the daily planning that emerges after each day is done.

"They sure need a follow-up on adjectives," the teacher muses.

Reflection.

"I am going to have to reteach whole and half rests," the music teacher thinks to herself.

Reflection.

"I wonder why Juanita was so quiet today?"

Reflection . . . My time to ponder the day's events.

"There has to be a better way to get the new attendance forms filled out faster."

Reflection. Thinking about what went on during your day is reflection. Reflection time could occur before school, during recess or prep periods, during lunch, after school, or in the evening. Using those thoughts to prepare for the coming days is using reflection to improve instruction. Noting that your learners had (or did not have) trouble understanding your presentation during the fourth hour (*Communication*). Making observations and looking for patterns in your *Learners'* behaviors. Remembering that your learners seemed to focus better after you restated the objective (*Execution*). Thinking that you need to ask more questions to check to see that your learners are understanding before you move on to the next concept so you can avoid all those mistakes on the homework (*Assessment*).

Everything that we have covered in the CLEAR Model now becomes an efficient structure for self-evaluation of your teaching. It helps you identify strengths and weaknesses of your instructional approaches by giving you a step-by-step sequence of behaviors and dispositions that effective teachers use and that learners say helps them learn. Going over the major components of the CLEAR Model after a lesson gives structure to your *Reflections* and will give you clues on how to improve your future instruction. This implies that reflection is not just thinking about the past. It is using past experiences to improve the future. By extension, as you become familiar with the components of the CLEAR Model, you can use a pause during a lesson to do a quick self-evaluation. You can ask yourself, "Have I been **C**ommunicating clearly? Am I accommodating my various **L**earners? Is this **E**xecution working well? Have I been **A**ssessing while I go? And, what you are doing is **R**eflecting during the lesson. That means that reflection can be past, present, and future. This is the essence of metacognition—thinking about your thinking, in this case, thinking about your teaching—while you are teaching. The CLEAR Model can help you plan, deliver, and debrief your lessons with the focus on improving your instruction from the perspective of your learners.

> *Teachers must think for themselves if they are to help others think for themselves.*
>
> —Carnegie Corporation of New York

Metacognition does not come naturally for everyone. Some of us have to work at it so that it becomes more natural. Some suggestions to improve metacognitive reflection about your teaching are:

- ➤ Take advantage of pauses and quiet time to think about your teaching.
- ➤ Write down observations, feelings, ideas, and questions that cross your mind.
- ➤ Use a teaching journal. Make an entry daily if possible. Don't let a week go by without making an entry.
- ➤ Try video stimulated recall. Videotape yourself teaching. Watch the video. Use the CLEAR Model to debrief your lesson and note places for improvement. See the inset on videotaping lessons.

> *It is not the hours you put in as a teacher that count. It is the teaching you put into those hours.*

Each of these suggestions is a solo activity. These are intended for you to do during **M**y time—time you have alone in which you can thoughtfully reflect on your teaching. The more time you spend reflecting on your teaching, the better you will get at reflection, and the more your teaching will improve.

# Invite Learner Input

There comes a time when you may need a second opinion. Who might be qualified to give a valid and reliable second opinion about your teaching? First of all, the entire CLEAR Model is based on student responses to questions about effective teachers and what they do to help learning occur. Why not invite your learners to give their input on a survey about your teaching? Here is a short, generic version:

> ➢ What do you like about my teaching?
> ➢ What do you NOT like about my teaching?
> ➢ What would you suggest to improve my teaching?

Be prepared—kids can be blatantly honest! But you will get feedback (with some comments which you can and should ignore) that can give you insights into your mannerisms, biases, prejudices, and discriminatory practices that you would not have thought of on your own. You need to be high on the intellectual honesty scale to try this. I recommend this to all my student teachers with a very high percentage of positive outcomes and excellent suggestions for improvement from their learners.

## HINTS FOR VIDEOTAPED LESSONS

> ➢ Set a camcorder on a tripod in a back corner of the room where no one will knock it over.
> ➢ Set the lens on wide angle.
> ➢ Point the camcorder toward the area of the room in which you will do most of your teaching.
> ➢ Test to see that both the audio and video recording functions are working.
> ➢ Do NOT perform for the camera. Try to speak, move, write on the board, etc., as you normally would.
> ➢ Record and evaluate at least THREE lessons.
> > • Lesson one: teachers tend to look at how they looked: their hair, how they were dressed, a spot on their shirt.
> > • Lesson two: teachers tend to notice their mannerisms, incorrect grammar.
> > • Lesson three: teachers begin to focus on their teaching.
> ➢ Use the CLEAR Model to help you reflect on your teaching.

# Read Supervisor Comments

Whether as a student teacher, or a full time, inservice teacher, you will have your teaching evaluated by a supervisor—either a university representative during your student teaching experience or a principal or vice principal during your in-service experience. Both are part of your professional development process. Your supervisors tend to have significant classroom experience, which frequently gives them insight for helpful evaluative comments. Read those comments carefully, and plug them into the CLEAR Model. Build suggestions into your next lesson plans to implement the next time you teach. We will address this more in the last section in chapter 7: Implementing the CLEAR Model.

# Reframe Your Teaching

As we talked about before, the purpose of reflection is to improve the effectiveness of your instruction. As you think back over your lesson, view videotapes of your lessons, read your learners' and supervisors' comments, look at your teaching from each of these perspectives. *Reframe* what happens in your classroom from your learners' perspectives. Look at the same lesson from a supervisor's perspective. Then look again from your perspective. Restructuring—looking at your teaching from multiple perspectives—will often give you new insights for improving your instruction, taking a new look at persistent problems, and coming up with reflective and thoughtful resolutions to the emergent issues in your classroom.

# Other Teachers: Peer Reviews

This strategy for reflection is more appropriate for seasoned teachers. If you are a new teacher wanting valid feedback on your teaching performance, it makes good sense to ask an accomplished teacher for a peer review, rather than another new teacher, or a close friend that may give you a socially acquiescent response and a pat on the back, but nothing substantive to help you improve. Seek out teachers in a similar content area and/or grade level whom you know to be an effective teacher, and ask for a peer evaluation. You might even give them a copy of the CLEAR Model and ask them to write comments as they observe you. Follow up with a debriefing after the lesson in a relaxed atmosphere and ask for suggestions to help you improve the effectiveness of your teaching and classroom management.

The point is that other teachers' teaching in a similar situation, grade level, content area, school system can give you insights to stimulate your reflection process.

# <u>R</u>esolve Problems Toward Improved Learning

Here is the bottom line for the **R**eflection process in particular, and for the CLEAR Model overall: *Resolve problems and improve your teaching.* Going through the process of evaluating teaching is a useless exercise unless the information gathered contributes to improved teaching and learning in your classroom. Not only is teaching a profession that demands continuous improvement, it is, by its very nature, a moral enterprise. We touch the future with every learner we teach. Teachers have the greatest responsibility and the greatest honor of all the professions—teaching is Life 101.

# Summary for MIRROR

**R**eflection is thinking about your teaching—before you teach, while you are teaching, and after you have taught a lesson. It is psychologically looking in a mirror for the purpose of improving your teaching and your learners' learning. You need to take time for yourself to engage in this professional development activity—*My time. Invite* your students to give written comments, compliments, and suggestions regarding your teaching. *Read comments from your supervisor* after a lesson observation. *Reframe* how you look at your own teaching—consider the perspectives of your students or an outside observer. Ask *other teachers* to observe you and give you their feedback on your teaching. Finally, *resolve* problems and weaknesses in your teaching performance, using the CLEAR Model to help you identify and work on those areas that need improvement.

That brings us to the next section. How do you implement the CLEAR Model for the purpose of personal and professional development? Please read on.

# Implementing the CLEAR Model

With 23 elements in the first four components of the CLEAR Model, and another six elements in the Reflective component of the Model, self-assessment and evaluation toward professional improvement can be overwhelming tasks. We have used this model with hundreds of teachers and supervisors, and have developed a very manageable process for implementation. There are three basic steps.

> **❝** What we hope to do with ease we must learn first to do with diligence. **❞**
>
> —Samuel Johnson

## 1.  Identifying strengths and weaknesses

Use the CLEAR Model to assess your strengths and weaknesses over several lessons. You can self-assess with videotapes, journaling, or personal reflection, or you can ask for an observation from a supervisor, administrator, or peer teacher. Student survey comments as outlined above may also be useful. Place a colored check mark by each effective teaching principle that you are doing successfully. Next, use a different color marker to highlight the principles that need improvement. Check with your supervisor, student comments, or peer teacher to validate your observations. Use this information for the next step.

## 2.  Prioritizing for improvement

Rank the effective teaching principles you have selected for improvement from most needed to least needed to improve your instruction. This ranking is very important. Validate your ranking with your supervisor, administrator, or a peer teacher. Take the effective teaching principle at the top of your list and write it on your notes or lesson plan for your next lesson. Exactly what will you do to improve the effectiveness of your next lesson? Be specific. Include accommodations in your lesson plan. Edit your PowerPoint™ show or your transparencies that you will use to teach the upcoming lesson to include the teaching improvement. Write it down in plain sight.

## 3. Reminder to Help You Implement

Because many teachers leave their lesson plans or notes at their desk, in a plan book, or at a lectern while they teach, your note to yourself about which effective teaching principle of the CLEAR Model you plan to implement may not be visible. You will need a reminder that will be effective while you are teaching. Here are some suggestions:

➢ Create a mnemonic or visual reminder for the effective teaching principle you want to work on and write or draw it on the board. Create a mnemonic that will work for you—one that is meaningful, relevant, and personal. For example, if you want to remember to watch your learners' eyes to see if they are understanding your presentation, draw an eye on the board to help you remember to watch their eyes. Or draw an eye on a sticky note, and stick it to the back wall in a place you will be sure to see it.

➢ Write a reminder on the overhead transparency you will use during the lesson.

➢ Put an object on your desk, table, lectern, or some other place in your line of sight to remind you to implement the CLEAR teaching principle. For example, put a baseball on your desk to help you remember to engage your kinesthetic learners during the lesson.

➢ Have an observer watch to see if you do what you say you will do. The observer may be a supervisor, peer, parent, or a student.

➢ Hang a reminder from the ceiling, on a window, on a wall—somewhere in your line of sight to remind you.

> **❝** If at first you don't succeed, you're probably just like the teacher in the next classroom. **❞**

## Baby Steps

Whatever you do, do a little bit well rather than trying to fix everything at once. Teaching is a complex task. You have to think about administrative tasks, content, teaching, organization, room management, behavior management, not to mention the usual and too frequent interruptions over the intercom. Choose **ONE** element to work on and improve at a time. Use the reminders and mnemonics. Practice the planned improvement until it works every time. Sometimes just the simple reminder is all it takes, and you will need only one time to implement a new teaching principle that will become automatic after the first implementation. Other principles will take many trials and practice before they become part of your routine.

The key point here is to take *baby steps.* Practicing a new element until you are proficient will also contribute to your own self-efficacy, and will increase the probability that you will continue to improve your teaching effectiveness toward your overall professional development.

# Summary

Implementing the CLEAR Model is a lifelong process. *Identify* which effective principles you will implement based on careful observation and input from reliable sources. *Prioritize* which principles you will implement first. Plan to *implement one principle at a time.* Write the plan into your lesson plan or presentation notes, your presentation software, or on your overhead transparencies. Create a reminder. Practice it until it becomes automatic. Implement it in small, manageable steps—*baby steps.*

> **❝** Better to do a little well than a great deal poorly. Life's greatest adventure is in doing one's level best. **❞**
> —*Arthur Morgan*

# Reflection Questions

1.  Describe three strategies for private reflection on your teaching.
2.  How can student and supervisor comments help you reflect on your teaching?
3.  What does "Reframing your teaching" mean? What are the results of reframing your teaching?
4.  What are other sources of input for reflecting on your teaching?
5.  How does reflecting on your teaching help solve problems with your teaching and classroom management?
6.  What are the steps for implementing the CLEAR Model?

# References

Cruickshank, D. (1987). *Reflective teaching: The preparation of students of teaching.* Reston, VA: The Association of Teacher Educators.

Floden, R., & Klinsing, H. (1990). What can research on teacher thinking contribute to teacher preparation? A second opinion. *Educational Researcher* 19 (5): 15–20.

Hatton, N., & Smith, D. (1994). *Facilitating reflection: Issues and research.* Paper presented at the Conference of Australian Teacher Education Association. Queensland, Australia, July 3–6, 1994.

Leinhardt, G. (1988). Situated knowledge and expertise in teaching. In J. Calderhead (Ed.), *Teachers' professional learning,* pp. 146–168. London: Farmer Press.

Pugach, M. C. (1990). *Self-study: The genesis of reflection in novice teachers?* Paper presented at the Annual Meeting of the American Educational Research Association. Boston, MA, April 17–20, 1990.

Smith, L. R. (1982). *Training teachers to teach clearly: Theory into practice.* Paper presented at the Annual Meeting of the American Educational Research Association. New York, NY, March 19–23, 1982.

Sparks-Langer, G. M., & Colton, A. B. (1993). Synthesis of research on teachers' reflective thinking. In A. Woolfolk (Ed.), *Readings and cases in educational psychology.* Boston: Allyn & Bacon.

Zeichner, K. M. (1987a). Teaching student teachers to reflect. *Harvard Educational Review* 57 (1): 23–48.

Zeichner, K. M. (1987b). *Action research and teacher thinking: The first phase of the action research on action research project at the University of Wisconsin-Madison.* Paper presented at the Annual Meeting of the American Educational Research Association. Washington, DC, April 20–24, 1987.

# Preventive Component

**Comprehensive**

**Classroom**

**Management**

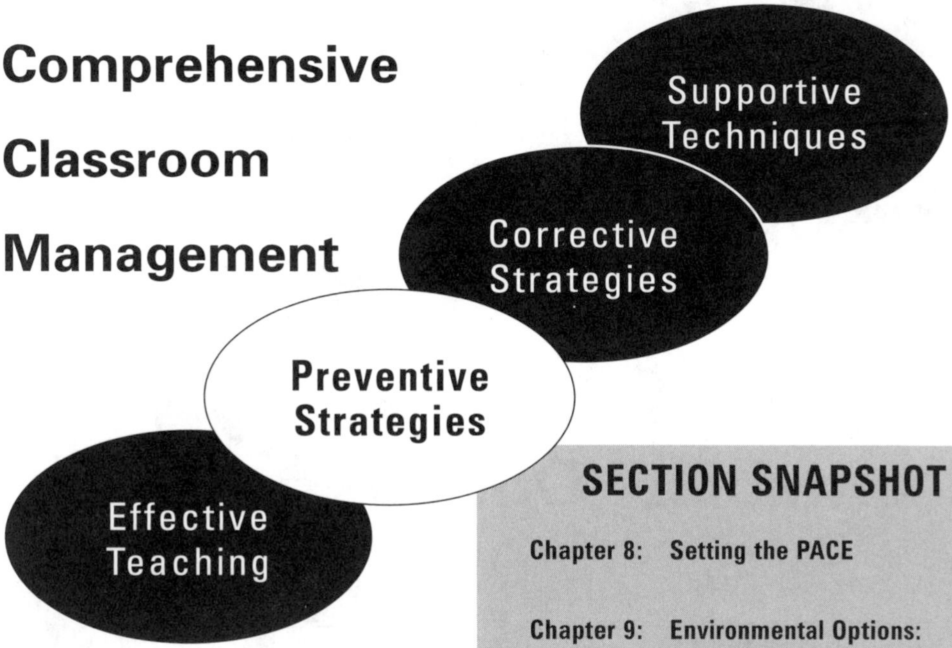

Supportive
Techniques

Corrective
Strategies

Preventive
Strategies

Effective
Teaching

## SECTION SNAPSHOT

Chapter 8:  Setting the PACE

Chapter 9:  Environmental Options:
Implementation

# Setting the Pace

## Using PACE for Prevention

**P**roactive Options

**A**ccountability Options

**C**hoice Options

**E**nvironmental Options

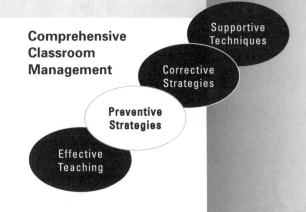

Comprehensive
Classroom
Management

Supportive
Techniques

Corrective
Strategies

Preventive
Strategies

Effective
Teaching

The learners will be able to describe strategies to prevent problems in their classroom through organizing and designing the class ahead of time and in the first week of school to avoid problems developing in the first place.

**CHAPTER SNAPSHOT**

- <u>P</u>roactive Options
- *Kounin's Approach*
- <u>A</u>ccountability Options
- <u>C</u>hoices
- <u>E</u>nvironmental Options: Introduction

Preventing problems in your classroom by setting the **PACE** is an integral aspect of success in the classroom. The old adage "an ounce of prevention is worth a pound of cure" is relevant for today's classroom. The more you organize and design the classroom to avoid discipline problems developing in the first place, the fewer classroom disruptions you have. Planning and preparing are essential. Emmer, Evertson, and Worsham (2000) have done extensive research with thousands of teachers indicating that effective classroom managers have well-developed, well-thought-out, well-implemented, and well-maintained prevention strategies in place (also Evertson, Emmer, and Worsham, 2000).

Your prevention component will not completely eliminate classroom problems, but it will surely make a difference in how many day-to-day discipline problems come up where you need to rely on your corrective interventions for the moment of misbehavior.

Setting the **PACE** focuses on the main aspects of prevention needed in your prevention component:

<u>P</u>roactive Options: You plan, organize, and design the class at the beginning so that you are being proactive and not reactive. Planning and preparing reaps many benefits. You manage your lessons so that things run smoothly with little down time. You clarify expectations of all with the students.

<u>A</u>ccountability Options: You plan, organize and design how you will hold students accountable for their learning tasks. How will you

structure things so that students can be successful in your class? What standards (how well something has to be done) will you set for their work? Your challenge is to manage student work so you and the students can keep track of it. You decide what to do about missed work. You plan techniques to have all students responding simultaneously at times. This will assist you in checking if they "all" understand the learning.

Choices: You involve your students in appropriate curriculum decisions, so they feel ownership of what they are learning. You provide them with structured choices as to how they do their assignments, which assignments they may choose from a list of potential assignments, or a combination of the two.

Environmental Options: You create a classroom climate that is conducive to learning. It needs to be predetermined, jointly constructed, taught to the students, and adopted and maintained. Establishing the environment includes:

➢ Rules or Code of Conduct
➢ Procedures
➢ Arranging the Room
➢ Working the Room

When you put all four together—**P**roactive Options, **A**ccountability Options, **C**hoices, and **E**nvironmental Options—you have set the **PACE** in your classroom and you have a well-developed prevention component. You avoid many problems before they even develop. You need to use less of the corrective intervention strategies for the moment of misbehavior. Let's look at all of your options for preventing problems so you can create learning opportunities in your class.

# **P**roactive Options

Using PACE for Prevention

Proactive Options
Accountability Options
Choice Options
Environmental Options

Proactive means preparing—being ready for what comes in the classroom, anticipating problems, and addressing them before they happen rather than reacting to them afterwards. The **ACE** (Accountability Options, Choices, and Environmental Options) in **PACE** will help you be an **ACE** teacher through helping you with the specifics that need your planning and preparing. In later sections of this chapter and into chapter 9 you will work on preparing and planning how to:

Hold students **A**ccountable for their schoolwork
Incorporate **C**hoices for the students

Establish your classroom **E**nvironment
- ➤ Classroom Climate
- ➤ Room Arrangement
- ➤ Rules or Code of Conduct
- ➤ Procedures
- ➤ Working the Room

Starting out with the attitude that planning and preparing are essential is what the **P** in **PACE** is all about.

**P**roactive Options are:
- ➤ Planning and Preparing to Prevent Problems
- ➤ Preventive Lesson Management
- ➤ Clarifying Expectations of All with the Students

Effective prevention—being proactive—entails avoiding problems before they even develop. An integral aspect of prevention is to make sure that your lessons are well planned and thought out and that the materials are prepared and ready for the next activity. The more time spent planning your lessons, the fewer disruptions you have.

> **FROM A META-ANALYSIS OF 50 YEARS OF RESEARCH**
> Teacher classroom management choices are the main influence on student achievement. Management choices have even a greater influence than student aptitude.
> —Wang, Haertel, and Walberg (1994)

## Planning and Preparing to Prevent Problems

The amount of time you put into planning and preparing will actually save you time in the long run. The time saved will come from dealing less with disruptive situations. Down time in the classroom is time in which the students are not actively engaged in learning activities. Down time comes from a variety of sources:

- ➤ Not having materials ready
- ➤ Passing out materials
- ➤ Non-instructional tasks, like attendance, late or missing assignments, lunch count, or book money
- ➤ Interruptions

Down time is a breeding ground for classroom disruptions. Once a new teacher asked me to figure out what the reason was that she was having a lot of classroom discipline problems. After observing her class, what I discovered was that she had a long, complicated process for handing out and collecting papers. While she was busy with that drawn-out process, the students found a great opportunity to start talking with one another and the teacher could never really get them back on-task again. Once we worked to tighten up her procedure for passing out and collecting papers, her discipline problems were largely gone.

Please notice that I said largely gone. As stated before, planning and preparing minimize problems, but do not eliminate them entirely. There will always be a need for the practical corrective strategies at the moment of misbehavior, but the less you need corrective interventions, the better. Ways to minimize down time will be illustrated throughout this section of the book. Let's look at some ways that lesson management can help with that.

## Preventive Lesson Management— Withitness

Managing your lessons well so you are keeping things moving smoothly from one part of a lesson to another part or from one lesson to another is a great way to minimize down time. Jacob Kounin (1977) was a pioneer in emphasizing the importance of lesson management to prevent problems in the class. He espoused that teaching was closely linked to discipline. You really can't separate the two. Managing your lessons, in Kounin's opinion, is more important than being able to handle discipline. If you manage your lessons effectively or in other words, implement effective teaching, you won't have as many discipline problems. We concur with Kounin's ideas. That is the reason this book started with the CLEAR Model to help you examine and fine-tune your instructional choices.

According to Kounin, in order to have well-managed lessons, you need to:

---

**KOUNIN'S PREVENTIVE STRATEGIES**

| | |
|---|---|
| 1. Plan your lessons well | 6. Be able to multitask—*overlapping* |
| 2. Have *variety,* interest, *and novelty* in the lessons | 7. Have materials ready |
| 3. Keep the *momentum* going—pacing | 8. Utilize the *ripple effect*—behavior spreads |
| 4. Focus group attention—*group alerting* | 9. Have smooth *transitions* |
| 5. Call on all students regularly—*accountability* | 10. Develop *"withitness"* |

---

The first four strategies in the first column are all addressed in Section II—The CLEAR Model: **E**xecution.

## Call on all students regularly (Accountability)

In order to hold students *accountable* during the lesson, you need to call on each of them often. This keeps students attentive when they do not know when their turn is coming. Calling on students randomly or in an unpredictable pattern helps keep them focused on the lesson. This focuses their attention and keeps students alert. You want to avoid going around the room in a pattern, as students figure out when their turn is coming and do not listen to the rest. (The exception to this is for very young learners who have not learned about the culture of school. Taking turns in a predictable order acts as a cue for the next student to participate.)

Having them give group responses is another strategy for keeping them accountable. You also make sure that you pose a question and give some think time before mentioning anyone's name. If you start with any student's name, then the rest cease to listen to or think about the question that was asked.

You want to concurrently make sure that you are providing a safe environment for making mistakes so students do not feel put on the spot. The purpose is to keep them involved, not to zap them for not paying attention. This will be discussed more in the supportive component—Section V.

## Be able to multitask (Overlapping)

For you to be able to do more than one thing at a time in the classroom helps to manage the lesson. When you are working with a small group, you still need to periodically scan the room, so you are noticing what behavior other students in the class are choosing. You do not want to get so focused on the small group that mayhem in the rest of the class is missed. A new teacher whom I worked with would get so focused on the reading group that she was working with that the problems going on in the rest of the room were completely missed by her. We worked together on her looking up every couple of minutes or so and scanning the room, briefly saying the name of any student who was making a poor choice and going right back to her group again. Once her "not in her small group" students realized that she was monitoring them, the need for the "name dropping" strategy (described in the next section) diminished.

## Have materials ready

Having materials ready to go is critical to avoiding down time. When you are looking for or preparing materials while the students are waiting, misbehavior is usually the result. A new teacher whom I worked with would get her construction paper ready and passed out for an activity while the students sat waiting. There were lots of misbehaviors that began while she was fumbling with the paper. Then it was hard for her to pull them back in and get them refocused on the lesson. Once she had a pile of paper ready for each group and had a material monitor from each group come to get one of the pile, her day went much smoother.

### *Utilize the ripple effect—behavior spreads*

The *ripple effect* lets us know that behaviors are contagious. Realizing this helps you to be timely in dealing with misbehavior before it has a chance to be "catching." We want to nip it in the bud. The ripple effect works with responsible behavior as well. We want responsible behavior to spread, so focusing on it in class is critical. The focus on responsible behavior is done in a more low-key manner with secondary students, but is still essential with students of all ages. John, who envisions himself as the class comedian, started making horse noises during a reading assignment related to horses. His teacher did not use the "Target Stop Do" strategy (described in the next section): "John, please stop making horse noises and get refocused on our story." The teacher did not use any strategy to deal with the horse noises and John got the laughter he was after. The horse noises continued. The next thing you know there were horse noises popping up all over the class, which was really hard to deal with. If John's teacher had only nipped the noise in the bud, it would have been much simpler to deal with.

### *Have smooth transitions*

Having materials ready is one aspect of maintaining *smooth transitions,* but it also involves having thought out what you are going to be doing next and what the students need to know and have in order to work on the lesson. The opposite of smooth transitions is jerkiness, vagueness, or forgetting key points that you will have to reteach later. Each of these is to be avoided. Examples of jerkiness would be the teacher starting the students on an assignment and then saying, "Wait a minute, I forgot to tell you an important part of your assignment." Or, "Oh, I forgot to give you the papers you need."

The teacher above could have done the following:

> ➤ Thought through what the instructions were that he needed to give for the assignment.
> ➤ Communicated the instructions while he was modeling the assignment.
> ➤ Prepared the necessary materials ahead of time.
> ➤ Assigned students to help to pass them out.

If he had done the steps above, the transition from the whole group demonstration to the students working on the assignment in groups would have gone smoothly instead of the jerky "I forgot" manner in which it unfolded.

## Develop withitness

Developing *withitness* is also important. This is when the students feel that you are on top of the situation in the classroom. You are aware of what is going on and deal with situations in a timely manner. You need to know that "withitness" is not a skill that necessarily comes naturally to teachers. You develop it over time, when you become comfortable with the content you are teaching and with the process of teaching.

> **''** Treat people as if they were what they ought to be, and you help them to become what they are capable of being. **''**
> —*Johann von Goethe*

When you first start teaching or when you switch to a different grade level or content, a great deal of your energy is tied up with the lesson and thinking about what you were going to say and do. Once you have some experience with the grade level, you are able to release energy to be aware of all of the many things going on in a classroom. Practicing all of the other aforementioned strategies of Kounin will help you to become "withit" sooner.

## Clarify expectations of all with the students

Being clear about expectations is an important aspect of being proactive. Clarifying expectations "with" the students rather than "to" the students creates a situation where you and your students are working together to create a classroom conducive to learning. As you explore the next three aspects of **PACE**—**A**ccountability, **C**hoices, and **E**nvironment—please think of what ways and in what areas you can include students in the decision-making process. You want to do some pre-thinking and some pre-planning, so you are clear on what you can live with and not live with in your classroom, but leave room to finalize your plans and preparation with student

> **FROM RESEARCH**
> Teacher expectations greatly affect both classroom behavior and the learning environment.
> —*Proctor (1984)*

input. This all-important way to have students take ownership of the classroom will be looked at in more detail in the supportive component—Section V.

It is critical that you examine your expectations of the students. What you expect has bearing on what you get. Having positive expectations and high expectations gets you better quality and quantity of results. Students have a tendency to live up to our expectations.

Based on research (Rosenthal and Jacobson, 1968) we know that you can create a self-fulfilling prophecy where a student ends up acting a certain way because that was what was expected of him or her. I worked once with a boy, Jacob, who came to school in the shadow of his older brother who had struck fear in the hearts of all through his bullying behaviors. Jacob started out very cooperative with others, but, unfortunately, others expected him to be like his brother. Down the road Jacob was just like his brother. He had responded to

**FROM RESEARCH**

Problem behavior is related to teachers having negative perceptions about the ability of learning disabled children.

*—Bender and Golden (1989)*

what was expected of him. You need to be careful what expectations you project to students.

Another thing to be cautious of is the tendency that once you form a not-so-positive expectation of a student, it is possible that the students could make some positive changes and you might not notice them. This is called the sustaining expectation effect. Even though some students make some pretty poor choices, you need to work hard on not forming negative expectations of them. If you

## KOUNIN'S APPROACH

**Assumptions**
➤ Prevention is more important than handling misbehavior.
➤ Teaching is closely connected to discipline. Lesson management and variety are integral to a well-managed classroom.
➤ Effective teaching influences discipline more than discipline strategies. The key is keeping students actively involved.

**Main Points**
➤ Withitness: Being aware of what's going on in the classroom and on top of the situation.
➤ Overlapping: Dealing with more than one thing at a time—multitasking—working with a small group, but still knowing what is happening in the rest of the classroom.
➤ Smooth Transitions: Keeping things running smoothly in the classroom to minimize down time and keeping the momentum going—things moving along.
➤ Ripple Effect: Behavior ripples or spreads. A teacher needs to be timely at dealing with negative behavior and encourage positive behavior.
➤ Accountability: Keeping students involved and attentive through calling on them regularly.
➤ Variety and Interest: Implementing lessons that are enjoyable, varied, and actively involve the students—keeping up teacher enthusiasm.
➤ Group Alerting: Gaining and focusing students' attention and communicating expectations.

**Implementation**
➤ It is important to organize and design the class to prevent problems. How integral is effective teaching to effective management and discipline? Lesson management and smooth transitions are key. Kounin's ideas are used by most of the other approaches.

**Limitation**
➤ Mainly prevention strategies—need more answers when problems develop despite the focus on prevention.

do form negative expectations, be very cognizant of attempts to make positive changes on the part of the student lest you fall into the trap of just not noticing the positive progress of that student. Students should also be clear on what they can expect from you. Communicate to students about what they can expect from you.

## Summary for Proactive Options

Your *Proactive Options* involve all the *pre-planning* and *preparing* you need to do to *prevent problems.* You also incorporate strategies of *preventive lesson management* recommended by Kounin, like *withitness, overlapping, smooth transitions,* the *ripple effect,* keeping students *accountable* by *calling on then regularly,* utilizing *attention focusing strategies* to keep your students *alert,* and having *variety, interest, and novelty* in your instruction. It is also important to *clarify the expectations of all* with the students. "All" includes you as well.

# Accountability Options

## Structure for Student Success

The purpose of having an accountability system is to help students to learn. You want to have a way to motivate students to follow through on their learning tasks and for you to keep track of it all. You want to design your accountability procedures with bringing about student success as being the main goal. "How can I help students learn?" needs to be the overarching question. You need to structure your accountability system for student success. What standards (how well something needs to be done) will I communicate to the students to aid them in being successful?

Using PACE for Prevention

Proactive Options

Accountability Options

Choice Options

Environmental Options

Student involvement in this process with an emphasis on self-management helps to bring about success. We don't want to set up a system in which students are destined to fail. Keep that in mind as you plan and prepare and then finalize the ways you are going to hold students accountable for their schoolwork, and thereby their learning. You had an opportunity to contemplate assessment issues as you explored the assessment A's in the CLEAR section of this book, but you need to make sure you have products to assess. How will you make sure that students follow through with their responsibilities? How will you help students to be responsible for their schoolwork?

Accountability
Options

# Managing Student Work

Emmer, Evertson, and Worsham (2000) in their research on effective classroom managers discovered that teachers whose classes ran smoothly had in place accountability procedures for managing students' work (also Evertson, Emmer, and Worsham, 2000). You need to do some planning and preparing in these areas:

> ➤ What standards will you set to guide students in succeeding?
> ➤ How will you post assignments?
> ➤ How will you collect and hand back student work?
> ➤ How will you keep track of completed assignments?
> ➤ How will you and the students keep track of work in progress?
> ➤ How will students make up missing work?
> ➤ How will absent students know about assignments?
> ➤ How will you give feedback to the students?
> ➤ How will your students self-manage?

> **FROM RESEARCH**
> Positive strategies, such as instruction for success, student decision making, and acceptance, are important to use in order to be effective with behavior disordered students.
>
> —*Rockwell (1993)*

## *What standards will you set to guide students in succeeding?*

You need to be clear about what expectations you have for the students' work. You need to communicate specifically what your standards are. Your standards let students know how well things need to be done. What parameters will you establish as to how you want their assignments done? Setting standards does not mean that you will not allow for individual choices in the mode of the assignment. It is important that you do give students options, but being clear about your expectations within those predetermined options sets the standard for what is successful work in your classroom.

## *How will you post assignments?*

You need to have some visual back-up for students to be able to remember and follow the assignments. Will you post the assignments on the board or in a special place in the room? Will you have students record the assignments in a certain place—a notebook or assignment sheet? Will you use the overhead to post or demonstrate assignments? Will you have the assignments posted on a web site or on a spreadsheet that students have access to through a computer in your classroom or possibly from their home computers?

## How will you collect and hand back student work?

You need to have a system for collecting and handing back student work. What system will you use to collect student work? Will you have certain bins for particular assignments or subjects or periods in the room? Will each student have a place that she hands in work? Will you have a student from each group or row who will collect assignments? Will you have student numbers to identify work and use numbered folders to put work in and hand it back? Will the students have special places (bins or mailboxes) in the room to pick up scored assignments? Will you use students to pass out scored papers to members of their group?

## How will you keep track of completed assignments?

You need to be able to keep track of students' assignment completion. Will you have a color-coded system for various groups or periods? Will you record all assignments in your grade book or just selected ones? Will you have a class check-off sheet for assignments? Will you have students correct their mistakes? Will you keep track of corrected assignments?

## How will you and the students keep track of work in progress?

When students are working on longer assignments you need to have a way to check on the progress they are making. Will you have different points at which they will hand in the work for feedback? Will you have a system where they self-monitor their progress toward completion? Will you have them meet with an assignment buddy to report on progress? It is a good idea to break an assignment that goes over a long period of time into smaller chunks or certain stages of the project that students can get feedback on as they continue to work on the bigger picture. This can help keep them on track.

## How will students make up missing work?

You need to decide what you will do about missed assignments. How long will the students have to make them up? Will there be points off for being late? Will you have a specific place to hand in make-up work? Will you put the students in charge of keeping track? Will you modify assignments for students who have trouble keeping up? Will you schedule a catch-up time within class? Will you send work home to make up missing assignments?

### How will absent students know about assignments?

You will need to decide how you will get information about missed work to absent students. Will you have a notebook where each day's assignments are recorded so absent students can check it when they come back? Will you have an assignment buddy for each student or an assignment monitor for the class that will inform the absent student? Will you post assignments on a web site? Will you have a make-up folder that you keep, particularly, for young students?

### How will you give feedback to the students?

It is important that you give feedback as soon as possible to the students. What will be your system for grading each day's work and getting it back to students in a timely manner? Will you check some assignments as they are working on them? Will you have parents help with grading? Will you have students involved in grading? Will you have the students use different colored pens or a self-scoring station in the class to score their own paper or will you have them switch papers to score another's paper?

When you have students involved in scoring assignments, do not ever have them call out scores. Either collect them yourself to look at or have the students leave them on the corner of their desk while you go around and look at them. This practice of having students call out scores tends to be embarrassing for some and, unfortunately, that has resulted in some recent legal cases seeking to ban this public way of recording scores.

### Students scoring each others' papers

There has been a lot of national discussion, including some in the courts, about students switching papers for grading. The consensus is that it is alright to have students trading papers and scoring each other, if the assignment is in the initial stages of learning, when it is for practice of new material, and the scores are not going to be averaged into their grade for the class. You do not want to use this practice when it involves a score that will be averaged in the student's grade. The Supreme Court has recently decided that trading papers for grading purposes rather than just for practice and feedback violates students' right to privacy.

We recommend that you do not record scores that will be averaged into their grade in the initial stages of new learning. It is important that students have a chance to work with new learning, sort out what they know and don't know, and learn from their mistakes before scores become a part of their grade. It is a natural part of new learning to make mistakes, and you want this to be part of the feedback system for students.

Now, for those of you working with older students (from about fourth grade on), they will have a tendency to not do work if it doesn't "count." So work does need to count, even if you are not recording scores for the grades in the initial stages of new learning. It can count as a completed and "corrected" assignment, as a nominal point value, or even a pass/fail grade in the record book.

## *How will your students self-manage?*

Encouraging students to self-manage their own schoolwork is vastly better than your being in charge of monitoring all. You want students to take responsibility for themselves. Involving them in the decision-making process and having the students help to develop self-management strategies that will work for them is a good idea. Even younger students can have some ideas and input as to how they will self-monitor. Taking the time to teach students to manage themselves will be time well spent. Having students keep track of their scores on assignments and tests can help them become responsible for their own progress.

## *Many questions for you to answer*

As you can see, this section has raised a lot of questions for you to answer. There is not one right answer for every teacher. You need to think about these questions and answer them for yourself. You can discuss them with colleagues in class and with teachers in schools. You need to make sure your decisions are consistent with your school policies as well. Research shows that effective classroom managers answer these questions for themselves, but that they answer them in different ways (Emmer, Evertson, and Worsham, 2000). Find ways to involve your students in this decision-making process as well. Do come up with some initial answers for yourself while you are developing your management plan as you read this book. (See form on pages 302–303 in the appendix.)

# Simultaneous Response Modes

Another great strategy for students' accountability is to utilize simultaneous response modes. You get an immediate check as to whether or not students are learning the information. Choral responses, where all of the students answer in unison, are one option, but there are others modes as well. Using individual whiteboards where the students write down their answer and hold it up for you to visually see can be used with students of all ages who can write. Using whole class signals like thumbs up and thumbs down or other appropriate gestures are ways to keep all students involved and to give a quick check of understanding. You can have all students in a group write down their answers simultaneously and then show group members all at once. The goal is to focus the attention of the students on the lesson at hand.

## Summary for <u>A</u>ccountability Options

You *prevent problems* from developing when you hold students accountable for their schoolwork on an on-going basis. You *structure* things so they are geared *for student success.* In conjunction with the students, you establish *accountability procedures* designed to keep students on track with their schoolwork and so both you and the students can manage their assignments.

Accountability procedures need to be developed and clarified with the students in the first week of school. When the foundation is laid for prevention in the first week, many future problems are avoided. Research shows that when teachers devote ample time to prevention strategies in the first week, they are more effective classroom managers the rest of the school year (Emmer, Evertson, and Worsham, 2000).

You also incorporate *simultaneous response modes* that actively involve all students at the same time giving responses to questions in order to check their understanding of concepts on an on-going basis. All are accountable, including you. Keep in mind that the main purpose of <u>A</u>ccountability Options is to help in the process of developing *independent learners* in your classroom.

# <u>C</u>hoices

## Student Involvement in Curriculum Choices

Using PACE for Prevention

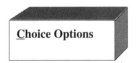

<u>C</u>hoice Options

Having students involved in appropriate curriculum choices is a great way to get students actively engaged in the learning process. Appropriate is an important word there. It would not be appropriate to have students decide if we were going to learn math or not. They just might decide "no." But we could have them decide how we will structure the math curriculum. With younger students they could decide if we are going to work on money before time or time before money. In other curriculum areas you could have older students decide which Shakespearean plays they are going to read or what specific historical figures will be researched. There are numerous ways in which students can be involved in curriculum decisions in an appropriate manner. You want to make sure that you are following your district curriculum, but find as many ways as you can to involve students.

William Glasser (1992 and 1993) emphasizes the importance of involving students in both curriculum decisions and assignment choices. He was one of the initiators of the Quality Schools movement which espouses that we need to be meeting students' basic needs in schools and delivering a quality curriculum to them. Glasser contends that schools that deliver unsatisfactory curriculum that has no relevance or usefulness are a major factor in the increase of discipline problems. Students must be actively involved in what we teach and how we teach it so we can solve discipline problems.

> *CC* Only a discipline program that is also concerned with classroom satisfaction will work. *))*
> —*Glasser*

## Structured Choices in Assignments

Giving students choices in how they do their assignments is another critical strategy for preventing classroom problems. When students have a choice of two or three ways in which they can do their assignments, they are much less apt to choose not to do their assignments. Assignment choices are also a valuable tool for engaging students in the assignment. Structured choices about how to do assignments give students an opportunity to make it relevant and interesting for themselves. Glasser and Dotson (1998) emphasize that students' having choice in classrooms is integral to meeting their needs and having school be a satisfying place to be. Students are more likely to learn when school is a satisfying place to be. Glasser hypothesizes that a majority of our students, particularly older ones, are not learning because schools are not satisfying places for them to be. The lack of relevance or connections with the students' interests are major factors.

Structured choices in assignments can vary according to your teaching style and the needs of the content, but having choices does pull students into the learning. You might have two or three modalities in which the assignment could be completed—could it be written out or acted out or built? Being creative to engage students and have them learn from the activity is the important issue.

More and more teachers are using Gardner's (1983) multiple intelligences as a tool for giving students options about assignments. Kagan and Kagan (1998) have created a great resource for teachers to design assignments and activities that appeal to the eight multiple intelligences developed by Gardner. Their book

> Academic success is reached by matching instruction to students' multiple intelligences. Development of intelligences is reached through stretching students' multiple intelligences. Asking not how smart we are, but how we are smart celebrates students' diversity in multiple intelligences.
> —*Kagan and Kagan (1998)*

connects Kagan Cooperative Learning structures with teaching to each of the eight multiple intelligences:

- Verbal/linguistic intelligence
- Math/logical intelligence
- Visual/spatial intelligence
- Musical/rhythmic intelligence
- Bodily/kinesthetic intelligence
- Interpersonal intelligence
- Intrapersonal intelligence
- Naturalistic intelligence

Here are some examples of various classroom activities that connect with each of the multiple intelligences. This can spark your thinking about how you can incorporate multiple intelligences into structured assignment choices or just give students more than one choice as to how an assignment is enacted.

**Verbal/Linguistic Intelligence**
- Write a poem or a play
- Create a story
- Write about a topic
- Discuss a book
- Conduct a debate

**Math/Logical Intelligence**
- Measure distances
- Compute a statistical analysis
- Estimate probability
- Solve story problems
- Input data into a spreadsheet

**Visual/Spatial Intelligence**
- Create different kinds of maps for the same place
- Make a sculpture
- Make a map
- Draw a picture
- Illustrate someone else's story

**Musical/Rhythmic Intelligence**
➢ Compose a tune
➢ Compose a piano piece
➢ Create new words for a familiar song
➢ Create a drum beat
➢ Listen to music of cultures

**Bodily/Kinesthetic Intelligence**
➢ Role play a character from history
➢ Perform a play
➢ Create a dance
➢ Make up a sport
➢ Create movements for a song

**Interpersonal Intelligence**
➢ Work on a team project
➢ Present with a partner
➢ Write a group report
➢ Share articles in a group
➢ Interview someone else

**Intrapersonal Intelligence**
➢ Reflect about milestones in your life
➢ Record journal entries
➢ Describe your feelings about injustice
➢ Write an autobiography
➢ Record your feelings for a week

**Naturalistic Intelligence**
➢ Observe things in nature
➢ Take a field trip in the country
➢ Watch videos about nature
➢ Classify animals
➢ Sort rocks and minerals

> **FROM RESEARCH**
> High school students were engaged and highly motivated and learned complex content when they were given choices about how they wanted to complete their work. Their opportunity for self-expression within the assignments was a key factor.
>
> —*Geocaris (1996/1997)*

## Summary for Choices

Finding ways to give students *choices* within the *curriculum* or as to *how they implement their assignments* not only hooks them into the learning process, but they are also great strategies to prevent classroom problems. The exact way you would implement these would vary according to grade level, teacher style, and content, but we encourage you to design your own ideas that will fit for you as to how you will allow curriculum and assignment choices to *motivate students.*

# Environmental Options: Introduction

## Conducive Classroom Climate

Using PACE for Prevention

Proactive Options

Accountability Options

Choice Options

Environmental Options

Creating a classroom climate that is conducive to learning is an essential preventive strategy. Establishing an environment where learning can take place takes planning and preparation. It is most effective when students are actively involved in the process of creating it. An environment that supports learning is introduced in this chapter and then delineated in detail in chapter 9.

You should take an opportunity to think in depth about your options related to classroom rules or code of conduct and classroom procedures. Your rules or code of conduct encompasses what are acceptable and unacceptable behaviors in your class, whereas procedures relate to the activities that go on in the classroom (how to do everyday tasks). "This is how we do things in this class" is what procedures are all about. Typical procedures spell out: how we come into the room and leave; how we get a drink; how we sharpen pencils; how we pass out papers, and so forth. You will also get to do some planning related to how you will arrange your classroom and use that arrangement to prevent problems by "working" the room.

Environmental Options

Many aspects of establishing a class climate—creating a class where everyone wants to be—will be explored in Section V, the supportive component, as those are the supportive aspects of classroom climate.

## Pre-planned

Even though the recommendation is to establish the environment with the students and have them give very real input into its creation, it is still important that you do a lot of pre-thinking before you enter the classroom and work on the environment with the students. You need to make a choice as to what you can live with and not live with in classroom behavior choices. Student involvement is crucial, but you need to guide the process and be the ultimate authority as to what will be compatible with creating an environment conducive to learning. So doing some pre-thinking as to what you would and would not be comfortable with is necessary. You also need to think about what procedures you want in your classroom and what your parameters are so that you can share that information when you involve the students.

> **FROM RESEARCH**
> Good climate, defined as an environment that fosters student learning, is actually synonymous with good discipline.
> —*Baker (1985)*

## Constructed jointly, adopted, and taught

For the environment to really work, it needs to be a collaborative effort. You need the students to cooperate with you in establishing an environment conducive to learning. Without their assisting in that endeavor your efforts may not be as effective. You need to create an environment where the atmosphere is: "This is our classroom and we all need to work together to make it a place where everyone can enjoy teaching and learning." The next step is to adopt the rules or code of conduct and the classroom procedures, so we have all agreed to them. Then it is important to teach the rules and procedures to the students. Even with older students you cannot assume that they will know what it means to abide by the agreed-upon rules or how to enact the classroom procedures. You need to clarify it through the teaching process, just as you would teach any of the classroom content you wanted them to know. The implementation of Environmental Options will be addressed in chapter 9.

> **Rules:**
> Do's and don'ts for the classroom.

> **Procedures:**
> How to do activities in your classroom.

**SETTING THE PACE**

**P**roactive Options
**A**ccountability Options
**C**hoice Options
**E**nvironmental Options

# Summary for PACE

You need to set the *PACE* in your classroom through utilizing *Proactive Options, Accountability Options, Choice Options,* and *Environmental Options.* **P**roactive Options implies that you are *planning and preparing* to prevent problems. You also use *preventive lesson management* strategies originated by Kounin so you can develop *"withitness."* It is important that you *clarify expectations of all* with the students. The **A**ccountability Options emphasize *structuring for student success, managing student work,* and utilizing *simultaneous response modes.* **C**hoice Options focus on actively involving students in *curriculum choices* and giving *structured choices in assignments.* **E**nvironment Options help you to create a *classroom climate conducive* to learning. Your environment is *pre-planned, constructed jointly* with the students, then *adopted* and *taught.*

# Reflection Questions

1. How is effective teaching linked with preventive classroom management?
2. What would "withitness" look like in your classroom?
3. How does communicating your expectations of student behavior affect your students?
4. Give examples of how you will hold students accountable for their work and their classroom responses by creating your accountability procedures (see form in appendix).
5. Brainstorm ways in which you can give students structured choices in their assignments.
6. How does structuring the classroom environment affect student behaviors?

# References

Baker, K. (1985). Research evidence of a school discipline problem. *Phi Delta Kappan* 66 (7): 482–487.

Bender, W., & Golden, L. (1989). Prediction of adaptive behavior of learning disabled students in self-contained and resource classes. *Learning Disabilities Research* 5 (1): 45–50.

Egeland, P. (1996-1997). Pulleys, planes, and student performance. *Educational Leadership* 54 (4): 41–45.

Emmer, E. T., Evertson, C. M., & Worsham, M. E. (2000). *Classroom management for secondary teachers.* Boston: Allyn & Bacon.

Evertson, C. M., Emmer, E. T., & Worsham, M. E. (2000). *Classroom management for elementary teachers.* Boston: Allyn & Bacon.

Gardner, H. (1983). *Frames of mind: The theory of multiple intelligences.* New York: Harper and Row.

Geocaris, C. (1996–1997). Increasing student engagement: A mystery solved. *Educational Leadership* 54 (4): 72–75.

Glasser, W. (1992). *The quality school.* New York: HarperPerennial.

———. (1993). *The quality school teacher.* New York: HarperPerennial.

Glasser, W., & Dotson, K. (1998). *Choice theory in the classroom.* New York: HarperCollins.

Kagan, S., & Kagan, M. (1998). *Multiple intelligences.* San Clemente, CA: Kagan Publishing.

Kounin, J. (1977). *Discipline and group management in classrooms,* Revised edition. New York: Holt, Rinehart, & Winston.

Proctor. (1984). Teacher expectations: A model for school improvement. *The Elementary School Journal* 84 (4): 469–481.

Rockwell, S. (1993). *Tough to reach, tough to teach: Students with behavior problems.* Reston, VA: Council for Exceptional Students.

Rosenthal, R., & Jacobson, L. (1968). *Pygmalion in the Classroom.* New York: Holt, Rinehart, & Winston.

Rosenthal, R. (1995). Critiquing Pygmalion: A 25-year perspective. *Current Directions in Psychological Science* 4: 171–172.

Shockley, R., & Sevier, L. (1991). Behavior management in the classroom: Guidelines for maintaining control. *Schools in the Middle* 1 (12): 14–18.

Wang, M., Haertel, D., & Walberg, L. (1994). What makes children learn? *Educational Leadership* 51 (4): 74–79.

# Environmental Options: Implementation

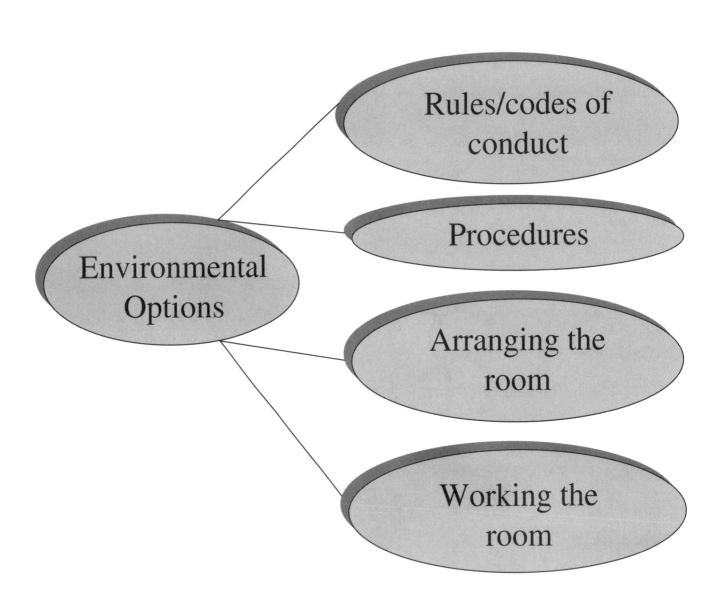

**OBJECTIVES**

The learners will be able to:

- Describe strategies to prevent problems in their classroom through pre-planning and establishing in the first week of school the rules and procedures needed to avoid problems.
- Explain factors to consider in arranging the room in a way that facilitates teaching, management, and working the room.

**Proactive Options**

**Accountability Options**

**Choice Options**

**Environmental Options**

**CHAPTER SNAPSHOT**

- Rules or Code of Conduct
- Environmental Options— Activity Procedures
- Arranging the Room
- *Evertson, Emmer, and Worsham's Approach*
- Working the Room

# Rules or Code of Conduct

**Environmental Options**

Your rules or code of conduct are implemented on the first day of school. You want to establish with the students from the very start the parameters needed, so teachers and students can all have a classroom conducive to learning. Involving the students in creating the rules or the code of conduct on that first day helps to make it "our classroom" and creates student ownership of the rules. A code of conduct is a variation of rules, which are phrased in the "I will" or "We will" form, in order to emphasize individual or class agreement and commitment to the class rules.

**FROM RESEARCH**
Student involvement in classroom rules is more than a useful management tool. It is a valuable way to help students understand and gain meaning from daily living, thereby impacting their life decision-making skills.

—*Boostrom (1991)*

**FROM RESEARCH**
There is a significant difference in student achievement, on-task behavior, and amount of disruptive behavior for good classroom management practices versus poor management practices.

—*Evertson and Emmer (1990)*

# Pre-Thinking and Pre-Planning

As stated in the previous chapter, you need to do some pre-thinking about your rules, so you are clear as to what you can live with and what you cannot. Since it is ultimately your responsibility to create an environment conducive to learning, you need to guide the rule creation process as it unfolds. Pre-thinking and pre-planning prepare you to do that. If there is a suggestion made by a student that you aren't comfortable with, then you are ready through your pre-thinking to process the student-generated suggestion with the class and give your rationale for not including it. Involving students in the creation of your rules or code of conduct does not entail accepting any rule they offer, just that you consider and discuss all responsible suggestions made by the students. If they suggest something that you can't live with or are uncomfortable with, you say so, but share with the students the reason. I emphasize during this process my responsibility as teacher to create a positive learning environment. I want them to be part of that process, but I need to make sure that it happens. Your pre-thinking and pre-planning prepare you to know what is negotiable with the students and what is non-negotiable. Keep in mind as you are preparing that the rules need to apply to you as well as the students.

# Getting Started

On the first day I usually start by saying something like, "This is our classroom and we all need to work together to make it a place where we can all enjoy teaching and learning. Would you be willing to help with that?"

You can change the words to suit your style or grade level, but do plan what you want to say to get the process started. Various teachers proceed differently at this point. You could have students think about:

> What would make this classroom a good place to learn?
> What rules do you think are important for a class to have?
> What choices do responsible students make?
> What agreements should the class make?
> What would a pleasant class be like?
> What would this class need to be like so everyone can learn?

You can structure this conversation any way that makes sense to you. Some teachers start with the whole class discussing. Others like to have the students meet in small groups first to do some pre-thinking. Others like giving the students an opportunity for individual reflection before the whole group discussion.

When we are discussing rules as a whole group, I like getting all of the students' ideas recorded on the board, chart paper, or overhead. Then we do some fine-tuning to come up with the actual rules or code of conduct for the class. What involvement will your students have in creating the rules? The level of involvement is a judgment call on your part.

# Guidelines for Creating Rules

Different teachers make very different choices about their rules and how they are worded. Elementary rules are often a little different from secondary ones. Rules have different names in different classes: code of conduct ("I will"; "we will"; or "we agree" format), class policies, class guidelines, class agreements, class charter, class expectations, or class constitution. As you work with the students to develop the rules, make them fit for you and your class. There is no one right way to design your rules, but some guidelines to consider when creating the rules are:

- ➢ Three to Eight Rules
- ➢ Focus on the Positive
- ➢ Understandable, Reasonable, and Attainable
- ➢ Posted in Classroom
- ➢ Student Involvement
- ➢ Consistent with School Rules
- ➢ Rules Should Support Effective Learning Principles

# Three to Eight Rules

The rationale for narrowing your rules to three to eight is that memory research says that our minds cannot hold too many bits of information at a time. If we have too many rules, some tend to slip away from our memories. Many specific behaviors will pertain to each rule. In whatever way you choose to phrase your rules, for example, "Respect Others," you will need to process with the students what behaviors are examples of following that rule and what are examples of not following that rule. Your rules will not address every specific behavior, but rather be life principles of good character that need to be defined and processed with the students.

You would define rules differently at the secondary level than at the elementary level. You might actually have the students practice a rule. The older students still need to have discussions that define examples and non-examples of the rules.

## Focus on the Positive

There are a couple reasons for the recommendation that rules should be stated in a positive manner. One is that then the focus is on what behaviors we "want" rather than what we "don't want." We assume that if students agree not to do something, they will be able to automatically fill in what we would want them to do, but that isn't necessarily true. Making behavioral expectations clear and very concrete is important.

The second reason is that it avoids what I call the "loophole kid." This is the student we find standing on his desk and when we say something about it, his answer is, "Well, the rules don't say not to stand on your desk." If the rule was "Respect School Property," then not standing on one's desk would be a logical example of following that rule. Certain students will tend to look for the loopholes in negatively stated rules.

## Understandable, Reasonable, and Attainable

This guideline seems almost self-explanatory, but you would be surprised at how "Un-understandable" some classroom rules are and how "un-doable" some are. I knew a student teacher in a second grade classroom who had a rule: "No Talking," and she would get very upset every time there was the slightest infraction to the point where there was a tense atmosphere in the room and her voice had a caustic note to it. I remember her telling me that if she had had those students from the beginning of the school year, they would certainly be doing what she wanted, which was to never talk. I very nicely explained to her that if she had had all of those students from birth on, they still would not be able to "never talk." Her seven-year-olds needed avenues to express themselves in appropriate ways and needed talking to be a legitimate aspect of the learning. Her "No Talking" rule was unreasonable and unattainable for her second graders.

The rules need to have some sense or rationale to them and not just seem arbitrary. Take a moment to reflect on whether or not rules that you have created or are going to create with students are clear and something that can be enacted. Reflect also on whether it would feel reasonable for you to follow that rule.

# Posted in the Classroom

For both elementary and secondary schools, it is a good idea to have a visual back-up and reminder in a prominent place to help keep everyone on track. Since student input may vary from period to period, various secondary teachers handle this posting guideline differently. Some secondary teachers come up with a general synopsis of what was discussed in each period and post that. Other secondary teachers choose to specifically honor the thoughts of each period and post rules agreed upon for each period. Do what seems best to you.

> **FROM RESEARCH**
> Student input into classroom rules and consequences is critical in order to give them a sense of ownership. This results in a commitment to responsible behavior even for difficult students.
> —*Curwin and Mendler (1997)*

# Student Involvement

We've discussed student involvement a lot already, but it is important enough for student buy-in to have "student involvement" listed here in the guidelines for creating rules. Just remember that you don't want the student involvement to be just perfunctory. You want it to be meaningful. Listen to students and their rationale for suggestions. In making your decisions about rules, have your guideline be "creating an environment conducive to learning." If a student's suggestion would interfere with that main goal of learning, then discuss that with the student. The bottom line as to why we have class rules is to establish an environment in which everyone in the classroom can enjoy teaching and learning. I am very up-front with students about that being the purpose, and we evaluate everything in light of that guideline.

# Consistent with School Rules

You need to make sure that your classroom rules are consistent with school rules. Every once in awhile, there is a school rule that I don't agree with. What I say to the students when that happens is: "I will be glad to take your input about the school rule to the faculty and work to bring about a change, but as long as that is a school rule, we will abide by it." It is tempting to undermine school rules you don't agree with, but this is not a good idea. It is better to use it as a learning opportunity for your students in that we can try to do something about it. As discussed in management styles, we want them to experience the democratic process through the ways we conduct our classes.

# Rules Should Support Effective Learning Principles

Think back to the CLEAR Model, particularly the Learners component. There are many documented learner differences including cultural, gender, learning style and preferences, cognitive style, mind style, personality style, and multiple intelligence strengths to name a few. Be careful that you do not make rules that might interfere with a student's learning. For example, a rule that prevents students from talking at all during seatwork may interfere with an auditory learner who needs to talk through a problem in order to solve it. The student needs to hear the problem in order for the mental processes to work effectively. The rule against talking during seat work effectively blocks the student from being able to think and learn.

When you develop your rules for your classroom with your students, consider your students' learning styles, cultural differences, social needs, and classroom communication structures.

# Examples of Typical Rules

Here are some examples of rules that are created in many classrooms. There is no one-size-fits-all when it comes to classroom rules or code of conduct. Do some pre-planning and pre-thinking about what you are comfortable with, but then create your rules with your students while you guide the process. The first seven examples could be used in an elementary or secondary classroom:

➢ Respect Yourself and Others
➢ Respect School Property
➢ Respect Others' Property
➢ Take Turns Talking
➢ Raise Your Hand to Talk
➢ Listen Quietly While Others Are Speaking
➢ Listen and Stay Seated During Whole Group Instruction
➢ Obey All School Rules

The next three examples are more typically found in secondary classrooms:

➢ Come Prepared and On Time
➢ Bring All Needed Materials to Class
➢ Be in Your Seat when the Bell Rings

All of those examples would work with slight modification to be restated in one of the code of conduct formats, such as "I will"; "We will"; or "We agree." For example:

- ➤ I will respect myself and others.
- ➤ We will listen quietly while others are speaking.
- ➤ We agree to listen and stay seated during whole group time.
- ➤ I will come prepared and on time.
- ➤ We will bring all needed materials to class.
- ➤ We agree to be in our seats when the bell rings.

## What If They Don't Cooperate?

Ninety-nine percent of the time students will cooperate in the rule creation process on the first day of school and make responsible suggestions. There is usually a "honeymoon period" at the very beginning of class, when even your more difficult students cooperate. That is one of the reasons that establishing your preventive component strategies in the first week is crucial. Just in case you get that one-tenth of 1 percent situation and the students are not cooperating in the rule creation process, let's discuss what you would do.

Anytime you are inviting the students to share in the decision-making process, you are offering to share classroom power with them. You need to make sure that they are participating responsibly in the process or you need to take the power back and decide yourself. You do it in such a way that you leave the door open to the students' having another opportunity to share in the decision-making process in a responsible way in the near future.

In the unlikely event that I was getting irresponsible or off-the-wall suggestions from the students during rule creation on the first day, I would say something like: "I think that it would be very productive for you to be part of the process of creating the rules in this class, but it is important that you take it seriously and give some responsible suggestions or I will need to decide for now." "For now" can vary from a short period of time to a longer one depending on your particular teaching situation. It just might be, for instance, in an inner-city school, that "for now" could last all semester. A teacher could re-negotiate rules at the beginning of the next semester after establishing the business-like classroom atmosphere, and after gaining the respect of the students. Later could be the next day for very young children.

Often students will respond positively to the choices I give them, but sometimes they continue with the irresponsible behaviors. In the case of continued misbehavior I would, in a very business-like, non-punitive manner, switch into my deciding about the rules "for now." Again the "for now" can be filled in with the amount of time that is appropriate to the situation. The more difficult the situation, the longer "for now" might be. Please use your teacher judgment based on your class.

If they then said, "We'll cooperate," in response to my deciding about the rules for today, I would say something like, "That's okay, your responsibility skills weren't in gear today, so I will decide for now. I'm sure that you will use your responsibility skills next week when we work on this again."

> **Encouraging Cooperation**
> ➤ Business-like tone
> ➤ Non-punitive focus
> ➤ Offer another opportunity to participate responsibly

It is most important that your students learn that you want them to be involved in the decision-making process in the classroom, but it is necessary that they take it seriously and participate responsibly or you will make the decisions for them. It is tempting to respond to their belated "We'll cooperate," by going ahead with involving them in creating the rules that day. What you really want, though, is for them to learn that in order for them to be part of the decision-making process, it is essential that they cooperate and participate responsibly. In order for this to be part of the process of teaching responsible behavior, the business-like tone and the non-punitive focus and the statement about trying again on another day are all important aspects. You also want to make sure that you come back to this and involve them on another day.

# **Environment Options—Activity Procedures**

The research of Emmer, Evertson, and Worsham (2000) also determined that effective classroom managers established classroom activity procedures in the first week of school with the students. Activity procedures encompass myriad examples of "this is how we do things in this class." The procedures that they found in place in the classrooms of effective managers were:

> ➤ Entering and leaving the room
> ➤ Beginning and ending the day or period
> ➤ Getting students' attention
> ➤ Student interaction
> ➤ Using areas of the room: drinking fountain, pencil sharpener, supply shelves, and centers

➤ Bathroom use
➤ Working individually and together
➤ Obtaining help
➤ What to do when finished
➤ Taking care of the room: class responsibilities
➤ Interruptions
➤ Missing materials
➤ Using areas of the school

# Entering and Leaving the Room

How will you have students come into the room? Will there be a line-up procedure for entering? Will there be something educational for students to work on when they first arrive, like bell work? How will you dismiss students when the day or the period is over? Will you dismiss them by rows or groups or some other criteria? Will they go as soon as the bell rings or will you be in charge of dismissing them?

# Beginning and Ending the Day or Period

What routine will you use to start the day or the period? Will you take roll or will students be in charge? Will you use cards or clips or magnets for them to move to indicate that they are present? Will you have assigned seats? How will you take lunch count? How will non-instructional tasks be kept as efficient as possible, so they do not detract from instructional time?

How will you get students ready to leave at the end of the day or period? Will there be a clean up or get ready warning? What tasks will you have students perform at the end? How will you keep transition time as short as possible?

# Getting Students' Attention

How will you get students focused for whole group instruction or discussion? Will you use a hand signal, an auditory signal or a light signal? Will you vary the signal? Which of those signals will you use to get the students refocused, if their attention strays?

**Hand Signals That Teachers Use Include:**
➤ The "Give Me Five" in which you raise your hand and the students all give your signal back and, of course, focus for whole group instruction at the same time
➤ Holding your hand out in a way that signals stop

➢ Utilizing sign language in various ways
➢ Putting a finger to the mouth indicating "shhhhh"
➢ Holding up a stop watch

**Auditory Signals That Teachers Use Include:**
➢ Chimes, bells, or other instruments
➢ Train or bird whistles (no playground whistles)
➢ Duplicating a clapping sequence
➢ Saying, "If you hear my voice, clap once. If you can hear my voice, clap twice, etc.
➢ Playing a piece of music
➢ Counting down
➢ Chinese gong

**Light Signals That Teachers Use Include:**
➢ Flicking the classroom lights (occasionally as a signal for whole group focus; don't overuse)
➢ Traffic light with green light for go, yellow for caution, and red for stop

# Student Interaction

Will students be able to talk during work time? What will the criteria be, if they are allowed to? Will there be times when there is no talking? How will students know the difference? Will you use a visual signal or possibly signs in the front of the room to indicate when it is okay to talk and when it is not? How will you describe the appropriate noise level? Would you call it inside voices, one-foot voices, whisper voices, or small group voices? How will you monitor the noise level?

# Using Areas of the Room: Drinking Fountain, Pencil Sharpener, Supply Shelves, and Centers

Will the students be able to use the drinking fountain, pencil sharpener, supply shelves, and centers whenever they want or will it be a one-at-a-time procedure? Would it be a one-student-using plus one-student-waiting procedure? Would they not be allowed access during whole group instructional time?

Will you have sharpened pencils for the students to borrow? Will supply shelves that are available for use be marked? Will centers be available when students have finished assignments or only when they are actually assigned to go to them?

# Bathroom Use

Will students be able to use the bathroom when they want or will it be regulated? Will there be bathroom passes? How many passes will you have? How will students use the passes? What will you do about students who abuse the bathroom privilege by disappearing for long periods?

# Working Individually and Together

How will students know when it is all right to work together and when they need to work individually? Will you have signs or signals to make it clear which is appropriate at different times?

# Obtaining Help

How will students get help when they need it? Will you have a sign up sheet or use a signal like a book turned on its end on their desk, so they can get help without holding their hand in the air for a long period? Will you have them ask three peers before asking you a question—3B4Me?

# What to Do When Finished

What choices will students have when they are finished with their work? Will they have books to read, centers, extension activities, be able to work on homework? How will you communicate to the students what their choices are?

# Taking Care of the Room: Class Responsibilities

What classroom jobs will you have? How will you assign them? Will they rotate? What tasks in the classroom will you turn over to students to free you up for more teaching?

# Interruptions

What will you tell students to do when there are interruptions from the intercom or visitors to the classroom? How will you deal with a student who interrupts you during class or while you are working with another student?

## Missing Materials

What will happen when students forget materials? They don't have a book needed or a pencil or paper. Will there be materials ready for that situation that can be borrowed? Will there be a consequence for borrowing?

## Using Areas of the School

Under what conditions will the students be permitted to go to the library, music class, study hall, or the office? Will you have passes? Can they go anytime or only at certain times?

## Your Answers About Activity Procedures

There are many questions for you to answer about "how we do things in our class." The questions direct you towards various choices other teachers have made. There is no one way that is best to design your procedures. It is again important that you do some pre-thinking and pre-planning. Then develop your classroom activity procedures with your students. Research demonstrates that teachers who have clearly defined activity procedures and address them in the first week of school prevent many problems from occurring and have smoother running classes. Please put some thought into these procedure questions. (See form in the appendix.) Use your colleagues in class and teachers in schools as your resources for ideas and feedback on your plans. *First Days of School* (Wong, 1991) is also an excellent source to help both new and experienced teachers with getting ready for the first week of school.

# Arranging the Room

**V**isibility
**A**ccountability
**C**ommunicability
**U**nderstandability
**U**sability
**M**ovability

You also need to put some pre-thinking and pre-planning into how you will arrange your classroom. A workable room arrangement prevents classroom problems. There is no perfect way to arrange a class, but there are "6 Abilities" to keep in mind when you are deciding how your room will be arranged. Does your room arrangement have the "ability" to meet the needs of learning? You want the **VACUUM of the 6 "Abilities" of Room Arrangement** to help you use your space effectively, so it will enhance your instruction and not detract from it.

**6 "Abilities" of Room Arrangement:**
- ➢ **V**isibility
- ➢ **A**ccountability
- ➢ **C**ommunicability
- ➢ **U**nderstandability
- ➢ **U**sability
- ➢ **M**ovability

## Visibility

You need to consider if visibility is facilitated for all students. Can they all see the board and the overhead? Are the students all visible to you so that you can see them and visually scan what they are doing?

## Accountability

You need to consider whether your room arrangement allows you access to all the students to hold them accountable for their schoolwork. Does your room arrangement allow you to easily monitor all of the students' schoolwork?

## Communicability

Does the room arrangement allow for good communication between teacher and students and among students in groups when communication is appropriate?

## Understandability

What message does your room give to others about what your class is like? Your room arrangement gives information about your teaching style and your classroom climate. Is your room arrangement giving a message consistent with what you want it to say about what it is like to learn in your class? Is your room giving the message you want it to give? Is the seating open? Closed? Collaborative? Individualized?

## Usability

You need to consider if areas and supplies that the students will need to use are accessible to them. Can they get to the supply shelves, the pencil sharpener, and the drinking fountain? Are areas you need to use accessible for you?

# EVERTSON, EMMER, AND WORSHAM'S APPROACH

## Assumptions
- Effective classroom management prevents problems.
- "Good management is based on students' understanding of what is expected of them."
- Classroom managers who are effective organize and design the class ahead of time and in the first week of school so expectations are clear.

## Main Points
- A carefully planned system of rules and procedures is the best way to communicate expectations.
- Both rules and procedures encompass your expectations concerning behavior.
- Rules focus on general expectations or standards of behavior.
- Procedures apply to specific activities aimed at accomplishing something rather than stopping something, such as collecting assignments, using the restroom, sharpening pencils, and coming into the room.
- Student involvement in creating rules encourages them to take more responsibility for their behavior.
- Accountability procedures are focused on managing student work, such as communicating assignments, monitoring student progress, and providing student feedback.
- Encouraging student self-monitoring and student self-evaluation and reflection is also important.

## Implementation
- It is important to implement and teach your rules and procedures during the first day/week. You teach your rules and procedures the same way as classroom lessons. It is important to get off to a good start. There is significant difference in student achievement, on-task behavior, and amount of disruptive behavior for good classroom and management practices versus poor management practices.

## Limitation
- Mainly prevention strategies—does not have an extensive focus on corrective strategies. Effective management does not stop.

*Movability*

You need to consider whether it is possible to move about the room easily. Can you walk near all of the desks? Can the students move around and get to one another? Can the students work in groups or individually if needed? If there is an emergency that requires evacuation, does your room set-up facilitate quick and safe exit?

## Room Arrangement Answers

Whether you currently have a classroom to examine or whether you are thinking about your future classroom, make sure that you consider the **"6 Abilities" of Room Arrangement**. Is your room organized in such a way that **V**isibility, **A**ccountability, **C**ommunicability, **U**nderstandability, **U**sability, and **M**ovability issues are addressed? What changes or adaptations can you make, if needed? Your classroom needs to have the "abilities" to facilitate learning.

# <u>W</u>orking the Room

A great, but simple and easy to use prevention strategy is one called "working the room." Fred Jones (1987) in *Positive Classroom Discipline* emphasizes this strategy. "Working the room" entails putting proximity to good use in your classroom on an on-going basis as a valuable prevention tool. To "work the room" you move around interacting with students and monitoring what they are doing. The more you use proximity in this way the more on top of the situation you will be—the more "withitness" you will have.

Using PACE for Prevention

Proactive Options

Accountability Options

Choice Options

Environmental Options

Sometimes teachers like to stick to the front of the room, because they think that is where they belong. They also might be glued to the front because they use the overhead a lot. Actually the more you move around the room, the better. Jones recommends that you circulate around the room in such a way that you are never more than two desks away from students in the path that you follow. His recommendation needs to be considered as you work on your room arrangement.

The power of proximity cannot be underestimated. Even if you use the overhead a lot, figure out how you can move in between changing overheads or writing on them, so that your proximity to the students will serve to prevent problems from occurring.

# Summary

To implement your *Environmental Options* you need to establish with the students *your rules or code of conduct* that focus on what are acceptable and unacceptable behaviors in this class. You also set the stage for preventing problems by developing *activity procedures* that delineate "this is how we do things in this class." *Student involvement* in rule and procedure creation is important so that they will have ownership of the environment. When you *arrange the room* you want to consider the *6 "Abilities" of Room Arrangement—Visibility, Accountability, Communicability, Usability, Understandability,* and *Movability. Working the room* entails using *proximity* as a valuable prevention strategy, so you are *monitoring* the students on an on-going basis.

# Reflection Questions

1. Create your list of rules or code of conduct for your classroom.
2. Discuss options for your classroom activity procedures. Develop a list for use in your classroom.
3. Draw a floor plan implementing the 6 "Abilities" of Room Arrangement.
4. Describe how you would use the power of proximity as a preventive tool.

# References

Boostrom, R. (1991). The nature and functions of classroom rules. *Curriculum Inquiry* 21 (2): 193–216.

Castle, K., & Rogers, K. (1994). Rule-creating in a constructivist classroom community. *Childhood Education* 70 (2): 77–80.

Curwin, R., & Mendler, A. (1997). *As tough as necessary.* Alexandria, VA: Association for Supervision and Curriculum Development.

Emmer, E. T., Evertson, C. M., & Worsham, M. E. (2000). *Classroom management for secondary teachers.* Boston: Allyn & Bacon.

Jones, F. H. (1987). *Positive classroom discipline.* New York: McGraw-Hill.

Wong, H., & Wong, R. (1991). *First days of school.* Sunnyvale, CA: Harry K. Wong Publications.

Using PACE for Prevention

Proactive Options

Accountability Options

Choice Options

Environmental Options

# Section Four

# Corrective Component

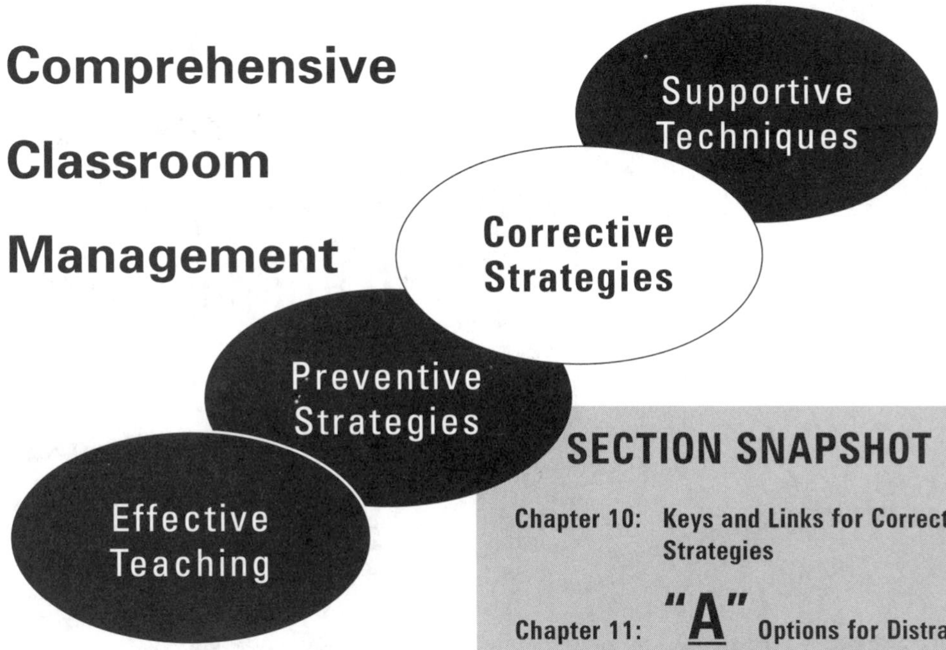

**Comprehensive**

**Classroom**

**Management**

Supportive
Techniques

Corrective
Strategies

Preventive
Strategies

Effective
Teaching

# Keys and Links for Corrective Strategies

Teacher attitude

Modeling self-management

Student factors

Keys and Links

Perspectives on power

Levels of misbehavior

## OBJECTIVES

The learners will be able to describe "how" to implement corrective strategies and "with whom" to use various strategies for the moment of misbehavior.

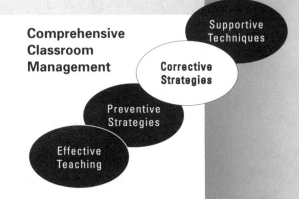

Comprehensive Classroom Management

Supportive Techniques

Corrective Strategies

Preventive Strategies

Effective Teaching

In this section we are going to focus on those all-important strategies for the moment of misbehavior. Chapter 10 will provide the global view. Chapters 11, 12, and 13 will encompass specific explanations and examples. We will address, "What do I do right now while this student is acting up?" Having a variety of practical strategies to deal with misbehavior helps you to feel confident that you are equipped to handle whatever happens. That is what this corrective section is all about—helping you feel confident that you are prepared. The more you are implementing effective teaching principles and preventive strategies, though, the less corrective action you will need to take. Being ready with the corrective interventions for the moment of misbehavior in conjunction with effective teaching and preventive strategies will help you be even more successful in your classroom. You will also need to pay close attention to the strategies in section V from the supportive component, as those strategies are critical to encouraging, supporting, and teaching responsible behavior to students.

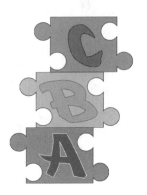

As important as it is to have practical corrective interventions when misbehavior occurs, without the strategies from the other three components, you would be stuck in an endless cycle of trying to put out one classroom fire after another. You need strategies from the other components to have more long-lasting solutions. Corrective strategies are short-term solutions only, designed to deal with the immediate situation. Corrective strategies are definitely needed, but they have limited value, if not used in combination with the other three components. We want you to have a complete management plan that will help you to enjoy teaching and your students to enjoy learning.

Several factors will impact your enjoyment of teaching and your students' enjoyment of learning. Your attitude toward the misbehaving students that you work with will affect whether the outcome is successful or not. Your ability to control your reactions when dealing with misbehavior, modeling self-management, has a great influence. Your consideration of which factors are affecting your students when they choose misbehavior, so the discipline strategies you use can also help meet students' underlying needs, is another crucial aspect. Your realization that power has more effectiveness when shared is another element. The last factor is recognizing that there are various levels of misbehavior and that you will be most successful when you match your strategies to the level of seriousness.

# Teacher's Attitude

Several of the Responsibility Model discipline approaches highlighted in this book are built on the premise that students can and do make choices about their behavior.

*—Dreikurs et al. (1982), Dreikurs and Cassell (1972), Glasser (1986), Albert et al. (1996), Nelsen (1987), Kyle, Kagan, and Scott in Charles, 2002)*

It is crucial that you approach all students you work with as though they have the ability to learn responsible behavior. Sometimes the field of psychology would have us think that our students are merely victims of what they were born with or victims of what they grew up with. The old nature vs. nurture argument (whether we are more determined by our genetic heredity or by the environment in which we are brought up) implies that our actions are driven by factors outside of our control. Actually the students we work with are greatly impacted by what they received through their genes at birth and by the kind of treatment they received as they were growing up, but despite being influenced by those factors we all have choices about our behavior. Dreikurs and his collaborators emphasized that your students choose their own behaviors (Dreikurs, Grunwald, and Pepper, 1982; Dreikurs and Cassell, 1972). We cannot choose what happens to us, but we can make choices about our reaction to what happens. Making responsible behavior choices is not necessarily easy, but we can develop the ability to do so. You need to go into your classroom with the attitude that every student can learn responsible behavior.

# Classroom Evidence

We'd like to point out to you some classroom evidence in the form of a scenario in which students do make choices about their behavior. Picture a student who behaves responsibly in one class, but then walks across the hall and behaves atrociously in another class. Can you imagine a student doing that? Do you know one? Perhaps it is you? Did that student's DNA change as she crossed the hall and cause the poor behavior in the second class? Did the negative effects of his or her homelife change to create the obnoxious behavior in the second class? No—the student was able to behave responsibly in the first class and neither of those nature vs. nurture factors changed as the student walked across the hall into the second classroom. What, then, did make the difference?

Did you think of the teacher, or the subject taught, or the peers, or whether that student thought she could not succeed in the second class as possible explanations? Any of those could have been the reason. If students can make different choices in different classes depending on what is happening in that class, then you have a lot more control over student behavior choices in your classroom than it might first appear. Students do make choices about their behavior based on what is happening in the class they are in. This is good news for teachers. Our students are not just puppets of fate with birth or circumstances pulling all the strings. They can learn responsible behavior and we can create a class that fosters that outcome.

> **"** Students need encouragement like plants need water. **"**
> —*Dreikurs et al. (1982)*

You can greatly influence the behavior choices your students make through the effective teaching strategies you use, combined with implementing prevention strategies and with creating an encouraging, supportive classroom climate. The next piece in the puzzle is to draw on practical corrective intervention strategies when students do misbehave. You implement corrective strategies that will hold students responsible for their poor behavior choices, but in a manner that maintains the students' dignity, so they can learn from their mistakes and be more likely to choose responsible behavior in the future. The "**way**" that you use corrective strategies for the moment of misbehavior is a critical piece of the puzzle. It is not just knowing lots of strategies that is crucial, but "**how**" you implement them.

# DREIKURS' APPROACH

## Assumptions

➤ Students can choose their behavior. One of the main jobs of the teacher is to help the students develop social interest, so they will be motivated to choose socially useful behavior and make a contribution to the classroom and to life in general.

➤ Encouragement is essential. Students need encouragement like plants need water.

➤ Teachers need to have a democratic, or collaborative, discipline style in order for discipline to flourish. Effective discipline does not work in an autocratic or permissive classroom.

## Main Points

➤ Students need to feel as if they belong in the classroom.

➤ When students do not feel as if they belong, they will misbehave to fulfill one of four mistaken goals: attention, power, revenge, or display of inadequacy.

➤ Students with a goal of misbehavior that is attention-seeking want everyone involved with them. Those students would benefit from more attention for their responsible behavior choices.

➤ Students with a goal of misbehavior that is power-seeking want to be the boss. Those students would benefit from some legitimate avenues for control in the classroom.

➤ Students with a goal of misbehavior that is revenge-seeking want to get even with others. Those students would benefit from learning to deal with their hurt feelings in more socially constructive ways.

➤ Students with a goal of misbehavior that is a display of inadequacy do not want others to know that they can't. Those students would benefit from lots of encouragement to know that they can do it.

➤ Teachers can help students to identify their own goal of the misbehavior, so they can find solutions with questions like: Could it be that you want some more attention? Could it be that you want to be the boss? Could it be that you want to get even with others? Could it be you don't want others to know that you can't do it?

**DREIKURS' APPROACH** (continued)

➢ Logical consequences should always be used instead of punishment.
➢ Classroom meetings are a vital strategy to practice democracy in the classroom and help students to feel that they belong.

**Implementation**
➢ Class meetings would be used to involve students in the decision-making process in the classroom. Rules would be created together and logical consequences established that connect with the rules. Encouragement strategies would be used frequently to help all students feel as if they were an important part of the class and could succeed.

**Limitation**
➢ Teachers sometimes find it hard to implement.

# Modeling Self-Management

Respectful, business-like interaction with students even when they are misbehaving is the missing puzzle piece. Is this easy? No. You are a human being and have emotional reactions when students misbehave. It is normal and human for you to experience some angry feelings inside when you have a controlling student battling you for power in the classroom. It is not appropriate, though, for you to act from that anger or spread that anger around in your class. You have a professional responsibility to get that anger under control and respond in a respectful, business-like manner despite how you are feeling inside. You need to do so not only because it is the right thing to do, but also because it is critical if you want students to respond to your strategies, learn from their mistakes, and make better choices in the future. Modeling self-management is an essential aspect of the "**how**" in delivering corrective strategies.

It is not easy to get your emotional reaction under control and respond in a respectful, business-like manner when students are misbehaving. If it was easy, we could end this book now and all go home. It can be done and it can be learned and that is what this corrective component is designed to teach you. It is essential that you learn to model self-management, not only so your immediate strategy will be effective, but also because students learn the most

**FROM RESEARCH**
Teachers dealing appropriately with their own negative emotions have a significant impact on classroom management.

—*Emmer (1994)*

from what you do. What you "do" speaks a whole lot louder than anything that you "say." How you conduct yourself in your interactions with students teaches them more than anything you say about actions in the class. If you want students to learn responsible behavior, then your modeling it is imperative. Your own personal mental health is an integral aspect of being successful at modeling self-management. Chapter 16 emphasizes some ideas for teacher stress management. Please pay close attention to them and make time for yourself and your mental health. Make time for your family and friends.

There are two **Keys of Effective Delivery** of corrective intervention strategies that are essential at the moment of misbehavior in order to model self-management:

---

      ⊶   **Use as Few Words as Possible**

      ⊶   **Control Your Reaction**

---

## ⊶ Use as Few Words as Possible

The first **Key of Effective Delivery** of corrective strategies is to *Use as Few Words as Possible* at the moment of misbehavior. If you give into the natural impulse to go on and on verbally, you fall into the trap of inadvertently reinforcing the misbehavior. What happens is that the student gets you all wrapped up focusing on him or her, while in the meantime you are letting the lesson lag. Some students like having that focus on them and delaying the lesson. It is not always in their awareness, but they respond to it nonetheless. Those students get hooked on the attention that nagging and scolding give them. They don't make the same distinction between positive and negative attention that our adult mind thinks they will. They just like the spotlight on them.

You, therefore, need to be as short and succinct as possible verbally while the misbehavior is occurring. If you need to discuss at length the implications of a student's behavior choices with him or her, you just do it a little later and not right when the misbehavior is happening. Sometimes teachers of very young children say to me that the young ones won't remember it later, but even five minutes later is fine—just not right while the misbehavior is going on.

Many of the corrective interventions are designed to help you to streamline your verbal interactions during misbehavior and use only enough words to get the job done.

**FROM RESEARCH**

When teachers practice themselves the conflict resolution strategies that they teach their students, the teachers benefit greatly.

—*Scherer (1992)*

## ⌐ Control Your Reaction

The second **Key of Effective Delivery** of corrective strategies is to *Control Your Reaction.* While it is normal to experience various feelings and impulses welling up inside you when you are dealing with misbehavior in the classroom, it is essential that you keep them internal. Since this is not necessarily the easiest thing to do, you need to develop your own strategies to help you appear cool on the outside even when you are boiling inside.

Think of what kinds of strategies help you to keep your cool in other aspects of your life. What strategy helps you to use respectful, business-like interaction with your boss, your spouse, your parents, your best friend? Seek out what works for you currently in other situations. You can also ask other teachers what works for them. You can use the teacher's lounge to let out those tensions later!

Some teachers I know think of something pleasant or take deep breaths—a whole lot of deep breaths—or some mentally go somewhere they would like to be. Fred Jones (1992) in *Positive Classroom Discipline* says that you should control your reaction by thinking of Queen Victoria. She was known throughout the lands as being able to deal with impertinent courtiers by looking them squarely in the eye with a business-like look on her face and saying, "We are not amused." Now, Fred Jones doesn't think that you should say this out loud, but rather just think it inside as a tool to calm your reactions. He also recommends deep breaths to control your physical reactions.

> **FROM RESEARCH**
> When teachers change their own behaviors in a positive manner, it has a positive effect on the behavior of low achievers.
> —*Hawkins, Doueck, and Lishner (1988)*

There are a couple of mental strategies that I use when students are pushing my buttons and I am tempted to lose my cool. First, I remind myself that for some students it is very powerful, heady stuff to be able to control the emotions of an adult. I remind myself if I give in to those natural human feelings and impulses and fail to control my reaction, I am giving this student exactly the pay-off he or she is after—controlling my emotions. If that isn't working my second mental strategy when I am feeling my temperature rise is to ask myself, if I give into these typical human responses inside of me and lose my cool, what am I modeling to the student? What will the student learn from what I "do"? I want to make sure that I am teaching the student that you can have negative feeling reactions inside and still get them under control and respond appropriately.

Come up with a "chill out" strategy that will work for you. The two important things are to recognize that all teachers need such a strategy and to develop one that will work for you. You can also seek out help from your school counselor or psychologist to develop a strategy.

Not only will your corrective strategies be much less effective if you violate this key and lose your cool with a student but an interesting side effect occurs. The fact that you are choosing inappropriate behavior gives the students full license to focus most of their attention on teacher behavior and not much on their own behavior. All they think about is how out of line and out of control you are. Little thought is given to their own behavior, which is what we want them to be thinking about. So it is critical for you to be modeling self-controlled emotions if we want students to think about their own behavior choices and what can be done about it and not be largely focusing on your personal behavior.

Many of the corrective strategies are designed to help you to get your reaction under control and respond in the business-like manner that will get you the results you want with students as well as help to teach self-management.

## Positive Perspective

> **❝** Teaching means helping the child realize his potential. **❞**
> —*Erich Fromm*

A positive perspective is a vital factor in being successful when dealing with misbehavior. When a student is distracting others from learning, pulling power plays or taking his or her anger out on others, it is sometimes hard for you to conjure up that student's positive qualities. The qualities that he or she is putting to a negative use at that time are much more evident. Without seeing the positive qualities of your misbehaving students, long lasting results will be elusive. You must be alert to the positive characteristics in all of your students, but especially those making poor choices. You must be able to focus on the plusses of your misbehaving students as well as those making responsible behavior choices.

You also need to be able to see the positive "potential" in the qualities that your irresponsible students are currently putting to poor use. Stubbornness has the positive potential of becoming determinism or perseverance. Power plays have the positive possibilities of becoming leadership skills or creative thinking. Even anger displays have the potential of that same emotionality being redirected into earnest learning endeavors.

Seeing positive potential can give you glimpses of future solutions. Seeing and building on the strengths of your misbehaving students gives you and your students some positive directions to work towards. Focusing on the strengths of your misbehaviors is not a quick fix, but does gradually help to realize the positive potential. Without a positive direction you and your misbehaving students will most likely keep going in circles with both of you treading the same negative ground, creating vicious circles that lead nowhere except to more frustration.

It is critical that you are able to mentally step out of any current problem situation and see possible positive outcomes. If you are so locked into a negative cycle with a student that you cannot even visualize a successful outcome, what chance do you have of ever bringing it about? Acting as if problems with students, even your most difficult ones, can eventually be solved helps to head things in that direction. What you think you are going to get does impact what you get. The impact of teacher expectations was explored in the CLEAR Model, in the LEARNERS component.

# Student Factors

Active involvement of students in the discipline process also helps to lead toward long-lasting solutions. As emphasized in *Win-Win Discipline* (Kyle, Kagan, and Scott in Charles, 2002), discipline in order to be successful needs to be done "with" the students, not "to" the students. Teachers and students working together to co-create solutions is important, if you want students to "buy into" the process and actually make some sustained changes in their behavior choices. Teachers need to ensure an environment conducive to learning for all of the students, but this is achieved more effectively when you and your students are allies rather than adversaries in the process.

> **" Help each student contribute to the solution rather than be a part of the problem. "**

Meeting the needs of students within the context of your discipline program is a thread that runs through several of the recognized approaches (Glasser, 1986; Nelsen, 1987; Albert et al., 1996; Coloroso, 1994; Kohn, 1996b; Kyle, Kagan, & Scott in Charles, 2002; and Charles, 2002). Each approach defines student needs a little differently, but the underlying theme is consistent with the basic premise of *Opportunities and Options in Classroom Management*. To create a classroom where learning is relevant and students and teachers both enjoy being there, you combine:

➤ Effective teaching that actively involves and engages students in the learning process.
➤ Prevention strategies to avoid problems or misbehaviors altogether or nip problems in the bud.
➤ Corrective strategies that hold students responsible for poor choices, while maintaining their dignity.
➤ Supportive strategies that build a positive classroom community.

You cannot control what happens to your students outside of school, but you can control what environment they experience in school. In *Synergetic Discipline,* Charles (2002) identifies seven main needs that students have: **Dignity, Enjoyment, Power, Security, Hope, Competence,** and **Acceptance.**

**STUDENTS' NEEDS CONNECTED
TO SOLUTIONS
(RESPECT Strategies—
From the Supportive Component)**

**Need:** **Dignity**
**Solution:** <u>R</u>esponsible behaviors intentionally taught

**Need:** **Enjoyment**
**Solution:** <u>E</u>stablishing classroom harmony

**Need:** **Power**
**Solution:** <u>S</u>tudent involvement

**Need:** **Security**
**Solution:** <u>P</u>arent involvement

**Need:** **Hope**
**Solution:** <u>E</u>ncouragement and effective praise

**Need:** **Competence**
**Solution:** <u>C</u>apable strategies

**Need:** **Acceptance**
**Solution:** <u>T</u>eacher/Student Relationship

# CHARLES' SYNERGETIC APPROACH

## Assumptions
➤ Students have basic needs that can be met in the classroom when teachers create a classroom community.
➤ Students have a need for Dignity, Enjoyment, Power, Security, Hope, Competence, and Acceptance.
➤ Teaching and learning need to be pleasurable and satisfying and compatible with students' basic needs.

## Main Points
➤ Teaching that actively involves students in the learning process results in little misbehavior.
➤ Methods for helping students to behave responsibly can be implemented in a gentle, but still very effective manner.
➤ Classroom conditions need to be established that increase motivation and energy.
➤ Teaching and discipline need to be approached from a unified perspective in order for them to be effective.
➤ Preventing and redirecting misbehavior are essential.
➤ Looking at the cause of misbehavior is important. Teachers need to prevent misbehaivor by limiting its cause and correct misbehavior by attending to its causes.
➤ The usual causes of misbehavior are probing boundaries, mimicking others, boredom or frustration, strong distraction, desire for attention, desire for power, no sense of belonging, residual emotion from an outside event, threats to personal dignity, disagreements that escalate and/or egocentric personality.
➤ The main purpose of discipline is to help students.

## Implementation
➤ Keeping students' seven needs in mind the teacher needs to entice cooperation, rather than force it. Students do cooperate for teachers whom they trust. The teacher needs to create a classroom with heightened enthusiasm and a sense of purpose. The tools to accomplish this are: teacher ethics, trust, charisma, communication,

> ### CHARLES' SYNERGETIC APPROACH (continued)
>
> and interest; class assignments; and procedures for problem resolution. When discipline problems occur, the teacher would say something, like, "Is there a problem I can help you with?" Or "Can you help me to understand why this is happening?" The focus is on helping the student to choose responsible behavior rather than punishing. Teachers keeping their reaction under control when conflicts arise is integral.
>
> **Limitation**
> ➤ This approach could take awhile to be implemented.

## Understanding Unmet Needs Leads to Long-Term Solutions

The premise that unmet needs underlie students' misbehavior choices does not imply that students should be able to misbehave so their needs can be met. This is not viewed as an excuse to continue on their path of misbehavior, but rather as a path to possible long-term solutions. If you only deal with the immediate situation, as important as that is when students are currently misbehaving, you do nothing to create sustained results. This corrective component focuses mainly on all-important strategies for "What do you do right now while the student is acting up?" But as you are gathering strategies for your management plan, continually keep in mind that the corrective interventions need to be implemented in concert with the other three components. When all components work together you can be addressing students' underlying needs, which helps students to make real changes in their choices. Actively involving students is an integral aspect of meeting their needs through the discipline process.

# Perspectives on Power

When you are actively involving students in the discipline process you are in essence sharing the power with your students. Some teachers have the misperception that sharing power means giving some away and therefore you will have less. Actually the opposite is usually the case. Through the process of sharing power with students you have more power in the situation than when you are attempting to hold on tight to power. When students share in the power in the classroom, it creates a sense of ownership and makes it more likely that students will work with you to create a positive classroom environment. In essence you are putting some of the responsibility on their shoulders. Most students will rise to the occasion.

Sometimes students do not currently possess the skills to participate responsibly in developing their own discipline solutions, and then it is important that you exercise your responsibility of holding them accountable for their choices. When you are offering to share the power with the students, if they do not participate responsibly, you take the power back. But you do it in a way that leaves the door open for future responsible interaction. You continue to help them to learn how to participate responsibly in creating solutions. You use the choice language to say something like:

> "It is important that you take this seriously and give responsible suggestions or I will need to decide for now."

If they continue to be irresponsible in the process, say something like, "I will decide for now. We will have an opportunity to work on this again next week. I am sure that you will be more responsible when we try again next week."

The more you say this in a business-like tone with controlled reactions on your part, the more effective it will be and the more likely the students will learn from it and make more responsible choices the next time. Resist the temptation to give them one more chance at this point. (They will ask for it!) They will have one more chance the next week (or the next day with very young children). Your main goal is to teach them that participation in the discipline process requires responsible choices. You really want them to be involved, but it is necessary for them to participate responsibly or you will need to take the power back and decide for now. Shared responsibility is what you are after, but it needs to be taught. It doesn't just happen. This works with individual students as well as with the whole class.

**FROM RESEARCH**
Actively involving students in the discipline process impacts greatly their ability to make responsible behavior choices and their attitude toward school.

—*Kyle (1991)*

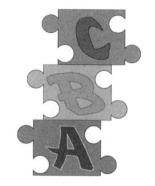

## KYLE, KAGAN, AND SCOTT'S APPROACH

### Assumptions

Win-Win discipline is built on three pillars:

➢ The teacher and the students need to be on the same side working together as allies, not as adversaries.

➢ Shared responsibility, the teacher and the students co-creating solutions, is integral for sustained results. Active involvement of students in the discipline process is key.

➢ The ultimate goal of discipline is long-term learned responsible behavior.

### Main Points

➢ You implement the Win-Win discipline process to deal with disruptive behavior while helping the students meet their needs through responsible behavior choices.

➢ You identify the Four Disruptive Behaviors: ABCD—aggressive, breaking the rules, confrontational, and disengaged disruptive behaviors.

➢ You recognize and validate the Seven Student Positions: AAA-BCDE—attention-seeking, angry, avoiding embarrassment, bored, control-seeking, don't know, and energetic.

➢ You ask the critical questions associated with the three pillars:
1. Can I relate to where the student is coming from?
2. Did we create the solution together?
3. Is it more likely that the student will act responsibly in the future?

➢ You implement structures for the moment of disruption that match where the student is coming from.

➢ You choose appropriate Win-Win follow-ups to involve the student later in the same day or the next day.

➢ You incorporate Win-Win preventive solutions for long-lasting results.

➢ You analyze and respond to four class patterns—ABCD—to find whole class solutions.

➢ You prevent discipline problems through curriculum, instruction, and management links.

**KYLE, KAGAN, AND SCOTT'S APPROACH (continued)**

➤ You create a school-wide Win-Win discipline program, so everybody wins—students, teachers, parents, and administrators.
➤ You invite parent and community alliances.

**Implementation**
➤ You use differentiated structures geared to the type of disruptive behavior and the position of the student. You view discipline as an opportunity for the student to learn responsible behavior.

**Limitation**
➤ It is not a quick fix.

# Empowering Students Through Involvement

Strategies for actively involving students and, thereby, sharing the power, will be explored more in-depth in the corrective chapters coming up. Strategies to use when students do not participate responsibly will also be practiced. You can involve students at a level that feels comfortable to you. There is no magic formula for the right amount of involvement. Just keep in mind that student involvement in the discipline process results in more ownership and follow-through and that is what you are after. Older students particularly respond well to involvement. They have a high need for control over their own lives and when you give them a positive way to meet that need, it can be very powerful.

Some teachers tend to think of power as something negative, as in having power over another person. Power has very positive uses when it is focused on empowering. It can be very empowering for students to be part of the class decision-making process and to be part of the process of solving classroom problems, whether they are whole class problems or individual problem situations. It is very empowering for students to have a legitimate sense of power in your class. When students have legitimate avenues for power, they are not continually battling you for power in inappropriate ways. Some empowerment strategies are:

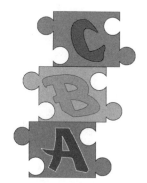

➤ Creating rules/code of conduct
➤ Creating activity and accountability procedures
➤ Choices in consequences for misbehavior
➤ Choices in mode of assignment

➤ Classroom responsibilities
➤ Helping to develop discipline solutions
➤ Sharing their expertise
➤ Being a peer mediator
➤ Self-managing their progress in academics or behaviors
➤ Participating in class meetings

# Levels of Seriousness of Misbehaviors: "ABC" Options

In the next three chapters we will focus on practical corrective strategies you can use at the moment of misbehavior. So far in this chapter we looked at "**how**" to use strategies. "**When**" to use strategies is another vital piece of the puzzle. There are various levels of seriousness of misbehavior. Knowing this gives you direction as to what strategies to use at what level.

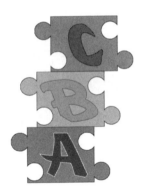

"A": Distracting Behaviors
"B": Controlling Behaviors
"C": Angry/Violent Behaviors

## Distracting Misbehaviors: The "A" Level

At the first level of seriousness of misbehaviors are distracting behaviors. These are the low-level, annoying behaviors that don't cause strong reactions in us, but do really irritate us. Distracting behaviors annoy us because they distract us and the students, and delay or interrupt the flow of the lesson. The smooth transitions that Kounin (1977) recommended that we use to prevent problems from developing are put at a standstill as we stop the momentum of the lesson to deal with one distraction after another.

Some common distracting behaviors are:

➤ Pencil tapping
➤ Calling out
➤ Sharpening pencils
➤ Roaming the room
➤ Playing with objects
➤ Weird noises

Since these are low-level misbehaviors, low-level strategies are appropriate. These distracting misbehaviors do cause distractions from the lesson, but they do not usually push our buttons and arouse strong reactions as the controlling and the angry/violent behaviors do. The distractions definitely bother us, but it would be "mild" on the reaction scale. *Controlling your reaction* is not as difficult with these distracting misbehaviors as it is with the controlling and angry/violent misbehaviors coming up, but to use *as few words as possible* is the challenge. Our natural impulse is to nag, remind, scold, and get after these students verbally. The "A" option strategies will help you to focus your verbal interaction and be as short and succinct as possible. This is critical so that you interrupt the lesson as little as possible and so you do not inadvertently reinforce the misbehavior through interacting too long with the students choosing distracting behaviors in your class.

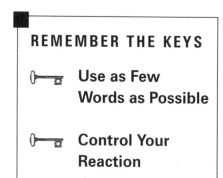

**REMEMBER THE KEYS**

- Use as Few Words as Possible

- Control Your Reaction

The corrective strategies that help you deal effectively with distracting behaviors are the "<u>A</u>" Options for Distracting Behaviors:

> <u>A</u>ctive Body Language
> <u>A</u>ttention Focusing Strategies

Explanations and examples of the "<u>A</u>" options for distracting behaviors will be detailed in chapter 11.

## *Supportive connections with distracting behaviors*

Students who choose distracting behaviors often have unmet needs for attention. They do not make the distinction that we would expect between positive and negative attention. Any attention will do and to have the whole lesson at a stall while everyone, including the teacher, focuses on them is reinforcing. Helping them to get their attention needs met through responsible behavior would be the path to solutions in that situation. Distracting behaviors can also be indicative of a learning modality or style that differs from the current instruction, in which case you would look toward adapting the instruction to meet their learning needs (Jensen 1998). In addition to utilizing the corrective strategies detailed in chapter 11 and looking back at effective teaching strategies, it is crucial that you also look to the supportive strategies in section V for long-term results that encourage and teach responsible behavior. With students choosing distracting behaviors, you would want to look particularly at the supportive strategies on the right (to be covered in detail in chapter 14):

**Supportive Solutions for Distracting Misbehaviors**
> Giving attention for responsible behaviors.
> Building positive teacher/student and student/student relationships.
> Using encouragement and effective praise.
> Incorporating capable strategies to adapt your instruction to meet their learning modality needs.

# Controlling Misbehaviors: The "B" Level

**REMEMBER THE KEYS**

🔑 **Use as Few Words as Possible**

🔑 **Control Your Reaction**

Controlling misbehaviors is the next level of seriousness. Some students resort to misbehavior to meet their legitimate need for a sense of control over their lives. Lacking a responsible way to feel in control, these students pull power plays and try to manipulate things to be the way they want them to be. They defy adults through words or actions or both. These controlling misbehaviors create a stronger reaction in us than the distracting ones. We feel angry and challenged. Our buttons are being pushed and our impulsive reaction is to want to push back and to show those students who is boss. We still need to be concerned about keeping our verbiage to a minimum, but the hard part now is *controlling our reaction*. We are at the "hot" level inside. It is increasingly difficult to keep those reactions inside and not to let them leak out in our voice, facial expressions, and body language, much less in our actions. We often experience physical reactions, like an upset stomach, a headache, a clenched jaw, or a red face. *Controlling our reaction* becomes the main challenge. The "B" option strategies are designed to help you accomplish that.

Some common phrases we hear from students choosing controlling misbehaviors are:

➤ "You can't make me."
➤ "I don't know why I have to do this."
➤ "This is stupid."
➤ "We shouldn't have to do this."
➤ "All the others kids are doing it. Why don't you talk to them?"

## Unmotivated or Apathetic Controlling Behaviors

Unmotivated or apathetic students often fall in this category of controlling misbehaviors. Because the problem is what they are "not" doing rather than what they "are" doing, we often don't recognize them as controlling misbehaviors. The student's behavior rather than her words is saying to us, "I don't want to be bothered doing this;" "This assignment is too much trouble;" "I don't want to put out the energy required to do this;" or "I don't want to do all the thinking needed." These students are into subtle non-compliance, but since they are not in our face, pushing our buttons as the more overt challengers are, we often don't recognize their behavior as controlling.

# Other Sources of Unmotivated Behaviors

## *"I Can't" messages*

Unmotivated behaviors can also come from students believing that they are not capable of performing the tasks. They have very loud "I Can't" messages in their heads that determine their behavior. These students are usually trying to avoid being noticed and are not doing their work. It is again what they are "not" doing that is the problem, not what they "are" doing. But the behavior is coming from a different place than for the student who just doesn't want to be bothered to put enough effort to do the work, as was the student choosing passive controlling behaviors described above. The behavior of these students is coming from what, to them, is a very real "I Can't" message. It is sometimes hard to tell the difference between unmotivated behaviors coming from passive controlling misbehaviors and ones coming from an "I Can't" messages, but recognizing that it can be either, and that the sources for solutions are different, can help. You will look at <u>C</u>apable strategies for helping students with "I Can't" messages in the supportive component.

## *Boredom*

Unmotivated behaviors can also come from students being legitimately bored. They just haven't connected with the instruction. It may be too easy for them or not seem relevant to them. This is often the case with your high ability students who are not being challenged by the material or the lesson presentation. When the unmotivated behaviors are coming from that source, you would look to the effective teaching component and the CLEAR Model for solutions.

The "<u>B</u>" options for controlling misbehaviors that help you to get your reaction under control and respond in a business-like, professional manner are:

---

### "B" OPTIONS FOR CONTROLLING BEHAVIORS

➢ <u>B</u>utton Pusher Escapes
➢ <u>B</u>rief Choices
➢ <u>B</u>usiness-like Consequences

---

Explanations and examples of the "<u>B</u>" options for controlling behaviors will be detailed in chapter 12.

*Supportive connections with controlling behaviors*

Students who choose controlling misbehavior often have unmet needs for power and a sense of control over what's happening to them. It is developmentally appropriate for students of all ages to want to have more and more control over their lives as they progress through grades, but these are students that have not found a positive way to meet that need. They end up meeting that need through misbehavior, controlling, and manipulating people around them. They often have an even stronger need for control than is typical. That strong need for control and power can translate into leadership skills, independent thinking, and creativity—if it can only be channeled in a positive direction. Some of the supportive strategies to help with this are:

---

### SUPPORTIVE SOLUTIONS
### FOR CONTROLLING BEHAVIORS

➢ Legitimate avenues for power in the class
➢ Classroom responsibilities
➢ Involvement in the decision-making process
➢ Choices, choices, and choices

---

# Angry/Violent Misbehaviors: The "C" Level

**REMEMBER THE KEYS**

⊶ **Use as Few Words as Possible**

⊶ **Control Your Reaction**

Angry/violent misbehaviors are the highest level of seriousness. These behaviors come from students who have angry feelings for a variety of reasons that usually don't have anything to do with you personally. You and/or the students in the class become convenient scapegoats for working off their angry feelings. Their misdirected anger spills out into the classroom sometimes in violent actions. Our reaction to them is often in the "sizzling" range. We feel outraged, fearful, intimidated, or indignant or even sometimes experience feelings of dislike toward them.

It is normal and human to experience feelings of dislike when we have a revengeful student taking all of his or her anger out on us, but we have a professional responsibility to get those feelings under control and respond appropriately, despite our internal turmoil. Sometimes teachers think that they need to take care of the feelings of dislike before they can do anything, but exactly the opposite is what is needed. Even if you are having trouble control-

ling your reaction, what you need to do is to take actions that demonstrate that you care about what happens to this student. Even when teachers are in the throes of feelings of dislike, they can tap into caring about what happens to that student. When you deliberately take actions that demonstrate that you do care, after awhile your feeling response will get in line with your actions.

Our impulse is often to want to retaliate and fight back. When we are at the "sizzling" level, *controlling your reaction* is even more of a challenge. The corrective strategies that are "C" options are designed to help both you and the student to control these strong reactions.

Students with angry/violent misbehaviors often exhibit one or more of the following:

> Hurting others physically
> Hurting others emotionally
> Destroying things
> Intimidation of others and other bullying behaviors
> Violent actions (intense physical harm)

The "<u>C</u>" options for anger/violent behaviors that help to keep you above the "C" level even though you are sizzling inside are:

> <u>C</u>hill Out Time
> <u>C</u>hoice Levels
> <u>C</u>onsequences
> <u>C</u>hat Time with Students
> <u>C</u>ontract
> <u>C</u>urbing Violence

Explanations and examples of the "<u>C</u>" options for angry/violent behaviors will be detailed in chapter 13.

## *Supportive connections with angry/violent behaviors*

The unmet needs of students exhibiting angry/violent misbehaviors revolve around an inability to deal with their angry feelings in a constructive manner. All they know is to act out their anger with hurtful consequences to others. Their primary need is to learn how to deal with the their feelings in a way that doesn't hurt others or themselves. Some of the supportive strategies that can be helpful to them are:

---

### SUPPORTIVE SOLUTIONS
### FOR ANGRY/VIOLENT BEHAVIORS

➤ Anger management
➤ Conflict resolution
➤ Learning pro-social responsible behaviors
➤ Stress management
➤ Forming positive teacher/student and student/student relationships
➤ Forming a connection and commitment to the school and extra-curricular activities
➤ Increased parent/child communication
➤ Expectations of success by the student
➤ School counselor and/or school psychologist help
➤ Effective teaching choices linking to learner interests
➤ Peer mediation
➤ Peer counseling

---

# Summary

The *keys and links for corrective strategies* help you with the *"how"* and *"when"* to use strategies. The teacher having an attitude that *all students can learn responsible behavior* is important for success. There are two keys to effective delivery of corrective intervention strategies: *Using as few words as possible* and *controlling your reaction.* These keys are the tools for you to model self-management. Helping students meet their *underlying needs* through your discipline program helps with long-term results. *Sharing power* with your students helps to empower them to make responsible behavior choices. The *levels of seriousness of misbehavior* connect with strategies appropriate for each level. There are *"A" options for distracting behavior* (detailed in chapter 11); *"B" options for controlling behaviors* (detailed in chapter 12); and *"C" options for angry/violent behaviors* (detailed in chapter 13). You will learn numerous corrective strategies to deal with misbehavior at the moment it is occurring and shortly thereafter.

# Reflection Questions

1. What evidence can you cite to support the notion that all students can learn responsible behavior?
2. What strategies will you use to manage your reactions to student misbehaviors? How will you model self-management?
3. How are unmet student needs and misbehaviors related? Give examples of how you will meet student needs in your classroom.
4. What are the results of sharing classroom power with responsible students? Give examples of how you can give your students legitimate power in your classroom. What is an appropriate teacher response if students are not sharing power responsibly? (Levels of misbehavior: "ABC" Strategies)
5. Describe each of the three levels of misbehavior. What are examples of supportive strategies that can contribute to the development of responsible behavior for each level?

# References

Albert, L., Kyle, P., Desisto, P., Maguire, M., Zgonc, Y., Smith, F., & Soriano, A. (1996). *Cooperative discipline.* Circle Pines, MN: American Guidance Service, Inc.

Coloroso, B. (1994). *Kids are worth it!: Giving your child the gift of inner discipline.* New York: Avon Books.

Charles, C. M. (2002). *Building classroom discipline.* Boston: Allyn & Bacon.

Dreikurs, R., & Cassell, P. (1972). *Discipline without tears: What to do with children who misbehave.* New York: Elsevier-Dutton.

Dreikurs, R., Grunwald, B., & Pepper, F. (1982). *Maintaining sanity in the classroom: Classroom management techniques.* New York: Harper and Row Publishers.

Emmer, E. (1994). Towards an understanding of the primacy of classroom management and discipline. *Teaching Education* 6 (1): 65–69.

Glasser, W. (1986). *Control theory in the classroom.* New York: Harper and Row.

Hawkins, D., Doueck, H., & Lishner, D. (1988). Changing teaching practices in mainstream classrooms to improve bonding and behavior of low achievers. *American Educational Research Journal* 25 (1): 31–50.

Jensen, E. (1998). *Teaching with the brain in mind.* Alexandria, VA: Association for Supervision and Curriculum Development.

Jones, F. H. (1987). *Positive classroom discipline.* New York: McGraw-Hill Book Company.

Kohn, A. (1996b). *Beyond discipline: From compliance to community.* Alexandria, VA: Association for Supervision and Curriculum Development.

Kounin, J. (1977). *Discipline and group management in classrooms,* revised edition. New York: Holt, Rinehart, and Winston.

Kyle, P. (1991). Developing cooperative interaction in schools for teachers and administrators. *Journal of Individual Psychology* 47 (2).

Nelsen, J. (1987). *Positive discipline.* New York: Ballantine Books.

Scherer, M. (1992). Solving conflicts—Not just for students. *Educational Leadership* 50 (1): 14–17.

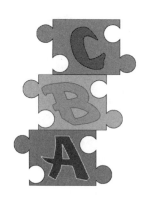

# "A" Options for Distracting Behaviors

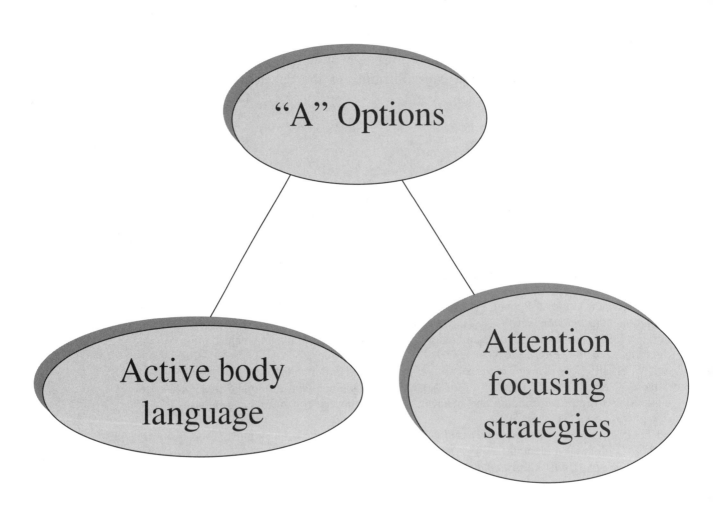

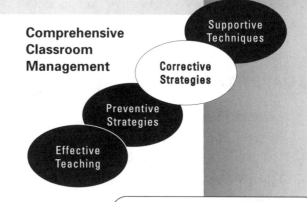

Comprehensive Classroom Management

Supportive Techniques

Corrective Strategies

Preventive Strategies

Effective Teaching

## OBJECTIVES

The learners will be able to practice strategies for the moment of misbehavior for the "distracting level" of seriousness.

## CHAPTER SNAPSHOT

- <u>A</u>ctive Body Language
- <u>A</u>ttention Focusing Strategies
- *Fred Jones' Approach*

Distracting misbehaviors are ones that sidetrack you, the teacher, from the lesson and divert the attention of the students from the learning. Jones (1987) discovered that the majority of misbehaviors that we deal with fall into this category. They interrupt the lesson, stop the momentum, and get the focus away from important matters and annoy us all at the same time. We all slip into distracting behaviors from time to time, but some students develop a pattern of one distraction after another. There is usually some kind of attention that is needed. Often the students exhibiting a pattern of distracting behaviors are after attention for themselves. They enjoy the focus being on them, either consciously or unconsciously. They like the spotlight on themselves, even if it is only briefly. With some students their need for attention is different in that their learning modality or learning style needs are not being met and they need attention given to meet their learning needs.

We will be exploring active body language strategies and attention focusing strategies that will help to deal with either type of distracting behaviors (personal attention or learning modality style) in the short run. We want to deal with the distraction in a way that interrupts our teaching and the flow of the lesson as little as possible and these strategies will help you to accomplish that. In the long run, though, we need to look at meeting the unmet need to have lasting results that go beyond the immediate situation.

Students who like the attention on them need to learn, through supportive strategies, to get their attention needs met through responsible behavior choices, rather than continuing the cycle of attention diversions. They will go along with you, when you use one of the "A" Options, in the immediate situation and say things like, "I'm sorry, I forgot;" or "Oops, I won't do it again." They won't argue with you and justify their inappropriate choices, as will the students choosing controlling or angry/violent behaviors. But they will only stop their distracting behavior for a short period of time unless you are also incorporating supportive strategies to deal with their underlying need for attention. You need to be weaning them away from getting their attention needs met through misbehavior into getting their attention needs met through responsible behavior. For those who have unmet learning

## "WHEN" TO USE CORRECTIVE STRATEGIES

### "A" Options for Distracting Behaviors

| | |
|---|---|
| **Examples:** | Pencil tapping, calling out, sharpening pencils, roaming the room, playing with objects in desk, making weird noises. |
| **Strategy Options:** | **A**ctive Body Language<br>**A**ttention Focusing Strategies |
| **Strategy Function:** | Focus your verbal interaction and be as short and succinct as possible |
| **Teacher Reaction:** | "Mild"—annoyed, irritated |
| **Teacher Impulse:** | Nag, remind, scold and get after these students verbally |
| **Student Unmet Need:** | Attention to student or attention to differing learning style needs |
| **Supportive Solutions:** | Attention for responsible behavior choices<br>Building positive teacher/student and student/student relationships<br>Using encouragement and effective praise<br>Incorporating capable strategies to adapt your instruction to meet their learning needs |

The "A" options detailed in this chapter are all appropriate for handling low-level distracting misbehaviors. You can choose from them based on which are appealing to you and which fit your current situation. Keep in mind, though, that corrective strategies are short-term solutions only designed to deal with the immediate situation.

Sometimes students who are controlling will exhibit some of the behaviors that are typical of students who are choosing distracting behaviors. A student choosing controlling behavior will not necessarily respond the same way to the "A" options strategies as a student choosing distracting misbehaviors. A student who is distracting would respond to the "look" by ceasing the behavior for at least a little while. A student who is controlling might say, "What are you looking at me for?" in a challenging tone of voice. That does not mean that your low-level "A" options are not effective. They are very effective with distractions, but may be ineffective with controlling behaviors and angry/violent behaviors. Look to the "B" options and the "C" options when students do not respond to "A" options.

needs, please look to the capable strategies in the supportive section and to the effective teaching component for long-term solutions.

Remember the supportive solutions options to use with students choosing distracting behaviors, if you want long-lasting results that go beyond the immediate situation:

➢ Attention for responsible behavior choices
➢ Building positive teacher/student and student/student relationships
➢ Using encouragement and effective praise
➢ Incorporating capable strategies to adapt your instruction to meet their learning needs

> **❝** Disciplinary problems become opportunities for conveying values, providing insights, and strengthening self-esteem. **❞**
> —*Haim Ginott*

# Active Body Language

Your body is a very powerful tool in dealing with discipline problems. Fred Jones (1987) in *Positive Classroom Discipline* emphasized the importance of using active body language to deal with the many distracting behaviors in your classroom. Active body language needs be utilized in a non-aggressive manner. It is a firm non-verbal message that communicates to the student choosing distracting behaviors the need to stop the misbehavior and to move on to responsible behavior. The nice thing about active body language is that it is very consistent with one of the keys—*use as few words as possible*—as you are getting the job done without words at all. At the same time it entails minimal disruption to the lesson. So don't overlook these simple, yet effective strategies with your low-level misbehaviors. Some of your non-verbal active body language options are:

> - The Look
> - Proximity
> - Body Carriage
> - Appropriate Touch
> - Signals and Gestures
> - Teaching Pause

---

**FROM RESEARCH**

Classroom discipline is an ongoing process of securing and maintaining student cooperation.

—*Doyle (1985)*

---

## The Look

Getting eye contact and maintaining it for a few seconds with a student who is distracting communicates the need to cease the behavior without resorting to words. Use a firm look, but not an angry or hostile one. A business-like demeanor is most effective. Even if the student does not respond immediately, maintaining the eye contact should bring results, if you are dealing with distracting misbehavior.

## Proximity

The power of proximity cannot be underestimated. When a student is choosing a distracting behavior, often the best thing to do is to walk over and continue teaching standing right next to this student. You want to make sure that you have arranged your room in such a way that proximity is possible. You also want to make sure that you are not anchored to the front of the room. Even when you are using an overhead, get in the habit of moving around the room or as Jones (1987) would say, "working the room," in between adding or changing things on the overhead. Proximity is both a deterrent (prevention strategy) and a valuable tool to deal with misbehavior while it is happening (corrective strategy). Fred Jones recommends that you arrange your room in such a way that as you "work the room" or move around it on an ongoing basis, you are never more than two desks away from any student in the path that you follow. Remember "movability" when designing your room. It can help you to maximize the power of proximity.

If the student is actually choosing controlling misbehaviors, even though it appears to be merely a distracting misbehavior, then she might not respond to the nearness of the teacher in a positive manner.

Active body language is firm, business-like, and supportive, but not attacking or mean. It is intended to transmit a clear message that responsible behavior is needed now, but not meant to intimidate the student. Intimidation may provoke future angry/violent misbehaviors. Teachers sometimes confuse disciplining with being mean. Discipline actually comes from a word that means "to teach." We are, therefore, teaching responsible behavior when we hold a student responsible for the choices he is making. Discipline, to be effective, needs to be firm and directed, but not mean and aggressive. Examine what your body is saying to your students.

Make sure that your body language is firm and deliberate, but not mean and aggressive. Is your voice tone consistent with your body carriage, with your facial expression? Mixed messages cause discomfort in students and are counterproductive to creating long-term solutions.

# Body Carriage

Jones (1987) emphasizes that the way you carry yourself is also a valuable discipline tool. When you are dealing with a discipline situation you want your body to be erect and to project an "I mean business" demeanor and that you are committed to bringing about responsible behavior choices. Again this does not mean aggressive. Aggressive body language tends to invite reciprocal behavior. You want to be projecting a message of firmness, not anger.

## Appropriate Touch

Using physical touch in an appropriate way is another non-verbal choice that you have. A light pat on the back can communicate "stop" to a student choosing distracting behavior. A hand gently touching the shoulder can say desist. Even though there is some concern nationally about teachers touching students, the touches just mentioned would not be misconstrued. Neither would a high five or a handshake be inappropriate.

Sometimes students who have experienced abuse will not respond positively at all to touch. They might flinch or overtly react to a touch, even one meant benignly as guidance to responsible behavior. If you have a student who reacts negatively to touch, use another strategy, but discuss any concerns you might have with your school counselor or school psychologist.

Some active body language strategies are appropriate to be used both with individuals and also with the whole class. Sometimes it is the whole class or large segments of the class that are choosing distracting behaviors. You need to have "whole class options" in your management plan as well as strategies to use with individual students.

## Signals and Gestures

Using signals and gestures is another choice you have for dealing with distractions in a non-verbal manner. This strategy can be used both as a "whole class option" and with an individual who is distracting. Thumbs down, hands crossing each other in a stop message, a finger to the mouth that communicates "shhhh," sign language that has been taught to the students are examples of how signals and gestures can help you. You can also meet with an individual student and agree on a signal that you will give that student to help him or her keep on track.

Signals and gestures can also be used to highlight responsible behaviors. A thumbs up signal or a silent cheer given with the hands can punctuate appropriate choices. Use your imagination.

> **FROM RESEARCH**
> Positive non-verbal teaching behaviors produce positive outcomes for students.
>
> *—Baringer and McCroskey (2000)*

Research shows that kinesthetic symbols (using hand gestures that translate the concept into a movement connected with the learning) aid students in remembering learned material. You can put that same finding to work in your discipline program by developing kinesthetic symbols that signal or cue the appropriate responsible behavior. You can also develop kinesthetic symbols that communicate ceasing and desisting unwanted behaviors. Using kinesthetic symbols not only aids memory, but also "uses as few words as possible" and interrupts the lesson as little as possible.

## Teaching Pause

To pause in your teaching for a few seconds can be a very effective way to have active body language communicate with your whole class. It also combines several of the previous active body language strategies. With "teaching pause" you give a non-verbal message: "What I have to say is important enough that I am not going to say it until everyone is listening."

Keep in mind that "teaching pause" is a non-verbal, active body language strategy. You do not deliver lecture #32 about the negative effects of wasting class time. It may be very appropriate to have that kind of discussion with your students, but you save it for later, so you don't fall into that trap of inadvertently reinforcing the misbehavior.

### Variation 1

You simply stop teaching, standing erect in your "I mean business" stance, and you scan the room getting eye contact with as many students as possible, giving a non-verbal message that you need students to focus and desist in the distracting behaviors. You don't have a scowl on your face. The "look" is firm, business-like, but not angry.

The moment all of the students are focused on the whole group interaction, you go right back into teaching again. Don't give into the temptation to have them suffer in silence for a while, since they wasted some of your valuable teaching time. What you want to do is reinforce the fact that the students are now making responsible behavior choices. The most I ever do at this point is to say, "I appreciate it when everyone listens," and then I go right back into teaching again.

## *Variation 2*

Sometimes, unfortunately, the students are so caught up in their distracting behaviors that they do not notice that you have stopped teaching. A more overt non-verbal message is needed at those times. You can sit down, maintaining your "I mean business" body carriage scanning the room getting as much eye contact as possible with a firm, but non-aggressive look on your face, giving a non-verbal message that you need the students to be focused. The sitting down makes the non-verbal message even more overt. Again the moment the students are all focused, you stand and resume teaching. "I appreciate it when you are focused on the lesson."

Sometimes you have a lot of students in your class who are choosing controlling behaviors. That often will translate into having "whole class" misbehaviors that are controlling rather than distracting. When this happens "teaching pause" will not be effective as described because versions one and two are relevant for distracting behaviors. A version of "teaching pause" used with controlling misbehaviors is needed. In this situation the students would owe back the time the class took to get themselves focused. Your nonverbal signal would be you keeping track of how much time the students owed (looking at your watch or clock while recording the time is a non-verbal message you give to the students). You would go right back into teaching as soon as they were focused on the lesson again.

# **A̲ttention Focusing Strategies**

There is a lot of power in the non-verbal active body language options that you have available to you when dealing with students who are distracting. Some of the attention focusing strategies are still non-verbal, but do not utilize active body language. Other attention focusing strategies are useful verbal strategies. If you can handle the situation with no words, great, but there are times when you want to add more information for the student and words are needed. You still want to *"Use as few words as possible."*

The verbal attention focusing strategies serve two vital purposes. They focus the attention of the distracting student, but they also help to focus your verbal interaction, so you do not go on and on. Remember our impulse is to use lots of verbiage. The verbal attention focusing strategies are designed to help you say only what needs to be said at the moment of misbehavior. If you need to discuss at length the ramifications of the student's choices, you do that later and not while the misbehavior is occurring. Your choices for attention focusing strategies are:

> **"** When you don't understand the rules, you cannot play the game of life successfully. **"**

> ➢ Signals—Auditory and Visual
> ➢ Refocus Notes
> ➢ Target Stop Do
> ➢ Voice Change
> ➢ Name Dropping
> ➢ Grandma's Rule
> ➢ Distract the Distractor
> ➢ Coupon Approach
> ➢ I-Statements

## Signals—Auditory and Visual

Auditory and visual signals are great ways to focus students' attention. You can use the "give me five," where you raise your hand as a signal, and the students are to give you the same signal back. The students returning your signal is an important aspect of this strategy. Not only does it have students acknowledging your signal, but also for the students who might have their backs to you, they see their peers returning the signal and then they respond also. Sign language can also be a great visual signal. Holding your hand out in a way that communicates stop is another option as well as just holding a finger to your mouth indicating "shhhhh." Please don't verbally make a "shhhhh" sound as that can get to be a bad habit on your part that is not usually anywhere near as effective as the silent signal "shhhhh."

Some teachers use flicking the lights as another option for a visual signal. You just want to make sure that you are not overusing it to the point where it seems like a strobe light and has a negative impact on your students. Some teachers like using a stoplight type of light signal, where green is go ahead with your behaviors, yellow is caution, and red is stop.

For auditory signals there are several options. You can use a clapping pattern that the students respond to by clapping back the same pattern. Another variation of clapping is to say, "If you can hear my voice, clap once. . . . If you can hear my voice, clap twice." Obviously, you want to keep the number down, so you teach the students how to respond quickly to that signal.

You can also use a variety of sounds as an auditory signal. Chimes are effective, a music snippet on an audiocassette, or playing a few notes on any kind of instrument. Unusual sounds are other options. Some teachers use rain sticks or train or bird whistles. Be creative.

Sometimes teachers who work with secondary students think auditory and visual signals are only for younger students, but anytime you have students involved in groups, projects, or experiments you have to have a way to get them all back together again for whole group instruction or discussion. No matter what the age is, it is needed. Auditory signals are used in training seminars for business executives. I suggest asking your students which signal they prefer, if you are uncomfortable with the idea.

I knew an inventive high school teacher who put a short snippet of the song *Respect* on an audiocassette. He would play that as a signal when he needed the students to focus on whole group instruction. It not only accomplished the focusing of the students, but also had an appropriate message for the students.

When using signals, it is vital that you allow "wait time" for the students to respond and get focused. Teachers are not always comfortable with waiting, so they give the signal and then start teaching before the students are actually paying attention. All they have accomplished is to teach the students that the signal really doesn't mean anything. Take the time to teach them that when it is whole group time, we need everyone focused in order to begin.

## Refocus Notes

A handy non-verbal way to deal with distracting behaviors is to use refocus notes. Instead of interrupting your teaching to deal with disruptions, you write what you want the student to cease doing on a refocus note. You walk over to the student's desk while you continue to teach and quietly put the note in front of the distracting student. If you are utilizing this strategy, it is important that you let the students know in the first week that this is one of the strategies you will be using and explain its rationale. That way the students aren't all wondering why you wrote a note. The strategy allows you to communicate with the distracting students using few words and with minimal distraction from the lesson.

Teachers of younger students will have refocus notes all made up ahead of time that might say, "Please stop _____" and a space to fill in the specific behavior. Teachers of older students find that post-it notes are just right for this purpose. Some teachers get quite inventive and also have "I appreciate _____" notes, which they spread around liberally.

A word of caution—Refocus notes are most effective with students choosing distracting behaviors. They sometimes work with students choosing controlling or angry/violent behaviors, but there is also the potential that one of those students might wad the note up and throw it on the floor. Again this does not mean that this isn't a good strategy, just that it might not work well in all situations. It is most effective with distracting behaviors.

It is a good idea to share your corrective strategies that you will be using with the students during the first week of school. You, of course, start with the rules and procedures as discussed in the previous section of this book. Sharing your corrective strategies, what they are, how they will be used, and their purpose is another important task in the first week of school.

We are not trying to put anything over on the students. Being open about your plan and its rationale is an integral aspect of eliciting their cooperation in creating a classroom environment conducive to learning. Your discipline is done "with" the students and not "to" the students. I let them know that it is my responsibility as their teacher to ensure a positive learning atmosphere, but I need them involved to make it really work. I put it on the basis that we all need to work together to create a classroom where everyone can enjoy learning and teaching.

## Target Stop Do

"Target stop do" is a very useful verbal structure as it effectively focuses your verbal interaction. The "target" is the student who is enacting distracting behaviors. The "stop" is the distracting behavior that needs to be stopped. The "do" is the responsible behavior that needs to replace the misbehavior. For example, "Juanita, please stop tapping your pencil and get busy on your math problems."

Now you may be wondering why we even need that strategy when it is so simple, but remember that our impulse is to go on and on verbally. Without "target stop do" I might say:

> "Juanita, how many times have I told you not to tap your pencil? You are disturbing the whole class. I can't teach, and the other students can't learn. You had better stop right now or else. I don't know what I am going to do with you."

Whew! That was a lot of words and look how long I was focused on that distracting student. She got a lot of my time and attention, which just might be reinforcing enough for her to tap her pencil a lot more.

## Voice Change

Changing your voice can be just the thing to refocus student attention. I know one teacher who broke into a very slow southern drawl to grab the students' attention and another who perfected an Arnold Schwarzenegger voice. Another teacher I know uses a computer voice. No matter what the age of the students, they do respond to new and different voices from their teacher.

Another effective way to change your voice is to speak in a whisper. The noise level of the students will often settle down quickly as they get quiet to hear what you are saying. This is vastly better than raising your voice to be heard over the students. When you talk exceedingly loudly, the students learn that yelling gets attention.

## Name Dropping

Name dropping is an attention focusing strategy in which you merely slip the student's name into what you are saying a time or two. It alerts the student to the need to make a change in her behavior with minimal disruption of the lesson.

# Grandma's Rule

Grandma's Rule is a verbal attention focusing strategy that you use when incorporating incentives. They are delivered as "When . . . Then . . ." statements. For example, "When you have finished with your report, then you may choose an educational game to play."

When you are using incentives, my advice is to actively involve the students in creating them. You also want to make sure that the incentives are helping to lead the students towards more intrinsic motivators, like solving a challenging problem or enjoyment of the learning process, rather than continuing an incentive forever. The goal for using incentives is to gradually wean the students off of them. You have to use lots of supportive strategies to accomplish that, because it takes a positive learning environment for students to move toward intrinsic motivation.

# Distract the Distractor

Sometimes the simple strategy of distracting the distractor can be just what you need. One way to distract is to ask the student a question. It is crucial, though, that the question not be used as an opportunity to embarrass the student. Unfortunately, sometimes a teacher will see that a student is not paying attention and will ask the student a question that he or she doesn't have a prayer of answering. This practice may lead to future angry/violent misbehaviors. You want to phrase your distracting question in such a way that the student can legitimately answer it.

Another way to distract a misbehaving student is to ask the student to perform a task for you. You need to be careful, though, in using this strategy with young children because they "love" to do things for the teacher. We don't want them learning that misbehavior is their ticket to help the teacher. Distracting the distractor from the misbehavior is what we are really after.

# Coupon Approach

The coupon approach is used to focus the attention of individuals in a different way. It is used when you want a student to reduce a particular behavior, but not eliminate it altogether. An example would be a student who meets her need for attention by asking an inordinate number of questions. We would not want that student to stop asking questions completely, but merely learn how to manage the multitude of questions asked and to develop the skill to think before asking the question or to seek the answer on his or her own.

What you would do is to meet with this student and discuss the rationale for self-monitoring of her question asking. You would then agree on the number of question coupons that the student would have to use for each day or period. One coupon is surrendered for each question asked. The student would know that when the coupons were gone, so was her question asking for the day or period. The hard part will be for you not to answer her questions after the coupons are gone on the first few days. You would say something like: "You'll be able to ask more questions tomorrow, and I am sure that you will think even more about which ones to ask. This plan is to help you get your question asking under control."

## I-Statements

I-Statements are an effective way to communicate about negative behavior. They have the following three parts:

I feel _____ (Feeling Word) _____

when you _____ (Specific Behavior) _____

because _____ (The Effect of the Behavior) _____

Examples of "I-statements" are:

"I feel annoyed when you come to class late because it disturbs everyone."

"I feel frustrated when you call out answers in class because other students don't get a chance to think about what the answer is."

"I feel irritated when you sharpen your pencil during whole group instruction because no one can hear the lesson."

A fourth optional part adds, "I would prefer that you . . ." or "I would appreciate if you would . . ." and then you fill in what the specific responsible behavior would be. This is not an original part of I-statements, but it adds a lot of power to them as you are redirecting them to the responsible behavior. You can also teach I-statements to your students. They are a nice tool for students to use when others are putting them down. They need to learn the fourth optional part for sure. School counselors and school psychologists often teach them to students of all ages. Students will sometimes use them with you, though, once they have learned I-statements. I encourage you to think of that as positive and respond accordingly. When students use strategies with you that you use with them, it is a good sign that your modeling of responsible behavior is having an impact.

I-statements only work as a corrective intervention with low-level distracting behaviors. They can be used with controlling and angry/violent behaviors as a way to initiate the interaction about their negative behavior. Then use a corrective strategy appropriate for the behavior. You need to be careful, though, using them with some students choosing angry/violent behaviors; they might be quite pleased that they have provoked a negative reaction in you.

I-statements serve several purposes. Like other attention focusing strategies in this chapter, they help you to focus your verbal interaction, so you don't go on and on. They also put the emphasis on your reaction to what the student is doing, rather than a "finger shaking," blaming perspective. This creates more receptivity on the part of the student to hearing about and doing something about his or her misbehavior. With the low level distracting behaviors that we have discussed in this chapter, I-statements can serve as a corrective intervention in that the student will often say "I am sorry" or some variation on that theme and stop the distracting behavior for at least a period of time.

# FRED JONES' APPROACH

### Assumptions
➤ Effective body language is one of your most valuable discipline tools.
➤ Effective teaching strategies can reduce misbehaviors.
➤ An incentive system will motivate students to choose responsible behavior.

### Main Points
➤ Preventing discipline problems is the most effective way to handle problems.
➤ Controlling your reaction so that you are calm and business-like is crucial.
➤ Preferred Activity Time (PAT) is a good way to motivate students. They earn time towards a preferred activity.
➤ Providing efficient help to students minimizes discipline problems.
➤ You need to actually teach responsibility.
➤ A major emphasis is on non-verbal body language—looks, proximity, facial expression, gestures, body carriage, and eye contact.
➤ "Working the room," or moving around monitoring the students on an on-going basis, is needed for prevention.
➤ You want to convey that you mean business through your firm, but non-aggressive body language. You use your body to set limits.

### Implementation
➤ Since you lose about 50% of your teaching time to off-task behaviors or disruptions to the learning, you combine the body language strategies with efficient help and an incentive system to counteract disruptions.

### Limitation
➤ You would need more strategies for the serious misbehaviors.

Remember that with all of the distracting behaviors, if you don't also incorporate supportive strategies, these corrective strategies will only be short-term solutions to deal with the immediate situation. The student will be back again doing it in a little while because the underlying need that is triggering the misbehavior has not been met. You will get long lasting results when students learn to meet their needs through responsible behavior rather than through misbehavior. This is such a crucial part of the process of being successful with your discipline plan, that I am going to repeat here the supportive strategies that are particularly relevant with students who are choosing distracting behaviors:

➢ Attention for responsible behavior choices
➢ Building positive teacher/student and student/student relationships
➢ Using encouragement and effective praise
➢ Incorporating capable strategies to adapt your instruction to meet their learning modality needs

> *What office is there which involves more responsibility, which requires more qualifications, and which ought, therefore, to be more honorable than that of teaching?*
> —*Harriet Martineau*

# Summary

When students are exhibiting *low-level, annoying distracting misbehaviors* the *"A" options for distracting behaviors* are your most effective tools. You have several *Active body language strategies* to choose from. These strategies have you using your own body as a valuable discipline tool and using no words at all. You also have several *Attention focusing strategies* to choose from that help you to deal with distracting misbehaviors, but at the same time keeping your verbal interaction at the moment of misbehavior to a minimum. Make your choices according to which strategies fit your style and the situation that you are dealing with.

Anytime that you are using corrective strategies be sure to remember the *keys to effective delivery of corrective strategies. Use as few words as possible* at the moment of misbehavior, so you won't fall into the trap of inadvertently reinforcing the misbehavior. *Control your reaction* while you are dealing with the misbehavior.

# Reflection Questions

1. Role-play active body language for the following situations:
   - Pencil tapping
   - Calling out
   - Sharpening pencils
   - Roaming the room
   - Playing with objects in desk
2. Describe a situation in which you would use each of the following attention focusing strategies:
   - Signals—Auditory and Visual
   - Notes
   - Target Stop Do
   - Voice Change
   - Name Dropping
   - Grandma's Rule
   - Distract the Distractor
   - Coupon Approach
   - I-Statements
3. Discuss the following scenarios and how you would handle them.

   **Elementary: Daydreamer**
   Josh is daydreaming. Again. As usual. As always! Any suggestions?

   **Elementary: Wanderers**
   Manuel and Sally try to race one another to the water fountain. Both of them tend to wander around the class whenever they feel like it. What will you do?

**Secondary: Talk-aholics**

Rosemary and Daniel are talk-aholics. You are aware of their reputation and know that they will be in your class this next term. Plan a hierarchy of strategies for curbing their habit.

**Secondary: Belcher**

Charles thinks that it is very funny to make loud belching noises in class. Unfortunately, the other students are laughing when he does it. What will be your strategies for dealing with this disruption?

# References

Baringer, D. K., & McCroskey, J. C. (2000). Immediacy in the classroom: Student immediacy. *Communication Education* 49 (2): 178–186.

Doyle, W. (1985). Recent research on classroom management: Implications for teacher preparation. *Teacher Education* 36 (3): 31–35.

Ginott, H. (1971). *Teacher and child.* New York: Macmillan.

Jones, F. H. (1987). *Positive classroom discipline.* New York: McGraw-Hill Book Company.

# "B" Options for
# Controlling Behaviors

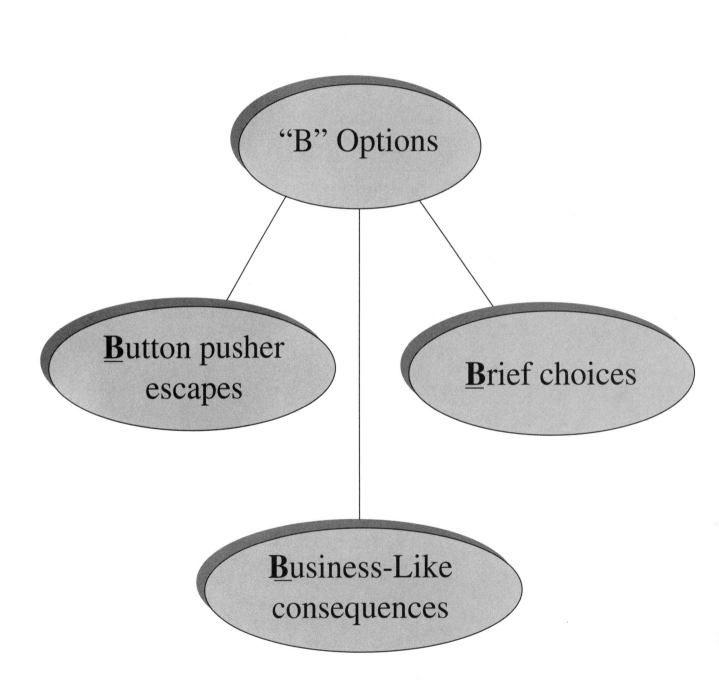

## OBJECTIVES

The learners will be able to practice strategies for the moment of misbehavior for the "controlling level" of seriousness.

**Comprehensive Classroom Management**

- Supportive Techniques
- Corrective Strategies
- Preventive Strategies
- Effective Teaching

### CHAPTER SNAPSHOT

- Button Pusher Escapes
- Brief Choice Language
- *Glasser's Approach*
- Business-Like Consequences
- *Albert et al.'s Approach*
- Unmotivated Controlling Behaviors
- *Coloroso's Approach*
- Unmotivated Gifted Students

### REMEMBER THE KEYS

🗝 **Use as Few Words as Possible**

🗝 **Control Your Reaction**

Students who are choosing controlling misbehaviors are quite adept at pushing our buttons. They seem to know instinctively what will get a rise out of us. Being prepared both mentally and with strategies to deal with their button pushing is the first step to being successful with students who engage in controlling behaviors. As with all corrective strategies we need to remember to *use as few words as possible* while the behavior is occurring. The biggest challenge, though, with controlling behaviors, is *controlling our own reaction*. It is normal and human to react when someone is skilled at pushing your buttons, but it is crucial that you do not. When you respond in a professional, business-like manner, it helps to defuse the situation rather than escalate the situation. The "button pusher escape" strategies are designed to help you deal with the initial situation when students are pushing your buttons to provoke a power struggle. These strategies help you to deal with a brewing power struggle in a manner consistent with modeling self-management. Linda Albert and her contributors (1996) call this type of strategy "Graceful Exits," because you are, in essence, offering the student a graceful way out of a problem situation, but we feel that "button pusher escapes" is more descriptive of the function they serve. Brief choice language and business-like consequences are also key ingredients to deal effectively with controlling misbehavior.

## "WHEN" TO USE CORRECTIVE STRATEGIES

**"B" Options for Controlling Behaviors**

| | |
|---|---|
| **Examples:** | "You can't make me;" "I don't know why I have to do this;" "This is stupid;" "We shouldn't have to do this;" "All the other kids are doing it. Why don't you talk to them?" |
| **Strategy Options:** | **B**utton Pusher Escapes <br> **B**rief Choices <br> **B**usiness-like Consequences |
| **Strategy Function:** | Control your reaction |
| **Teacher Reaction:** | "Hot"—angry, challenged |
| **Teacher Impulse:** | Push back, show 'em who's boss |
| **Student Unmet Need:** | Power and a sense of control over what's happening to them |
| **Supportive Solutions:** | Legitimate avenues for power in the class <br> Responsibilities <br> Involvement in the decision-making process <br> Choices, choices, and choices <br> Capable strategies |

Keep in mind that it is developmentally appropriate for students of all ages to want to have a sense of control over their lives. That process starts at age two when they say, "I want to do it myself" and continues until they go forth at eighteen to assume adult responsibilities. We want to nurture and channel the growth of positive control over their life and choices. We want to nip in the bud and rechannel the inappropriate manipulations and "You can't make me's." We want to provide legitimate avenues for power in the classroom, so they won't be battling us for power through misbehavior. Remember the positive perspective. Today's student choosing controlling misbehaviors is tomorrow's leader and creative thinker.

# **B**utton Pusher Escapes

Modeling self-management is critical when implementing "button pusher escapes." First of all, self-management impacts the current situation in a positive and defusing manner, but it also has an added long-term effect since students learn from what they see you "do." If you want the students to learn how to deal with it when their own buttons are pushed, then it is essential that they see that happening in your interactions with them. When anyone has a button pushed, he or she needs to have a way to respond to that individual to avoid escalating the situation. Having strategies to sidestep a power struggle when a student makes a provoking comment is a very necessary part of your management plan. Please equip yourself with several options to use when students push your buttons and you are tempted to lose your cool. Think of button pusher escapes as analogous to pushing the escape button on your computer to circumvent a problem that has developed. Here are your options:

**FROM RESEARCH**
Self-management and conflict resolution skills are valuable strategies for promoting responsible behavior with special needs students.
—*Dollard (1996)*

**FROM RESEARCH**
Being a positive role model is essential for positive behavior changes in students.
—*Peterson (1996)*

---

**BUTTON PUSHER ESCAPES**

➤ Acknowledge the Student's Power
➤ Table the Matter
➤ Let's Chat
➤ "To You To Me" Statements
➤ Humor
➤ Redirect the Student
➤ Responsible Thinking Questions

---

" The pessimist sees difficulty in every opportunity. The optimist sees opportunity in every difficulty. "

## Acknowledge the Student's Power

"Acknowledging the student's power" is a very useful "button pusher escape." When you are working with students who choose controlling behaviors, you sometimes hear "you can't make me." This definitely pushes teachers' buttons. I have asked hundreds of teachers what they think most teachers say at that point and their usual response is, "Oh, yes I can!" But let's really examine that. Can we make students do something? Well, we could put a pen in the student's hand and we could pick up that hand and move it around on a piece of paper. But could we really make that student engage his or her mind and actually do something? No, we couldn't. We can influence a student to choose responsible behavior, but we cannot make them. So why get into an argument about it? "Acknowledge the student's power" strategy is designed to sidestep a power struggle about whether or not you can make the student do whatever it is you would like him to do. You simply say something like, "You are right, I can't make you.

> Working out solutions with a controlling student does not imply that the student just gets away with any behavior. Students do need to be held responsible for their poor behavior choices. What we want, though, is for them to learn from their mistakes and to learn how to have a legitimate sense of power in the classroom where they don't need to be combative to feel in control. We will look at business-like consequences shortly as a viable way to accomplish holding students responsible for misbehavior, but doing so in a way that maintains their dignity and does not push back to "get" the students' buttons in exchange.

**FROM RESEARCH**

Teachers need to create caring classrooms in which students are honored, while correcting the behavior. This increases their academic performance.

—*Freiburg (1996)*

But remember what your choices are. You can either work on this now with the rest of us or you can work on it later during choice time. It is your choice."

You can change those words to fit your style and grade level, but the essence of the strategy is that you are not going to fight with students as to whether or not you can make them do something. Instead you calmly and in a business-like manner remind the students of what their choices are in the situation and leave it at that. I like to add something like, "I am sure you'll make a responsible choice." You can focus your remarks in a manner that feels comfortable to you.

## Table the Matter

"Table the matter" is a "button pusher escape" to indicate the need to close things down for now. You want to leave the door open to discuss the problem at a later time, but you indicate that now is not the appropriate time. You do want to discuss the problem with the student. You just don't want to do it when feelings are running high. "Table the matter" is a non-specific postponement of the discussion about what is bothering the student choosing controlling behaviors.

When the student makes a provoking, button-pushing comment, you say calmly and business-like, "This is not the appropriate time to discuss that. We

The key to being effective with "button pusher escapes" is the business-like manner in which they are delivered. If you lose your cool or bring a lot of emotion into your voice or your body language, the student will see that as an invitation to fight back (possibly on an instinctive level, not necessarily in their awareness level). What you want to do is to maintain a calm exterior (even if your insides are "hot") and indicate through a "button pusher escape" that you are not going to fight with the student. Your demeanor says, "I am willing to work out a solution, but I am not willing to fight." That is the message that you want your "button pusher escapes" to be giving—a congruent message that runs through the various parts of your body. As we've said before that is not necessarily easy but is essential to having positive results with students choosing controlling behaviors.

need to move on with our writing now;" or "We can discuss this later. Right now we need to complete our science experiment."

What we need to do is to take power struggles with the accompanying button pushing out of a win-lose situation altogether. We don't want to "lose" while the student "wins" nor do we want to "win" while the student "loses." So in a business-like manner we want to change the dynamics where we can work out solutions with students, but not in an adversarial or fighting manner. We want to hold them responsible for misbehavior choices, not in a combative manner, rather in a "you can learn from your mistakes" manner. We want to change the dynamics so the students are not continuing to challenge us with their choice of time and place, issue and audience. "Table the matter" strategy is a way to change the time, place, and audience. We are deferring the discussion to later when we are not on the spot, in front of the whole class, and feeling pressured.

Remember the keys to working through or defusing power struggles are to not take it personally, respond business-like, and to help the button pushing students to find a legitimate sense of power in the classroom. That way they are not always battling you for power in inappropriate ways. Meeting that need for control in a positive way is essential for a long-term solution.

One of the problems when students are using button-pushing comments aimed at instigating a power struggle is that the student is choosing the time, the place, the issue, and the audience. If we put power struggles into a win-lose situation, who do you think is going to win? I have asked that question to hundreds of teachers and their usual response is "the student." Yes, if we allow a power struggle situation to be win-lose, the odds are with the students. They are younger, have more energy, and have a lot invested in looking cool in front of their peers.

The next strategy—"let's chat"—is another choice for rescheduling the problem situation to a time and place when we are not pressured by the audience. We are deferring the discussion and problem solving to a later time so it is not happening in front of the class when feelings are running strong.

## Let's Chat

"Let's chat" is another "button pusher escape" that helps you to change the dynamics away from the student choosing the time, the place, the issue, and the audience. What you do is to acknowledge the student's frustration and offer him or her a definite meeting time. For example, Lorenzo says, "I hate this class. I am not doing this lousy assignment!"

You would say something like, "Lorenzo, you seem very frustrated about the assignment. I will be glad to meet with you and discuss it. I could meet with you at 9:00 or at 10:30. Which do you prefer?"

Giving the student a choice of times is important rather than mentioning just one time, since control is the issue here and having some control over the situation, as in choosing between two times, can temporarily satisfy the student choosing controlling behaviors. Notice, I said temporarily. You would, of course, need to meet for teacher-student chat time with the goal of working out a solution involving the student as much as possible in the decision-making process. You want the teacher-student chat time and any follow-up after that to give the student a sense of control in a positive way, not a confrontational one. With "let's chat" you are scheduling a specific postponement of the discussion about the problem and scheduling teacher-student chat time.

The next strategy "To you to me" is designed to deal with the immediate situation by focusing on what your view of the situation is and what you perceive to be the student's view.

**FROM RESEARCH**
New teachers' greatest need is practical discipline strategies.

—*Barrett and Davis (1995)*

Again the message is "I am not going to fight with you. I am willing to discuss, but not fight."

> I'll bet some of you are wondering, "What do I do if the student doesn't choose a time to talk about the issue when I use the "let's chat" button pusher escape." If you were thinking that way—great. It is always good to think critically about discipline strategies and how they would work for you. The answer to your "what do I do" question is coming up in the next chapter in the discussion of "chill out time" and "choice levels," options for dealing with angry/violent students.

## "To You To Me" Statements

"To you to me" statements are useful strategies in which you recognize the student's perspective in the problem situation, but then offer your perspective on the matter.

The student says, "This assignment is really stupid." You mentally step out of the situation, get your reaction under control, and respond, "To you this assignment seems stupid, but to me, it is an important part of learning how to solve story problems."

The "to you to me" statement gives you an opportunity to deal in the moment with the student's challenging remark without taking it personally and without fighting.

It would be very appropriate to pull this student aside a little later and process with the student her reaction to the assignment. You just don't want to do that when the misbehavior is happening.

Look to the discussion of "chill out time" in the next chapter for your choice levels when the student does not accept your offer of "pushing the escape button" on the problem, but pushes even more. Even though all controlling students will not accept an offer to push the "escape button," I would rather offer the button pusher escape first and see if they will accept it rather than jump in and engage in a power struggle. It takes two to struggle. Your "button pusher escapes" say, "I choose not to engage in a power struggle."

## Humor

Humor used appropriately can be very effective to seize the moment when a student is pushing buttons to provoke a power struggle. You deflect the button pushing with humor. Humor as an effective discipline strategy does **not** include sarcasm, harsh or bitter language, or intentionally cutting remarks. You can make fun of yourself or the situation; you should not make fun of the student in any way. Here are some examples that teachers have shared with me:

| | |
|---|---|
| Student button pushing remark: | "You don't know anything about coaching." |
| Teacher humor escape: | "Oh yes, I do. The instructions came with my Reeboks." |
| | |
| Student button pushing remark: | "This is a really dumb class." |
| Teacher humor escape: | "You need four dumb classes in order to graduate." |

Sometimes teachers say to me, "But sarcasm works." My answer is that it only appears to be working on the surface. If you could look below you would find anger and hurt lurking underneath that will come back to haunt you later. Sometimes a teacher can have an especially good relationship with the students and some low level teacher teasing does occur without too much damage. But there is always the risk that some student or students will be hurt by the stinging words. I implore you to leave sarcasm out of your discipline toolbox and put in appropriate humor that does not hurt any student.

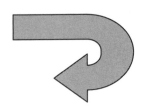

## Redirect the Student

Sometimes the best choice for a "button pushing escape" is to "redirect the student." The student says, "All the other kids are doing it. Why don't you talk to them?" Your answer would be something like, "We are talking about the choices you are making, not those of other students. I will talk to other students at other times. Please focus on your choices."

## Responsible Thinking Questions

"Responsible thinking questions" is a "button pusher escape" that has you asking the student questions to refocus when a problem situation is developing. Glasser (1986) emphasized utilizing questions that are directed at getting the student to think about what he or she is choosing to do and processing his or her own behavior. The goal is to redirect the student to choosing responsible behavior. You are helping the student to develop self-management skills. For example:

"What are you doing?"
"What should you be doing?"
"What could you be doing?"

**FROM RESEARCH**
Teaching social skills to students is important in promoting positive behavior. Teachers need to focus on teaching social skills with the same patience given to teaching writing skills.

—Stone (1993)

# Brief Choice Language

Shakespeare penned a phrase "brevity is the soul of wit." He must have been thinking of classroom discipline when he wrote that. Brief interaction combined with choices is just what is needed to deal effectively with students who are controlling. Brief choices are very appropriate, because choices can help to give students a sense of control over their lives, which connects nicely with their unmet need. Brief choice language can at first glance appear to be a matter of semantics, but it is more than that. It is critical that students make the connection that they do have control over their lives. You would be surprised at how many students, including secondary, have no clue that their actions directly impact whatever outcome they are going to experience. Brief choice language helps to make these connections for the students.

Brief choice language is deceptively simple, but actually packs a lot of power. When using brief choice language first you explicitly state the appropriate responsible behavior. Then you use the word "or," followed by what the consequence will be if the student continues to choose an inappropriate behavior. Sample statements are:

➤ "I need you to get busy on your math problems or you will need to work on them later during choice time." (See the Second "E" in RESPECT in the supportive Component, Section V, for an explanation of choice time.)
➤ "Please stop playing with things in your desk and get busy on your math problems or you will need to work on them during choice time."
➤ "I would like to see you putting some energy into your math problems or you will need to be working on them during choice time."

# GLASSER'S APPROACH

## Assumptions
➤ It is essential that we improve student satisfaction in school in order to motivate them to learn.
➤ Teachers must move from being a "boss" teacher to being a "lead" teacher.
➤ Quality in the curriculum and the instruction is of utmost importance. It needs to deal with what students consider to be important in their lives.

## Main Points
➤ Boredom or frustration with the lack of relevance or connections with the students' interests in school are major factors in most misbehaviors. School is dissatisfying for most students.
➤ In order to have effective and relevant curriculum, it must connect with students' lives, be useful and entail quality. Due to this lack, few students are currently doing their best work.
➤ Classroom meetings are critical to students being able to meet their needs for survival, belonging, power, fun, and freedom in the classroom. Students rarely misbehave when their needs are met in school.
➤ The importance of involving students in both curriculum decisions and assignments choices is emphasized.
➤ Students being actively involved in what we teach and how we teach it is needed for discipline solutions.
➤ You need to use non-punitive, non-coercive strategies to motivate students to work and learn. You should befriend students and offer encouragement, stimulation, and help.

## Implementation
➤ Implementing a quality education is most important. Actively involving students in the decision-making process is key. Quality schoolwork with quality self-evaluation are needed for students to find school a satisfying place to be. A warm supportive class environment is integral as well.

## Limitation
➤ His suggestions would take a lot of time to implement.

I used the same example—math problems and choice time—each time so you could see that there is no set way to phrase brief choice language. You can easily adapt it to your style and word choice.

The "brief" part is important because of one of the keys we have been talking about all along—the need to *use as few words as possible* when the misbehavior is occurring. This strategy is similar to the "target stop do" that we discussed using with distracting behaviors. The difference is that we did not need to add a potential consequence with "target stop do," since we were dealing with a low level misbehavior on the levels of seriousness of misbehavior. With controlling behaviors, the middle level of seriousness, we do need to let students know the logical consequence of their actions.

The power of the seemingly simple strategy brief choice language is in the structure. It focuses your interaction on just what is needed in the situation, and it emphasizes that students do have choices. Through the words that you use you are indicating that the responsibility for what befalls students rests squarely on their own shoulders. You are in essence saying, "By your current behavior choice, you are choosing to experience this consequence. You could at any given moment make different choices and have more preferred consequences as a result."

When you use brief choices, you are also empowering students to think about their choices and related outcomes. You are helping them to make the connection between their behavior and the outcomes. You are teaching them responsible behavior through the strategy you are using because you are having them experience the logical consequence of their own choices. With this in mind it becomes crucial, if we really want students to learn from their mistakes and be motivated to make responsible behavior choices in the future, that we fashion consequences in such a way that they are logical outcomes of what the student chose to do. Arbitrary, unfair, or disconnected consequences will not bring any of this about. Alfie Kohn (1996b) says that consequences are "Punishment Lite," but they do not need to be. The next section will make a clear distinction between consequences and punishment. A major factor is student involvement in the creation.

We will focus on business-like consequences shortly, but let's examine brief choice language and its usefulness a little more. In the last few years I have worked extensively with student teachers and with first year teachers supporting them in implementing effective discipline in their classes. We have met in schools and we have processed together what works and what helps them the most. You read in the CLEAR Model that it was developed from the voices of hundreds of learners who, through research, expressed what teachers do that helps them learn most effectively. Student teachers and first year

**FROM RESEARCH**
Every adolescent has latent leadership abilities. It needs to be recognized and nurtured for it to develop.

*—Fertman and van Linden (1999)*

" Punishment demands obedience, consequences allow choice. "

teachers who have read the discipline approaches highlighted in this book have let their views be known as to what strategies are most helpful to them. Their views are reflected throughout this section in terms of choices that were made about strategies featured in this book. Time and time again over the years they have expressed that using brief choice language was their most useful strategy. The new teachers reported that brief choice language:

> Created a different, more receptive reaction in their students than when they phrased a similar message differently.
> Helped the new teachers to feel more confident and prepared to deal with controlling behaviors.
> Could be used as another option for "button pusher escape."
> Could also be used to indicate a student's options about "chill out time" (see "chill out time" featured in the next chapter).
> Can be used to create choice levels when students are not accepting "button pusher escapes" (see "choice levels" featured in the next chapter).
> Could be utilized to create consequences on the spot when they had not been pre-developed (coming up next in this chapter).

> *Help each student contribute to the solution rather than be a part of the problem.*

Developing the skill to choose business-like consequences that will hold students responsible for their choices and be consistent with teaching responsible behaviors is something you need to put some thought and some pre-planning into. Let's focus on how to make consequences a part of the process of learning responsible behavior.

# **B**usiness-Like Consequences

I frequently have an opportunity to work with experienced teachers in solving discipline problems and many want me to create their consequences for them. Why can't I do that? There are several reasons. I do not know:

> The student
> The teacher and that teacher's style
> The situation
> The school culture
> With what the teacher would be willing to follow-through

# ALBERT ET AL.'S APPROACH

## Assumptions
➢ Behavior is based on choice. Students misbehave to fill their unmet need to belong.
➢ You can influence students to make responsible behavior choices. You use encouragement, intervention, and collaboration. Encouragment is your most powerful tool.
➢ Students need to feel "capable" of performing tasks, "connected" to the teacher and other students and that they can make a "contribution" to class. These 3 C's are integral.

## Main Points
➢ The goals of students' misbehavior are attention, power, revenge, and avoidance of failure.
➢ You need to develop a code of conduct with the students in which you agree on operating principles—"This is how we will interact with one another."
➢ Parents need to be partners in the discipline process.
➢ A 5 step action plan will help you deal with misbehavior.
➢ Teachers exhibit one of three discipline styles—hands-on (authoritarian), hands-off (permissive), or hands-joined (democratic). You need to use the hands-joined to be effective with students.
➢ Consequences need to be related, reasonable, respectful, and reliably enforced.
➢ Graceful exits help to defuse power struggles. They are verbal strategies that offer the student a graceful way out of the problem. For example, acknowledge the student's power, state both viewpoints and table the matter.

## Implementation
➢ The action plan process involves: 1. Describe the misbehavior. 2. Identify the goal of the misbehavior. 3. Choose an intervention strategy. 4. Select an encouragement technique. 5. Involve parents as partners in the discipline process.

## Limitation
➢ It may be difficult to determine the student's goal of misbehavior.

All of that and probably more is not known by me. How then would I be able to create a consequence appropriate to the situation? It is critical that all teachers develop consequences for their own classroom that will be comfortable for them. They also need to develop the consequences in collaboration with the students who will be affected by them. Student involvement leads to learning from the consequences.

> **" Punishment focuses on what is past. Consequences focus on the future. "**

For consequences to be effective and for them to help in this process of teaching responsible behavior they must be differentiated from punishment. Dreikurs, Grunwald, and Pepper (1982) and Dreikurs and Cassell (1972) got the educational world looking at the importance of utilizing logical consequences rather than punishment. Jane Nelsen (1987) espoused that in order to make that distinction between consequences and punishment we needed to follow the Three R's of Consequences in creating them. Her three "R's" indicate that consequences need to be "Related," "Reasonable," and "Respectful." Punishment would be defined as anything that violated those three "R's." Linda Albert and her contributors (1996) added a fourth "R" of logical consequences—"Reliably Enforced." All four of those are important for consequences to be effective and instructional. But we need to add a fifth "R" in order to emphasize an aspect that cannot be missing, if we truly want consequences to be part of the process of teaching responsible behavior. We will add "real participation" on the part of the students. The Five R's of Consequences are, therefore:

> ➤ Related
> ➤ Reasonable
> ➤ Respectful
> ➤ Reliably Enforced
> ➤ Real Participation

Without these critical R's of Consequences in place we have punishment, and punishment can have some undesirable side effects. Barbara Coloroso (1994) says that punishment is adult-oriented imposed power. It does not give students a sense of the consequence as being a logical outcome of what they chose to do. Learning responsible behavior choices means understanding the connections between behaviors and consequences. In addition to that, Coloroso says that punishment provokes one of these three F's: fear, fighting back, or fleeing. The student ends up afraid to make a mistake, wanting to fight the adult, or wanting to get away from the adult completely. Students may not like experiencing the consequence of the choice they made, but they do react to consequences differently than punishment. Dealing with logical consequences encourages them to learn from their mistakes.

# Related

Logical consequences need to have a clear connection between the behavior and the result. It should be clear to the student that "I chose to do this and this is happening to me because of what I chose to do." Having consequences directly related to the disruptive behavior makes that connection.

> ➣ I messed up the classroom, so I clean it up.
> ➣ I misused the computer, so I cannot use it the next day.
> ➣ I tore up a classroom book, so I must replace it.

# Reasonable

Logical consequences need to fit the level of the disruptive behavior. They need to be reasonable with regard to intensity and frequency of the disruptive behavior. Considering the examples above, it would not be reasonable to:

> ➣ Clean the whole school
> ➣ Lose computer time for the rest of the year
> ➣ Replace all the torn books in the class

Logical consequences must also be reasonable to you. If they aren't, then you most likely will not follow through with them. Teachers are sometimes reluctant to implement a consequence. But if they are reasonable to you, then you will follow through with the consequence and students will be able to accept them as a logical outcome of what they chose to do. I am not saying that students will be pleased to experience a consequence, just that reasonable consequences make them more accepting and open the door to students learning from the consequences.

# Respectful

Logical consequences need to be planned and implemented in a way that maintains the dignity of the student. The idea is to hold the students responsible for their disruptive behavior, but in a way that is going to make it more likely that they will choose responsible behavior in the future.

Consequences also need to be delivered in a respectful manner, if we want students to pay attention to them and to think about their own behavior choices. Remember the previous discussion in which it was pointed out that when we lose our cool, it gives the students full license to focus all of their attention on teacher behavior rather than their own. Students will not learn to make responsible choices in the future if they observe out-of-control teacher behavior and do not think about their own behavior choices. Respectful delivery and consistent modeling are crucial.

## Reliably Enforced

Are you thinking to yourself—how can all consequences be known ahead of time? If you were, you are on the right track again. You cannot anticipate everything. So you must be prepared to sometimes create consequences when the misbehavior is occurring. The brief choice language that has so many useful applications also allows you to create consequences in the moment. The student may know only a few minutes or seconds ahead of time, but it is a crucial difference that the student is then continuing the behavior when he knows the implications of his choices.

There is not a consequence in the world that will teach responsible behavior if it is not followed through and implemented. When you are designing consequences with the students, make sure that you can live with the consequences, as following through is integral to having positive results.

## Real Participation

For students to have ownership and learn from consequences, their involvement in the process of designing them is essential. During that first week of school after you have established the rules with your students, we recommend that you then work on consequences together. You would be surprised sometimes as to how effective students can be at designing logical consequences. You do need to do some pre-thinking and some pre-planning as we discussed before involving students in designing rules. You need to come into the interaction having thought of what you can live with and provide guidance for the participation process as it unfolds.

In order for students, though, to experience the consequences as logical outcomes their own behavior choices, the consequences need to be known ahead of time. That's where "real participation" comes in. When students are involved in the decision-making process, they know the implications of the choices they are making. Should they then choose misbehavior, they do so knowing the consequence of their choice. Knowing consequences ahead of time can often change their attitude about experiencing the consequence when they have made poor choices.

"I need for you to stop drawing on other group members' papers or you will need to be separated from your group for the rest of this period."

Now the student knows what will happen if he continues the misbehavior. If he continues, then the consequence of the choice is implemented. The brief choice language also gives students a warning, so please remember that another warning would only teach them that "I can have two warnings before I experience the consequence." It is wise to alert students to the implications and consequences of their choices, but we do not want to teach them to figure out how many warnings they can get away with. Remember that the more business-like your tone, body language, and demeanor, the more effective you will be. You could say something like:

> "I am disappointed that you have chosen to continue drawing on teammates' papers. You will be separated from the group for the rest of the period."

At that point, when they promise you that they won't do it again, you calmly reply, "I am sure you will make a more responsible choice next period, but by your behavior, you have already chosen separation this period."

## All Students Have the Ability to Learn Responsible Behavior

You want them to learn that you will follow through on the brief choice language and that they will experience the consequences of their choices. Please include a note of encouragement for the future and the expectation that the student will choose responsibly next time. This connects back to our initial discussion in the beginning of this section about how important it is to approach all students as if they have the ability to learn responsible behavior.

For secondary teachers, it is true that by the time students are in your classes, the misbehaviors may have become habits, and you have less time with each student in each day. So it is harder for you to have them undo years of getting a pay-off for their misbehavior. However, students can learn to make different choices in different places and they can still learn responsible behavior when they are in your secondary level class. Student involvement, though,

Please remember that when we say all students have the ability to learn responsible behavior, it is true that some students come to you with very low readiness skills for choosing responsible behavior and some come to you with very real learning challenges that impede learning responsible behavior. Notice that the word used was "impede"—not "stop"— them from learning responsible behavior. For some students it is harder to learn responsible behavior. It takes longer. It takes more support and follow-through, but they still have the ability to learn and make progress. Approaching behavior management from the perspective that all students can learn is integral to success.

> Natural consequences, rather than logical consequences, can sometimes be used and are very powerful when they are appropriate. They are consequences we do not have to create. They occur naturally. If you go outside in the rain . . . you get wet. If you skip a meal . . . you feel hungry. Use them when they will help you with teaching responsibility.

in the discipline process is even more critical with the older students. They won't buy-in to the process without it and developmentally they have a high need for having some control over their own lives. Involving them helps them to have a sense of control through responsible behavior choices.

## Business-Like Delivery

It is important to remember that "how" strategies are delivered is potentially half of their effectiveness. Consequences have been called business-like in this chapter because your delivering these consequences in a controlled, professional, business-like manner—despite your internal reaction to the controlling behavior—is essential to success.

## Many Options for Business-Like Consequences

> *" Logical consequences build conscience in children who misbehave. You actually use instances of misbehavior as teaching moments to rebuild in your child a proper sense of personal responsibility for the impact of his actions on other people and their feelings. "*
>
> —Taylor (2001a)

When the five R's of Consequences are followed and the logical consequences are Related, Reasonable, Respectful, have Real Participation, and are Reliably Enforced, they are one of your valuable tools for teaching responsible behavior. There are numerous options for logical consequences. You and your students just need to put some thought into what is related to the misbehavior. There are a few main types of logical consequences, but many specific examples that can fall under each type. Typical consequences that are associated with students choosing controlling behaviors are presented in the following paragraphs.

### Loss or delay of activity

One type of consequence that students can experience is a loss or a delay of an activity in school. An example of this would be students being delayed in going to a learning center, when their assignment was not completed because they were misusing the class time available to do the assignment. Think of more examples of when a loss or a delay of an activity would be related to a specific misbehavior.

## Denied or delayed access

Another type of logical consequence would be for students to experience denied or delayed access to areas of the classroom or areas of the school. If students were not using an area appropriately, losing access would be a related consequence of their choice. When they use class or school equipment inappropriately, then losing access to the equipment for a period of time is related. An example would be a student banging on the computer keys and then not being able to use the computer for the rest of the period. Take time to think of more examples of denied or delayed access.

## Denied or delayed interactions

Denied or delayed interactions would be a related consequence when students have abused the situation in their interactions with peers. If a student was to lose that interaction for a reasonable period of time, it would be a logical outcome of what the student chose to do. An example would be a student who was putting others down and then could not interact with those students for the remainder of the class period. Please generate more examples of denied or delayed interactions.

# Unmotivated Controlling Behaviors

> " To the power-hungry child, the only way to feel safe is to find a way to be one up and in control at all times. Any pressure that makes a child or teen feel more weak or vulnerable will result in renewed attempts at over-control. "
>
> —Taylor (2001a)

Students with a high need for control in their lives can also exhibit passive controlling behaviors in the form of not being motivated or engaged in the learning process. Unlike the active button pushers we have been focusing on in this chapter, with these students it is usually what they are "not" doing that is the problem rather than what they "are" doing. With these "unmotivated" students the issue is often "I don't want to be bothered doing all of this work that is expected of me in school. I just want to sit here and do nothing, at least certainly not the school work you want me to do. It is just too much trouble to expend all of the energy you want me to put out."

There could also possibly be other competing choices that are more reinforcing for the student than expending the time and energy needed to do

# COLOROSO'S APPROACH

## Assumptions
➢ It is important to treat students with respect and to give them both the power and the responsibility to make decisions.
➢ You need to provide guidance and support, so the students can learn inner discipline and learn to manage themselves.
➢ Students are worth the effort we expend on them.

## Main Points
➢ Only treat students the way you would want to be treated. Keeping their dignity intact is key.
➢ There are three categories of misbehavior—mistakes, mischief, and mayhem.
➢ Problems and disputes need win-win solutions.
➢ Students learn to make good decisions by having opportunities to make decisions and learning from the results.
➢ Consequences should not be punishing, but rather RSVP—reasonable, simple, valuable, and practical. Students learn positive control from logical, realistic consequences.
➢ The steps to solve problems are resolution, restitution, and reconciliation.
➢ There are three types of teachers and schools—brick wall, jellyfish, and backbone. Backbone teachers provide support and structure for students to learn responsibility.
➢ Don't give into the three cons of students—imploring, complaining, and sulking.

## Implementation
➢ You need to avoid punishment that is psychologically hurtful to students and provokes anger. Discipline helps students to see what they have done wrong and supports students in having ownership of the problem. It provides ways to solve the problem while leaving their dignity intact.

## Limitations
➢ It takes a while for some students to learn inner discipline.

Putting students' "names on the board" is an example of a consequence that does **not** follow the five R's of logical consequences. There is no logical connection with the misbehavior chosen, and it tends not to be respectful of students' dignity. The main reason it is usually not effective, though, is that students choosing controlling behaviors often find that they can take control of the strategy and seem to even enjoy doing so. Let us illustrate that for you.

Have you known a student in a class using the "name on the board" strategy that got two checks and then stopped? That student did not experience any consequence for the two checks. The next day the same student gets two checks and then stops. . . . The next day again two checks and then stops. Who is in control of that strategy? You are right . . . the student is. That student has figured out how many times he can misbehave before experiencing a consequence for his actions. The strategy is manipulated to work for him.

Now the point of this discussion is not to fix the "name on the board" strategy by adding a consequence at the first check—we still have the problem with it not being related or respectful. The point was to get you to think about how important the five R's of business-like consequences are. Please think about them as you plan and prepare and implement with student involvement the business-like consequences for your class.

school work. A negative reaction to the content being taught or the teacher who is teaching it and how it is being taught could also be a factor. The end result is passive, controlling, unmotivated behaviors that come from the students basically not wanting to do the work. Instead of openly defying us and pushing our buttons, like the students choosing active controlling behaviors, these students are not performing or not participating. They are not in your face saying "I don't want to do it," but rather saying it through their behavior.

Kick-starting these students—lighting a fire under them—is the challenge. They are trying to have some sense of control in their lives but are achieving it through lack of participation rather than overt challenging behaviors.

There is another type of unmotivated behavior that we will address in Section V, the supportive component, and that is the students who really believe that they can't do the work. They have a very powerful "I can't" message in their heads that is much louder than any "You can do it" that you are saying. The "I can't" message can be coming from various sources. The

> *No more than half of our secondary school students are willing to make an effort to learn.*
>
> —*Glasser (1986)*

## SUPPORTIVE CONNECTIONS WITH CONTROLLING MISBEHAVIORS

➤ Legitimate avenues for power in the class

➤ Responsibilities

➤ Involvement in the decision-making process

➤ Choices, choices, and choices

➤ Capable strategies

students could be perfectionists and since they can't really be perfect, they shut down and don't do very much of anything. They could have a pessimistic view of the world with very little hope that they can succeed and therefore do not try. They could be lacking in the skills to perform the task or lacking in ability. Telling the difference between unmotivated behaviors which are passive controlling behaviors (I don't want to be bothered doing it) and unmotivated behaviors that stem from an internal "I can't" is a little tricky.

Just be on the alert that there are two types of unmotivated behaviors and try to get at the heart of whether they have an "I can't" message that is very real in their eyes, or whether "I don't want to expend all that energy" is really the basis for the lack of motivation. With the "I can't" message, you would want to look to the supportive section with the "capable" strategies to work gradually on building up their capability level. With the passive controlling behaviors you would use the brief choice language strategies from this chapter as well as implementing business-like consequences that are appropriate to the situation. The "button pusher escapes" would not be as useful because these students are not openly challenging us. It is their seemingly lazy, apathetic behaviors that pose the problem and challenge us.

One thing that can be helpful is to observe the behavior of these students and not their words. They will often verbally indicate their willingness to do the work and catch up, but a look at their behaviors and what they really do will be the telling point. Utilizing lots of the supportive strategies highlighted in the box to the left. as well as looking back to the strategies in the CLEAR Model on linking to the learner would be effective choices to motivate these students who choose passive controlling misbehaviors.

# Unmotivated Gifted Students

Sometimes very able students choose the passive controlling behaviors because the instructional program is not meeting their needs. A gifted student can tune out and be very uninvolved when the learning is too easy, not relevant, or on a low level of Bloom's taxonomy (only addresses knowledge and comprehension levels of thinking). If you see unmotivated misbehaviors in very capable students in your class, please refer back to the CLEAR Effective Teaching Model for solutions. These students need challenging activities, relevance, and opportunities to think on a variety of cognitive levels. The solutions to their behavior choices are probably found in the teaching realm. If their needs do not get met through the instructional program, their behaviors could escalate into the active challenging, button pushing behaviors or even into the angry/ violent behaviors we will be looking at next. In our research we have discovered that a high percentage of the students committing terribly violent acts that we have heard about on the news had previously been identified as gifted students who were bored with school (Rogien and Anderson, 2001; Anderson and Rogien, 2002).

# Summary

You have numerous *"**B**" options for controlling behaviors.* You can choose one of the *button pusher escapes* that allow you to defuse a power struggle before it takes hold. You can use **B**rief *choice language* to communicate with students succinctly what their choices are and the implications of their choices with the accompanying **B**usiness-like *consequences.* *Business-like consequences* hold students responsible for their misbehavior choices, but they are *related, reasonable, respectful,* have *real participation,* and are *reliably enforced,* so that students can learn from their mistakes. Students can exhibit *passive controlling misbehaviors* as well as active controlling behaviors.

The *supportive solutions* that connect most effectively with students with *controlling behaviors* are to create *legitimate avenues for power* in the class, to give them *responsibilities* and *choices,* to use *capable strategies* and to actively *involve them in the decision-making* process.

Remember the importance of incorporating supportive strategies when working with students exhibiting controlling behaviors so that you can have more long-lasting results. You do not want to just deal with the immediate situation and neglect the long-term implications of what the supportive strategies will add to the resolution. Students who are choosing controlling behaviors have an unmet need for a sense of control over their own lives. Helping them to meet that need through responsible behavior is vital to success.

# Reflection Questions

1. Move into small discussion groups of no more than five participants. Discuss what "button pusher escapes" you think would work best for you. Justify why you think the strategy matches your personality or personal preferences.
2. For which of the scenarios below would the "button pusher escapes" be appropriate? For which of the scenarios would the brief choices strategy be most appropriate? Defend your choices.
3. Develop a set of business-like consequences to use in your classroom. Identify related misbehaviors that would match the consequences. Incorporate the five R's in your set of consequences:

- Related
- Reasonable
- Respectful
- Reliably Enforced
- Real Participation

4. Discuss the following scenarios and how you would handle them.

### Elementary: Cheating

It's achievement test time. You have tried to encourage all of your students to do their very best on their daily work, at home with their chores, and especially now on their annual achievement tests. You have been careful NOT to disproportionately increase test anxiety. However, during the reading comprehension section, you notice that Melissa is suffering from severe diagonal vision disorder (cheating). And at least two other students are well aware of her chronic disorder. What prescription would you recommend to treat her malady?

### Elementary: Mutiny on the Bounty

You have been chosen to direct the class play. Your charges range in grade level from first to eighth. There are three leading roles, 12 supporting roles, and a chorus that involves about 20 other students. Two issues have presented themselves as challenges on a particular day about two weeks into the practice schedule: 1) Several of the supporting actors think they are better qualified to fill the lead roles, and have made their opinions known to the rest of the cast, and 2) the unrest has precipitated subtle acts of sabotage which have resulted in lead actors "tripping" on the stage, "mistakes" in the scripts, and unrest among the ranks who are waiting for their cues off stage. Your challenge? How to avoid Mutiny on the Bounty!

### Secondary: Defiance

You have just handed back the exam results. Sean is NOT one of your outstanding students, and is not happy with his grade. You ask, "Sean, do you have any questions on the exam?" His retort challenges the validity of your test, compares your IQ to your shoe size, states his opinion about your heritage, and suggests a place for you to take an extended vacation. Sean uses descriptive language and explicit adjectives. Your response?

### Secondary: Speech

Sammy has had a bad day. You were busy during the passing period rearranging your notes and overheads for the next class and didn't see Sammy when she made her entrance, or you would have noticed the distraught look she wore on her face. The bell rings and you plunge into the lesson. Just as you are about to make point number two on your outline, Sammy stands up and blurts out, "What good is this _____ anyway? Who needs this _____? You're wasting our time making us sit hear and endure this mindless lecture. Why don't you just take the rest of the year off and let us do something fun? This class makes me hurl chunks!". . . Eloquent speech! . . . Your immediate thoughts? . . . your response? Remember you're on stage!

# References

Albert, L., Kyle, P., Desisto, P, Maguire, M., Zgonc, Y., Smith, F., & Soriano, A. (1996). *Cooperative discipline.* Circle Pines, MN: American Guidance Service, Inc.

Anderson, H., & Rogien, L. (2002). Gifted youth and aberrant behaviors: Searching for predictors. Paper presented at the Northern Rocky Mountain Educational Research Association Regional Conference, Estes Park, CO.

Barrett, E. R., & Davis, S. (1995). Perceptions of beginning teachers' in-service needs in classroom management. *Teacher Education and Practice* 11 (1): 22–27.

Coloroso, B. (1994). *Kids are worth it!: Giving your child the gift of inner discipline.* New York: Avon Books.

Dollard, N. (1996). Constructive classroom management. *Focus on Exceptional Students* 29 (2): 1–12.

Dreikurs, R., Grunwald, B. B., & Pepper, F. C. (1982). *Maintaining sanity in the classroom: Classroom management techniques.* New York: Harper and Row, Publishers.

Dreikurs, R., & Cassell, P. (1972). *Discipline without tears: What to do with children who misbehave.* New York: Elsevier-Dutton.

Fertman, C. I., & van Linden, J. A. (1999). Character education: An essential ingredient for youth leadership development. *NASSP Bulletin* 83 (609): 9–15.

Freiburg, H. (1996). From tourist to citizens in the classroom. *Educational Leadership* 54 (1): 32–36.

Glasser, W. (1986). *Control theory in the classroom.* New York: Harper and Row.

Kohn, A. (1996b). *Beyond discipline: From compliance to community.* Alexandria, VA: Association for Supervision and Curriculum Development.

Nelsen, J. (1987). *Positive discipline.* New York: Ballantine Books.

Peterson, T. (1996). Discipline for discipleship. *Thresholds in Education* 22 (4): 28–32.

Rogien, L., & Anderson, H. (2001). Gifted and aberrant behavior. Paper presented at the Northern Rocky Mountain Educational Research Association Regional Conference, Jackson Hole, WY.

Stone, S. (1993). Issues in education: Taking time to teach social skills. *Childhood Education* 69 (4): 194–195.

Taylor, J. (2001a). *From defiance to cooperation: Real solutions for transforming the angry, defiant, discouraged child.* Roseville, CA: Prima Publishing.

# "C" Options for
# Angry/Violent Behaviors

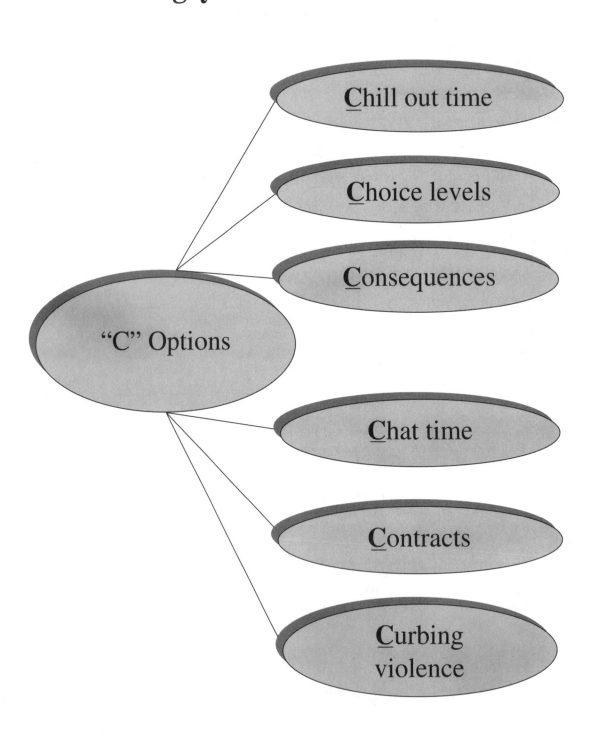

Comprehensive
Classroom
Management

Supportive
Techniques

Corrective
Strategies

Preventive
Strategies

Effective
Teaching

## OBJECTIVES

The learners will be able to practice strategies for the moment of misbehavior for "angry and/or violent level" of seriousness.

### CHAPTER SNAPSHOT

- **Keeping above the "C" Level**
- **<u>Ch</u>ill Out Time**
- **<u>Ch</u>oice Levels**
- **<u>C</u>onsequences**
- **<u>Ch</u>at Time with Students**
- **<u>C</u>ontracts**
- **<u>C</u>urbing Violence**
- *Curwin and Mendler's Approach*

# Keeping above the "C" Level

### REMEMBER THE KEYS

Use as Few
Words as Possible

Control Your
Reaction

Angry and/or violent behaviors are the highest level of seriousness of misbehavior. These are the behaviors that trigger the strongest reaction in us. These are the behaviors that sometimes provoke a reaction at the "sizzling" level. Our natural impulse is to strike back, to retaliate, or escape, as responding to angry and/or violent behaviors tends to kick in our flight or fight reaction. The challenge to *control your reaction* is at an all time high. It is even more crucial with angry and/or violent misbehaviors that you get your emotions under control and respond appropriately. Students' anger can be coming from a wide variety of sources, including: family stressors, school problems, media/entertainment impact, and various societal influences. Their choice of resorting to violent behavior is further impacted by peer influences, fear, drugs/alcohol, territorial squabbles, and perceived injustices. Despite varying sources and influences, what these students have in common is that their main unmet need is being able to deal with their anger in an appropriate way.

**FROM RESEARCH**
Positive, helpful teacher-student communication reduces the anger level of behaviorally disordered aggressive adolescents.

—*Crowley (1993)*

It is essential that we model self-controlled emotions in our interactions with these students if we are to have any hope of achieving our goal of students with angry and/or violent misbehaviors learning more constructive, prosocial ways to deal with their anger and alternatives to violent actions.

Your modeling of self-management is more important than ever. It is critical that angry and/or violent students see you modeling self-control and responsible behavior even if you are experiencing strong emotions. There are, of course, other supports that need to be in place in order to help angry and/or violent students to deal with their feelings constructively, but what you model in your interactions with all of the students is a vital piece of the puzzle.

Please think back for a moment to the discussion in chapter 10 about developing your own strategy for getting *your reaction under control.* I shared with you that one of my strategies to control my reaction, when I am tempted to lose my cool, is to ask myself, "What am I modeling for this student?" What will the student learn from what I "do"? If we want to make progress with students who are angry or violent, we have to consider how what we "do" impacts them.

If we want to have long-lasting results, then we need to combine strategies from all four components to help students with angry and/or violent misbehaviors learn how to deal with their angry feelings in more constructive ways. You need to look at the teaching choices you are making to connect the learning with the students. You need to set up a positive environment that will be perceived as fair through preventive strategies. You need to use practical corrective strategies that will maintain the student's dignity, while holding them accountable for poor, or even unacceptable, behavior choices they make. You need to look to the supportive strategies to create a school environment that counteracts some of the sources and influences of angry and/or violent behaviors and, of course, you need to model appropriate ways of dealing with emotions in your interactions. Let's start with exploring some of the corrective options you have to accomplish that.

# "WHEN" TO USE CORRECTIVE STRATEGIES

## "<u>C</u>" Options for Angry and Violent Behaviors

**Examples:**          Hurting others physically; hurting others emotionally; destroying things; intimidation of others and other bullying behaviors; violent actions (intense physical harm)

**Strategy Options:**    <u>C</u>hill Out Time
                         <u>C</u>hoice Levels
                         <u>C</u>onsequences
                         <u>C</u>hat Time with Students
                         <u>C</u>ontracts
                         <u>C</u>urbing Violence

**Strategy Function:**   Control your reaction

**Teacher Reaction:**    "Boiling"—outraged, fearful, intimidated, dislike

**Teacher Impulse:**     Retaliate, fight back

**Student Unmet Needs:**  Dealing with anger constructively

**Supportive Solutions:**  Anger management
                           Conflict resolution
                           Learning pro-social behaviors
                           Stress management
                           Forming positive teacher-student and student-student relationships
                           Forming a connection and commitment to the school and extracurricular activities
                           Increased parent-child communication
                           Expectations of success by the student
                           School counselor and school psychologist help
                           Effective teaching choices linking to learner interests
                           Peer mediation
                           Peer counseling

# <u>C</u>hill Out Time

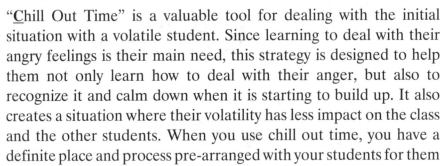

> **If you are patient in one moment of anger, you will escape 100 days of sorrow.**
> —*Chinese Proverb*

"<u>C</u>hill Out Time" is a valuable tool for dealing with the initial situation with a volatile student. Since learning to deal with their angry feelings is their main need, this strategy is designed to help them not only learn how to deal with their anger, but also to recognize it and calm down when it is starting to build up. It also creates a situation where their volatility has less impact on the class and the other students. When you use chill out time, you have a definite place and process pre-arranged with your students for them to calm down when they are losing control. Chill out time can also be used for students to process their misbehaviors and to work on their own ideas and plans for choosing responsible behavior in the future.

You implement chill out time with your students in the first week of school. If you are reading this and it is past your first week of school, you can act as if this week were your first and start establishing it now. It is best to have chill out time implemented in the first week when you are laying the groundwork for your entire teaching and discipline program—when you are processing and developing your prevention strategies with the students and sharing with them what corrective strategies you will be using and your rationale.

You let students know that we all get angry and upset at times, but we all need to learn to deal with those feelings in a way that doesn't hurt anyone, including ourselves. You say something like, "We are going to have a way that students in this class can take the time to get their act together when angry or upset feelings are building up. We will have chill out time. Sometimes you will have the opportunity to choose going to the chill out area, if you feel that you are about to lose control. At other times I might see you starting to get upset and I will give you the choice of calming down or going to the chill out area until you have calmed down. The purpose of this will be to give you a chance to chill out before you choose misbehavior as a way to deal with your anger or upset feelings."

"Unfortunately, sometimes we won't catch it in time and you may lose control and make a poor choice of behavior before you get calmed down. In those instances we will still use chill out time as a way to help you calm down after you have lost control. You will, of course, be responsible for poor choices that you make in anger and experience the appropriate consequence. We will work together tomorrow on designing consequences for the class. But the main focus of chill out time after you have lost control will be to think about the choices you have made and plan how you can make more responsible choices in the future."

You want to make sure that the students see chill out time as an opportunity to exercise their choice and self-control, not as a punishment.

As usual you can change the words to fit your style and your grade level, but you want to get across the idea that chill out time is a non-punitive time to get your act together. It can be self-selected by the students following a certain process you have outlined, or it will be a choice offered by you when they seem to be losing self-control. Furthermore you have the option of using a chill out refocus form (see the appendix for examples) designed to help your students think through choices that they are making and how they can avoid losing control and choosing misbehavior in the future. In cases where students have "really" lost control, calming down enough to fill out the chill out refocus form responsibly would be their ticket for coming back to class.

## Chill Out Time Connection with Time-Out

If "chill out time" is beginning to sound like time-out to you, please think only of examples in which time-out was a very effective, proactive time to allow students a process and the space to calm down when they are losing control in the class and to think about the choices they are making. We have chosen the name "chill out time" to emphasize the purpose of the strategy—to regain self-control.

Time-out, unfortunately, is often misused, and when used inappropriately, does not work very effectively. For some teachers, time-out is merely parking the student unsupervised in the hall for hours almost forgetting about him or her. The time is not used well and the focus is not on calming down and better choices in the future, but merely removal. The focus is not on holding the student accountable for poor behavior choices, but on getting rid of the problem, at least temporarily. When there is a dangerous situation in the class, removal is definitely needed, but for most classroom problems, the time can be used more constructively. If implemented from the first week of school as a cooling off, getting-your-act-together time, that is a proactive part of the problem solving process, chill out time becomes a valuable tool for working more effectively with students exhibiting angry or violent behaviors.

Time-out is also usually not effective when used as a consequence, even though that is how it is often used, because most of the time the student doesn't want to be in class anyway. Time-out then can be at best a ticket out of an unwanted situation and at worst, very reinforcing for the student's misbehavior. Please think of chill out time as a reframing of time-out, so it becomes a

useful tool to calm down classroom difficulties and a time for students to process their choices in a problem-solving mode.

## Chill Out Time Is Not a Consequence

"Chill out time" is not intended to be a consequence. It doesn't work effectively as a consequence. It is a calm down period before the consequence is implemented. In situations where your student went to the chill out area and calmed down before a consequence was warranted, or in other words, before the student lost control and misbehaved, the consequence after chill out time would merely be holding that student accountable for work that missed while in the chill out area. Being held accountable for work missed while in chill out time is very important, because we want chill out time to act as a pressure relief valve for students losing control in class. We want it to operate as a proactive, cooling off, getting-your-act-together time, but we don't want it misused as a way for a student to get out of something he or she does not want to do in class.

If students' behavior before going to the chill out area does warrant a consequence, then chill out time acts as a way for the students to calm down enough to accept the consequence as the logical outcome of what they chose to do. They may not want the consequence, but they will be more accepting of the logical consequence after they have calmed down and feelings are not running strong. Consequences come after chill out time. Chill out time is not the consequence. Sometimes chill out time can be just a few seconds or minutes. Sometimes students, and maybe even you, are "sizzling" enough to require a longer chill out time.

## The Need for Chill Out Time

"Chill out time" is beneficial for all involved. It is beneficial for the students with angry or violent behaviors because it gives them a legitimate way to deal with emotions stemming from their angry feelings. It benefits the other students, because it creates a class safety valve. It benefits the teacher because it is a proactive way to deal with volatile students with the emphasis on strategies for calming down. It is also helpful for the teacher as far as implementing consequences are concerned. What kinds of consequences do we implement in the heat of the moment when our own feelings are running strong? The answer I've heard from hundreds of teachers is consequences that are "too severe."

We can go overboard and implement consequences that are way out of line, too severe, or ones we really can't follow through with. "You are going to stay after school for the rest of your life!!!" Then we either need to stay after school for the rest of our life with that student or we have to back up and renegotiate. Chill out time not only lets the student calm down, but also helps you *get your reaction under control,* so you can effectively implement consequences that fit the situation. When you are calm, you can be more successful at utilizing consequences that follow the five R's—Related, Reasonable, Respectful, Real Participation, and Reliably Enforced.

# Options for Choosing a Place for Chill Out Time

"Chill out time" needs to be in a pre-arranged place with the process for going there clearly understood by the students. We don't want students just walking out of class and going who knows where to calm down or just going anywhere in our classroom. When you are setting the stage for chill out time in the first week of school, you make sure that students know, in addition to the rationale and purpose, where the chill out area is and how they get there. You would also talk to them about the chill out refocus form (see the appendix for examples), if you are going to use that. You would emphasize the problem-solving, getting-your-act-together focus of the chill out refocus form. They also need to know the process you want them to use, if they are going to be able to self-select chill out time.

Being able to self-select chill out time is particularly essential for angry or violent students. We encourage you to allow for this option when setting up chill out time. You want your volatile students to learn to recognize what sets them off and what triggers their anger and violent choices. You especially want them to be able to do something proactive to deal with brewing feelings before students lose control. When students self-select chill out time, you would, of course, hold them responsible for schoolwork they missed while in chill out time, so they will not abuse this option. Options for chill out time include an area in the school, an area in your own classroom, or create a partnership with another teacher in another classroom in the same building.

> **OPTIONS FOR CHILL OUT TIME**
>
> ➢ Chill out room in the school
> ➢ Chill out area in your own classroom
> ➢ Chill out partner with another teacher in the building

## *Chill out room in the school*

More and more schools are realizing the value of having a supervised room in the school where students can go to calm down and to work on processing their misbehavior choices and to plan for more responsible choices in the future. I have encountered schools that have called their version of a supervised chill

out room several different names, including opportunity room, refocus room, safe school room, and responsible thinking room. The main goal of this investment some schools choose to make is to provide a place for students to calm down out of their classrooms, where an adult will supervise and support them in processing their own misbehavior choice using that school's version of the chill out refocus form (see the appendix for examples). If you want to know more about chill out rooms, a practical resource for creating "responsible thinking rooms" (a version of the "chill out room") in schools that empower students to be part of the solution process is Ford's (1996) *Discipline for Home and School,* based on Glasser's (1992) work with *Quality Schools.*

If your school has such an opportunity, use it to create a version of chill out time that will work for you. It should be a proactive, problem-solving part of your discipline program. In some schools this room also serves as a detention or in-school suspension room. Those are situations when the room is used as a consequence for poor choices. The chill out time aspect of it needs to be kept as a getting-your-act-together period that comes before consequences are implemented to fit the situation.

## Chill out area in your own classroom

When special supervised rooms are not available, some teachers prefer to have a chill out area in their own classroom. You need to designate an area that is out of the mainstream and gives students an opportunity to calm down. They can also process their behavior choices and plan for future choices in this area if you are using the chill out refocus form. Having chill out time in your own room is often effective, but sometimes students' classmates pay too much attention to the student in the chill out area. If this happens, and a special supervised room is not available in your school, we recommend the next choice.

## Chill out partner with another teacher

More and more teachers are asking another teacher to be a chill out partner with one another. This would be all pre-arranged in collaboration with the students in the first week of school. The students in my class would know that our chill out area is in Mr. Fernando's class and the chill out area for Mr. Fernando's class is in our classroom. The students would all know ahead of time the problem-solving, calm-down focus of this strategy, where to go in the other classroom, and what to do with the chill out refocus forms waiting there for them to help process their behavior choices.

It is one of the mysteries of classroom discipline, but the chill out partner option usually works more effectively than chill out time being in your own classroom. When the students who need to chill out are in their own classroom, their behavior is sometimes captivating to their own classmates, but when they go into another class to chill out, it doesn't interest the students in the other class in the same manner. Usually it has little to no impact on the other class.

> One thing you do not want to do is to have a wide discrepancy in grade levels with your chill out partner. You would never say something like this to a sixth grader, "Well, if you are going to act like a kindergartener, go to the Kindergarten room." We do not want this to humiliate the students, but rather be aimed at helping them to make more responsible behavior choices after calming down and experiencing the consequences of their own choices.

### The office and chill out time

In general the office is the least effective option for chill out time. Remember that chill out time is designed to be a proactive part of the problem-solving process to give students an opportunity to get their act together and to process their choices. The office is the heart and center of the whole school with a lot going on and various adult conversations to listen in on. Have you ever watched a student parked in the office during ineffective use of time-out? People walk by and will say things to him like, "Oh, you are in trouble again, are you? What did you do this time?" Between the attention and the activity, the time in the office may be reinforcing. Save the office for when you need strong back up and support. (See the section in choice levels coming up for a more complete rationale.)

## Implementing Chill Out Time

When a student appears to be getting emotional and possibly losing control, you should say something like:

> "Teachers need to actually teach self-control to their students."
> —Brophy (1987)

> ➤ "I need you to calm down and get busy on your work or go to the chill out area until you are ready to cooperate."
> ➤ "I see that you are getting really frustrated. I think that some chill out time would be very helpful to you to keep your cool."
> ➤ "I need you to get yourself together immediately and stop putting others down or go chill out until you can."

Brief choice language gets put to good use when implementing chill out time. As usual you can vary the words to fit what will work for you.

## What If the Student Refuses to Go to Chill Out Time?

You have implemented chill out time in the first week, explained the rationale and its non-punitive, getting-your-act-together focus, and all of the students know what the chill out options are. Most of your students are cooperating in this strategy and it is helping to calm things down when students get upset. Then a problem situation develops with Jackie. You say "Jackie, you seem really upset, but I need you to chill out now or go to the chill out area until you can get it together," and Jackie says in reply, "No, I am not going anywhere. I am angry and you can't make me!"

What do you do now? The choice levels strategy is your best option when a student is refusing to cooperate in chill out time or does not accept your "button pusher escape" (described in detail in chapter 12).

# Choice Levels

In the context of all four components of management and discipline (effective teaching, preventive, corrective, supportive) being implemented in your class, combined with your students being actively involved in both the learning and the discipline process, most students will respond to the strategies we've been exploring together. Most of them will cooperate with your use of chill out time to calm things down and "button pusher escapes" to defuse difficult situations, but reality says that not all students will respond positively. You need to be prepared mentally and with strategies for refusals.

When you are implementing chill out time and you have given Jackie the choice of calming down or going to the chill out area and she refuses, the choice levels is a tool to respond in a business-like manner, even though your insides are churning at this point. With choice levels you are applying the brief choice language that we practiced in chapter 12. Instead of fighting or arguing with the upset, uncooperative student, as calmly as possible, you use brief choice language to keep narrowing the choices available to the student who is refusing. The real secret to choice levels working is a controlled, business-like delivery.

# Example of Choice Levels with Button Pusher Escapes

We'll look back now at the "button pusher escapes" that we discussed in chapter 12. We addressed the fact that sometimes a student will not accept your "button pusher escape" and alluded to the fact that a strategy would be coming up in this chapter to help you with the more difficult situations when a student is not responding to your attempt to defuse the situation. We had an example in the last chapter of using the "let's chat" button pusher escape when Lorenzo was upset. Let's see what your choice level options would be if Lorenzo refuses to accept your "let's chat" strategy.

Lorenzo says, "I hate this class. I am not doing this lousy assignment!"

### First choice level

You start with the "let's chat" button pusher escape. You would say something like:

> "Lorenzo, you seem very frustrated about the assignment. I will be glad to meet with you and discuss it. I could meet with you at 9:00 or at 10:30. Which works for you?"

> Lorenzo does not accept the "button pusher escape." He says, "I don't like either of those times. I'm not going to meet with you. I want to talk about it now. This assignment is lousy."

### Second choice level

> "Lorenzo, I know that you are upset about something, but now will not work. We are in the middle of a lesson. I need for you to choose a time to meet or go to the chill out area until you have calmed down and can choose."

> Lorenzo's next reply is, "I told you I wasn't going to choose a time and I am not going to the chill out area."

### Third choice level

> "Lorenzo, I am sorry that you are so upset, but at this point your choices are to escort yourself to the chill out area or I will need to call someone from the office to escort you. I'm sure you can make a responsible choice."

It is hard for you, the teacher, to remain calm, controlled, and business-like in the face of continued defiance, but that is the path to resolution of the problem. Most students will respond to one of those three choice levels, particularly if you are successful in being non-combative in your tone-of-voice and body language. With the very small percentage (I call them the "Three Per Centers") that will persist beyond level three in refusing or creating a danger to others, taking action is what is needed. This is the time to involve the office and follow through with the last option of calling the office to escort the student to the chill out area or detention. We strongly recommend saving the office as a deterrent only for serious situations, when you need strong back-up and support.

---

Often teachers overuse the threat of sending a student to the office on trivial infractions, so that when the office is needed, when a student is totally uncooperative or creating a dangerous situation, the office option doesn't have the power left to deter the persistent, out-of-control angry and violent student. Save the office for when you really need it. Sometimes when I am working with experienced teachers, they tell me that they don't have a system in their school for strong back-up and support to implement with students who go past level three and are creating very difficult, or even dangerous situations. My recommendation to those teachers is to go back to their schools and initiate dialog about what the teachers' lines of support are when that small percentage of students creates a major problem. It is crucial that every school work out those details as part of their crisis management plan.

---

# Example of Choice Levels with Chill Out Time

Sometimes there is only room in the problem interaction for two choice levels. Let's go back to Jackie and her refusal to cooperate in chill out time.

*First choice level*

Your original statement indicating need for chill out time:

> "Jackie, you seem really upset, but I need you to chill out now or go to the chill out area until you can get it together."

> Jackie's reply is, "No, I am not going anywhere. I am angry and you can't make me!"

*Second choice level*

Brief choice language narrows her choices.

> "Jackie, I can tell you are very upset, but you know how we handle anger in this class. Your choice now is to take yourself to the chill out area and work on calming down there or I will need to call someone from the office to take you there. I hope you will make the responsible choice."

We do hope that Jackie will make the responsible choice and most students will respond to one of the levels, if the choice levels are delivered in a calm, business-like manner. If Jackie continues being totally uncooperative, that is the time to get the office involved and tap into your school's crisis plan for completely uncooperative or dangerous students.

## Time to Take Action

Choice levels are not appropriate when a student is creating a dangerous situation. When there is the potential of harm to people or things, you need to take action. Immediate removal is warranted in those situations without utilizing choice levels. I once dealt with a student who lost control so much he started throwing chairs in the class. Action was needed at that point, and not choice levels.

I called the office to send for the individuals designated to remove students when they are creating a dangerous situation. Later after the student had calmed down we met to implement the consequence for his actions, but also to work on solutions in the future. For a lasting solution, this student needed to recognize what triggered his angry reactions, so he could get it under control before things got so bad. His consequence was to be isolated from the other students for a period of time in the chill out room, which at that school doubled as an in-school suspension room.

# Consequences

Consequences are an excellent tool to help angry and violent students experience the logical outcome of what they have chosen to do. The five R's of consequences are critical with these volatile students as well as the controlling students in the last chapter. For the students to learn from the logical consequences of their choices, the consequences need to be related, reasonable, respectful, have real participation, and be reliably enforced. All of the pre-

viously discussed options of consequences apply when you are dealing with students choosing angry or violent behaviors. Loss or delay of activity consequences, denied or delayed access consequences, denied or delayed interactions consequences (described in chapter 12) are often related to the misbehavior, when you are dealing with volatile students. It is important to have the consequence connect with the behavior that the student enacted, so that the student can experience the consequence as a logical outcome of what she chose to do. There is another category of consequences that needs to be added, which is often the most relevant when you are working with angry and violent misbehaviors. We need to add restitution consequences.

## Restitution Consequences

Restitution consequences are often relevant when students are choosing angry or violent behaviors, because these consequences focus on repairing the damage that was done. Since students who are angry or violent usually exhibit hurtful, destructive behaviors, making reparations is both appropriate and necessary. If the student messes something up, it is cleaned by the student. If the student breaks something, then it is fixed by the student. If the student destroys something, it is replaced by the student.

Replacing can be difficult sometimes, if the object destroyed has much value, but you want to make sure that the student is in some way involved in undoing the damage. You don't want a situation where the parents of the student are the only ones responsible for replacement. You want the student to be making restitution at some level. It might even entail the students doing community service for the school to contribute to his debt of restitution.

The hardest type of restitution is repairing the damage done to another person. Hurtful words or hurtful actions are the most difficult damage to

repair. Forcing the angry or violent student into insincere reparation with someone else does not accomplish much. Undoing the damage of harm to others cannot be forced. Healing relationships is more difficult than fixing or replacing material things. The most effective way to bring about restitution for hurt to others is to first wait until after chill out time, so the angry or violent student has calmed down and is more receptive to accepting responsibility for his or her actions. Then the reparation with the offended person becomes one of the choices for consequences. When chosen from two or three possible consequences, sincerity in making amends with another student or adult is much more likely. Teacher-student chat time can be a great tool to facilitate this process.

---

### CHAT TIME OPPORTUNITIES

➢ Define the problem with the student
➢ Focus on the student's strengths
➢ Have the student hear the teacher's perspective on the problem
➢ Hear the student's perspective on the problem
➢ Explore solutions together
➢ Select a viable solution(s)
➢ Discuss how to make solutions work
➢ Teach a replacement behavior
➢ Practice responsible behavior
➢ Settle on a consequence for the misbehavior
➢ Create incentives for responsible behavior
➢ Encourage future responsible behaviors
➢ Actively involve the student in the discipline process
➢ Build positive teacher-student relationships

---

# Chat Time with Students

Chat time is a very valuable problem-solving tool for you to use. It is one of your options for working on long-term solutions with angry and violent students. It is simple in that it involves getting together with the student and having a chat about the problem. But it is also complex because it is one of your primary choices for being able to actively involve the student in the discipline process. Chat time can be as simple as pulling a student to the side, while the other students are working, and having a short chat, or you can schedule a time to have a more in-depth chat.

All of the chat time opportunities above are relevant options for making the most of chat time with students. You may not be able to accomplish all of those in one chat, especially if it is a pulling-aside, short chat, but these are all important aspects of having long-term results with angry or violent students or with any students.

Remember that having or scheduling chat time is a great option for mis-behaving students. It is your best tool for involving the student, which makes it more likely that you will get buy-in, and that makes it more likely that the student will actually follow-through and implement appropriate responsible behavior changes. Use chat time often. But do remember that listening is a major part of it.

**FROM RESEARCH**

Involving students in the decision-making process and promoting student reflection about their own behavior is the key to effective discipline.

—*Wade (1997)*

Creating a situation during chat time where your students feel as if you are actually listening to them does not mean that you are excusing or letting them get away with the misbehavior. Rather you are listening for the purpose of working on the same side and looking for solutions together. Remember that "**real participation**" is one of the **five R's of consequences** (related, reasonable, respectful, have real participation, and be reliably enforced) and participation is a prerequisite for consequences to be part of the process of teaching responsible behavior. We want our students to learn from their poor choices and to be motivated to make more responsible ones. Chat time is one of your best options to accomplish that.

## What If the Student Doesn't Cooperate in Teacher/Student Chat Time?

Like many of the other strategies that we have talked about, sometimes students will make poor choices and not cooperate in the chat time process, even with its problem-solving focus and even with its opportunity to be involved in the discipline process. It is critical that you handle it in the same manner as other poor choices of students and be as business-like as possible. Students may be non-participatory, sidetracking, offering silly suggestions, or even being disrespectful in the chat time process. Being prepared to deal with uncooperative responses and knowing what to say will help you to handle it effectively.

## Non-participatory

These students just don't make suggestions. Their typical responses when asked for suggestions for solutions are, "I don't know" or "I can't think of anything" or possibly they will just hang their head and mumble. This can be frustrating, since you are trying to give them an opportunity to be empowered to make responsible choices and it just seems like their batteries are dead. Some possible phrases you could use with non-participatory students are:

"Some of the students that I have worked with have tried _____ and some have tried _____ . What do you think might work for you?" (You are giving them some choices that have worked for their peers.)

"I'd like you to be involved in the decision making, but if you can't think of any ideas, I will need to decide what happens." Sometimes that can spark them into thinking and contributing, but if it doesn't, then you decide. You cannot do more than invite students to be part of the process.

## Sidetracking

These students want to get you off in every direction except the one that entails looking at the choices that they are making. They might say to you, "I'm not the only one doing it. Why are you just picking on me?" With sidetrackers you could say:

"We are talking about the choices you are making. Let's focus on that. I'll be chatting with other students at other times."

"You sure are trying to get me off on a sidetrack. Let's focus on the problem we are having." (You are redirecting them back on track.)

## Silly suggestions

These students just come up with any off-the-wall suggestion just to divert things. They might say something like, "Well, what I think should happen is that we shouldn't have assignments in class anymore." Examples of how you could reply to silly suggestions:

"I need you to take this seriously and give me some responsible suggestions or I will need to decide."

"That won't help us to solve the problem we are having. Let's focus on that." (You are indicating the need to participate responsibly.)

### Disrespectful

Even though it is recommended that you invite students to be a viable part of the discipline process, that doesn't mean that you need to persist, if they are being disrespectful. Some of your options with disrespectful students would be to say something like:

Note the use of brief choice language in the chat time strategy. Brief choice language is useful in a wide variety of discipline situations.

"I am treating you with respect and I expect the same back from you, or we will need to end this chat time now."

"I am disappointed at the choices you are making. I will decide what happens this time. I hope that you will make better choices next time."

# <u>C</u>ontracts

**FROM RESEARCH**

Teachers need to encourage students to deal with their own behavior and have them be part of the process of identifying solutions. This is significantly more effective than imposing solutions.

—*Dowd (1997)*

Contracts are another useful tool with many misbehaving students, but especially with students choosing angry or violent misbehaviors. There is something about writing an agreement down and signing it that makes it more real and more likely that there will be follow-through, both from you and the students. You can use a more formalized contract (see the appendix for examples). Formal contracts would be appropriate used in conjunction with the more in-depth chat time. With more difficult problems the more in-depth contract is needed. Building in consequences, if the student does not stick to the agreement, is important, as well as incentives to encourage responsible behaviors. Don't overlook the power of focusing on the student's positive qualities. It is hard to see positive qualities sometimes when students are choosing angry or violent behaviors, but finding those strengths is critical to eventual success. Notice I said eventual success. These are more difficult students to work with, so the progress might be slower. Setting realistic goals for both the student and for yourself is essential.

When having a short chat with a student, you can still use a short version of a contract. What I like to do is to come to an agreement with the student and then ask him or her to rephrase what we agreed on. Then I just jot it down, read it back to the student for confirmation, and then we both sign it. I do that with six-year-olds and sixteen-year olds. I make sure that each of us has a copy. Even that simple version of a contract helps make our agreements more real and more likely to be upheld and honored. Try out the full version in a more in-depth chat and see how it works for you. I use contracts often and find they contribute positively to the chat time process. As I said before, it also helps me keep on track with holding the student responsible.

# <u>C</u>urbing Violence

Unfortunately, we are seeing more and more students come to school with angry and violent behaviors. We are having more students experiencing angry feelings for a variety of reasons, and not knowing how to deal constructively with the anger. The outcome is all too often violence (intense physical harm) or violent tendencies. We are seeing more and more bullying behavior. We are also experiencing more violent reactions to bullying behavior. Even some of our very able students are turning to violence, because their needs are not being met in school. Unfortunately, even though the triggers of anger and violence are starting outside of school, our educational system does contribute to the problem through large class sizes, more and more demands being put on teachers, inconsistent or arbitrary discipline policies, and a focus on suppressing negative behavior with little reinforcement given to positive behavior. Since research points to a positive school connection being a major factor in counteracting school violence, we need to focus more on the proven ways that our educational system can contribute to the prevention of angry behaviors and violence in school. On the next page are some of the strategies from the upcoming supportive component that we can implement in our schools to prevent bullying and violence.

> **FROM RESEARCH**
> Violence is prevented when students have a positive connection to the school.
>
> —*Furlong, Morrison, and Pavelski (2000)*

Let's also look for and build on the strengths of these angry and violent students. Let's look for ways to augment our corrective strategies with strategies that will help them learn to deal with their emotions and help them learn more pro-social behaviors. Incorporating the RESPECT strategies from the supportive component coming next is integral. Below are some options that are particularly relevant for the students with angry or violent behaviors. Use them to create opportunities, both for the students choosing angry or violent behaviors and for yourself and your class.

➤ Anger management instruction
➤ Conflict resolution skills
➤ Social skills instruction
➤ Stress management
➤ Forming positive teacher-student and student-student relationships
➤ Forming a connection and commitment to the school and extracurricular activities
➤ Increased parent-child communication
➤ Expectations of success by the student
➤ School counselor and school psychologist help
➤ Effective teaching choices linking to learner interests
➤ Peer mediation and bully prevention programs

If you find yourself concerned about eruptions of violence in schools, please remember that you have been gathering many options to help you be prepared to deal with difficult situations, options that you can turn into opportunities. When you notice violent tendencies or violence coming out in writings and drawings, schedule chat time with the student and try to open doors. They won't open easily, but developing a caring teacher-student relationship with students who are hurting is the only long-range path. Identify who you least feel like developing a caring relationship with. That is probably who needs it the most in your class. Get your school counselor or school psychologist involved as well. You are not alone. Draw on available resources. Create a positive learning environment in your class where students can feel positive connections.

Angry and violent students build up walls and do obnoxious things to push you away. Don't let them push you away. Sometimes teachers will just say to themselves, "It is not fair to the other students (or to me) to have this student in my class!" Well, of course, it isn't fair. It isn't fair to anyone. It isn't even fair to the students who are so angry that they are taking it out on all those around them. But the reality is that those students are included in our classrooms and it is our professional and ethical responsibility to help them succeed in school and to help them learn responsible alternatives to their angry and violent behaviors. The alternative is likely more and more individuals in our criminal system.

---

## WHAT TO DO WHEN VIOLENCE OCCURS

1. **Control your reaction:** This is paramount. You cannot defuse a situation if you lose control.

2. **Use button pusher escapes:** Distract the antagonists with humor or questions. You can use responsible thinking questions (what should you be doing right now?), Socratic questioning (look back to the CLEAR Model and Execution for information on Socratic questioning, which is especially effective with bright students), or distracting questions to take the focus away from the violent or hostile behavior. Your motive is to divert the student(s) creating the violence.

3. **Send for help, back-up, and support:** Get students in possible danger out of the way and send someone for help. Know what your back-up and support are in your school, so you can get help quickly.

4. **Use slow, deliberate, authoritative language:** "STOP NOW!" Our impulse is to move and speak more quickly when violence is occurring, but actually a slow, emphatic delivery will be more effective.

5. **Schedule follow-up chat time to develop a contract:** You implement the consequence that is appropriate in the situation, but you plan for preventing violence in the future. (See the description of contracts in this chapter and see the appendix for examples.)

6. **Choose follow-up supportive strategies:** Help these students learn to control their anger and violence. Using positive supportive strategies is not necessarily easy when students have created violent situations, but supportive strategies are key to finding some long-lasting results. Try to work through your natural reaction to these students and think of the benefits to everyone—the other students, you, the violent student, and society—of them learning to curb their anger and violence.

> Remember in violent situations you have a right to protect yourself and a responsibility to protect other students. We don't like to think about it or even to discuss it, but sometimes physical restraint is needed in dangerous situations. The Mandt System is approved in most states as a non-violent restraint program that incorporates compassion and self-control. We encourage you to find out if this is an approach that is approved by your state and your district.
>
> —*Herr, D. E., and others (1996)*

Consider the alternative to working at retrieving these students. They could be out vandalizing or stealing from our houses or worse while we are in school.

## Options for Curbing Violent Behaviors

We have been discussing numerous ways to prevent violence, but what if you don't prevent it all and have a violent outburst in your class? You need to apply many of the strategies we have already been discussing to deal with and defuse the violent situation before anyone gets hurt.

Curwin and Mendler (1988, 1997) in *Discipline with Dignity* espouse the concept that we need to focus on reclaiming students who are at risk of failing in our schools due to their misbehavior. They contend that we can find long-term solutions to angry and violent misbehaviors.

> **FROM RESEARCH**
> Teaching students a legitimate process for cooling down and dealing with their own emotional reaction is a valuable strategy to prevent violence.
>
> —*Kyle (1999)*

We are by no means saying that these students should not be held responsible for the choices they are making. They need to be accountable for the sake of others and for their own sake too, but let's do it in a way that will lead to solutions. We need to give a lot of credit to teachers who work in alternative schools. They work with these difficult situations every day. I have had opportunities to share the strategies we have been exploring with teachers from alternative schools and they find them quite appropriate for their setting as well. We need to learn from these special teachers. We need to be bringing alternatives into all schools, so we can find more solutions, options, and opportunities.

## CURWIN AND MENDLER'S APPROACH

### Assumptions

➢ Discipline must be based on dignity and hope. Chronic misbehavers have usually lost all hope that they will encounter anything worthwhile at school.

➢ Teachers must work at reclaiming students who are currently destined to fail, who are behaviorally at risk.

➢ It is possible to find long-term solutions, even to angry and violent behaviors. Short-term solutions are usually not effective.

### Main Points

➢ Responsibility is more important than obedience. Some discipline approaches are responsibility models (the students learn self-discipline); others are obedience models (the students do what the teacher says). Responsibility results in long-term behavior changes; obedience does not.

➢ Students misbehave when their personal dignity is threatened. They will do anything to preserve their self-worth.

➢ Teaching students to behave in an appropriate manner is an essential part of teaching.

➢ You should not use discipline strategies that interfere with students' motivation to learn.

➢ The number of students who are at risk of failing because of their misbehavior is increasing.

➢ Pre-planned consequences are necessary in discipline. They are best when the teacher and the students work together on them.

➢ You need to de-escalate potential confrontations. I-statements and keeping discipline private helps.

➢ Interesting lessons that are personally relevant to the students improve the behavior of difficult students.

➢ Consequences need to be clear and specific, have a range of alternatives, be related to the misbehavior, and not be punishment.

## CURWIN AND MENDLER'S APPROACH
### (continued)

**Implementation**

➤ You need three dimensions of discipline—the prevention dimension (avoid problems); the action dimension (actions you take to deal with misbehavior); and the resolution dimension (actions you can take with out-of-control students). You develop a social contract with the students in a class meeting that establishes how we will interact together, or what rules we will follow. You also establish with the students what will happen if the rules are broken.

**Limitation**

➤ Strategies are not always explained in detail, so it is sometimes hard to know how to implement them.

# Opportunities for Curbing Violent Behaviors

**FROM RESEARCH**

Creating a positive classroom environment combined with teaching replacement behaviors reduces aggression in emotionally and behaviorally disordered students.

*—Abrams and Segal (1998)*

There are many resources available for teachers who focus on needed anger management instruction, conflict resolution skills, and social skills instruction, in which the students can be taught more pro-social behaviors and replacement behaviors for their angry or violent choices. The school counselor or school psychologist is a valuable resource and support person in these areas. Often one of them can come into your classroom and teach needed pro-social skills to augment and reinforce what you are teaching in that area. Work together with the school counselor or school psychologist to help students with angry or violent behaviors to see the possibility of their own success in school, academically, socially, and emotionally. Often these students are trapped in a cycle of hopelessness where they can see no light at the end of the tunnel. Their lack of hope can lead to these students finding justification for their violent choices and not only do they not fear the consequences of their actions, they almost rush headlong into them (Trotter and Walker 2001, 2002). Hope of success is paramount for them.

You also need to reflect back, or even look back, to the effective teaching component in this book. What teaching choices can you make that will engage these difficult students? How can you make the learning relevant for them and connect with them? There is an incredible power in hooking these difficult students into the learning in your class. Let the effective teaching component help you with that. Spencer Kagan (1999) has incorporated some valuable research demonstrating that the goals of character education can be achieved through utilizing cooperative learning structures in your class into a very practical video. (Character education will be discussed more in chapter 14.) Put the power of your teaching to work toward building responsible character in your students.

> **FROM RESEARCH**
> At-risk youth need to be taught coping skills.
> —*Mazza and Overstreet (2000)*

Engaging students in helping each other through peer mediation and peer counseling is a great strategy to give extra, but different, help to your students choosing angry and violent behaviors. Often their peers can relate to them on a level with which they can connect even more so than with a teacher, school counselor, or school psychologist. A really nice side benefit of peer involvement is that it also gives the students with controlling needs a legitimate avenue for gaining a sense of control in your class.

Building positive teacher-student relationships and also focusing on positive student-student relationships are valuable for curbing violent behavior. Remember the power of a connection to school. Encouraging the parents of your students to communicate frequently with their children will enhance your efforts in school.

The supportive component will have many "options" that will also help with difficult situations. See what will help you create "opportunities" for your students with angry and/or violent behaviors. We will explore bringing RE-SPECT into your classroom:

- ➤ **R**esponsible behaviors intentionally taught
- ➤ **E**stablishing classroom harmony
- ➤ **S**tudent involvement
- ➤ **P**arent and staff involvement
- ➤ **E**ncouragement and effective praise
- ➤ **C**apable strategies
- ➤ **T**eacher-student relationship

# Summary

You have many practical strategies for *"C" options for angry and violent misbehaviors.* You can utilize *chill out time* to let things calm down prior to problem-solving. *Choice levels* can help you when students are resistant to chill out time options you give them or "button pusher escapes." *Consequences,* especially *restitution consequences,* help to hold angry and violent students responsible for their choices, but in a way that allows the students to learn from their mistakes. *Chat time with students* is a great way to actively involve students in the discipline process. The goal of chat time is finding solutions to problems. *Contracts* are a valuable tool to help with following through on plans. *Curbing violence* strategies, including effective teaching, anger management classes, and teaching pro-social behaviors and conflict resolution strategies, help angry and/or violent students move toward responsible behavior choices.

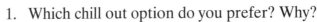

# Reflection Questions

1. Which chill out option do you prefer? Why?
2. Would you use a chill out refocus form (see the appendix for examples)? If so, how would you use it? Which form do you prefer? Why?
3. Describe when to use choice levels with a student. Give examples.
4. How are "B" level (business-like) consequences different from "C" level consequences? Explain why.
5. What is the purpose of chat time as an option? When would you use chat time with a student? Why would you use chat time?
6. Under what conditions should contracts be used? How would you involve a student in the development of a contract?
7. Discuss the following scenarios and how you would handle them.

**Elementary: Bully**
Most kids in your class know Craig as the second grade bully. You have heard rumors that he has at least three first graders fearing for their lives, if they don't supply him with lunch every day. It has also been discussed in the teachers' lounge that he was responsible for the snake in the vice principal's briefcase, the cherry bomb in the boys' toilet, and the silicone glue on the girls' toilet seats. Some even say he is connected with organized crime. What a professional opportunity! You just found out that Craig will be in your class this fall, and school starts tomorrow. Sounds like it's time to do some strategic planning. Suggestions?

### Elementary: Etiquette

You are midway through your lecture in your class on etiquette. Because of their talking you have used "the look" on Katie and Cassie several times during the lecture with less than adequate results. Suddenly Cassie has Katie by the hair and Katie is scratching and swinging for all she is worth. Sam looks at you and shouts, "Do something, quick!"

### Secondary: Vandalism

What would you do if a student destroyed several textbooks in your classroom?

### Secondary: The Big Game

Part of your duties is to help supervise intramural sports after school. This is the week before tournaments begin, and spirits are running high. During your supervision, you notice one particularly dynamic game, apparently between the top two teams. You hear a whistle from a student referee, which is immediately followed by shouts of "Unfair!! You're playing favorites!!," which is followed by physical punctuation marks to the nose of the referee. A full scale fist fight has developed right in front of your very nose! Guess who gets to try to calm the waters? What will you do?

# References

Abrams, B., & Segal, A. (1998). How to prevent aggressive behavior. *Teaching Exceptional Children* 30 (4): 10–15.

Atherley, C. (1990). The implementation of a positive behaviour management programme in a primary classroom: A case study. *School Organization* 10 (2,3): 213–228.

Brophy, J. (1987). Classroom management as instruction: Socializing self-guidance in students. *Theory Into Practice* 24 (4): 233–240.

Coloroso, B. (1994). *Kids are worth it!: Giving your child the gift of inner discipline.* New York: Avon Books.

Crowley, E. P. (1993). A qualitative analysis of mainstreamed behaviorally disordered aggressive adolescents' perceptions of helpful and unhelpful teacher attitudes and behaviors. *Exceptionality: A Research Journal* 4 (3): 131–151.

Curwin, R., & Mendler, A. N. (1988). *Discipline with dignity.* Alexandria, VA: Association for Supervision and Curriculum Development.

Curwin, R., & Mendler, A. (1997). *As tough as necessary.* Alexandria, VA: Association for Supervision and Curriculum Development.

Dowd, J. (1997). Refusing to play the blame game. *Educational Leadership* 54 (8): 67–69.

Ford, E. E. (1996). *Discipline for home and school.* Scottsdale, AZ: Brandt Publishing.

Furlong, M., Morrison, G., & Pavelski, R. (2000). Trends in school psychology for the 21st century: Influences of school violence on professional change. *Psychology in the Schools* 37 (1): 81–90.

Glasser, W. (1992). *The quality school.* New York: HarperPerennial.

Herr, D. E., and others (1996). *Training teachers for troubled times.* Paper presented at the Annual Convention of the Council for Exceptional Children, Orlando, FL (ERIC Document Reproduction Service No. ED395406).

Johnson, D., & Johnson, R. (1996). Peacemakers: Teaching students to resolve their own and schoolmates' conflicts. *Focus on Exceptional Children* 28 (6): 1–11.

Kagan, S. (1999). *Cooperative learning and character development* (video). National Video Resources.

Kyle, P. (1999). Cooperative discipline and violence prevention. In W. Bender, G. Clinton, and R. Bender (Eds.). *Violence prevention and reduction in schools.* Austin, TX: Pro-Ed.

Mazza, J., & Overstreet, S. (2000). Children and adolescents exposed to community violence: A mental health perspective for school psychologists. *School Psychology Review* 29 (1): 86–101.

Trotter, T., & Walker, W. R. (2001 and 2002). *Violence and at-risk youth.* Workshops conducted at the Idaho Counseling Association Annual Conference, Coeur d' Alene and Idaho Falls, ID.

Wade, R. (1997). Lifting a school's spirit. *Educational Leadership* 54 (8): 34–36.

# Section Five

# Supportive Component

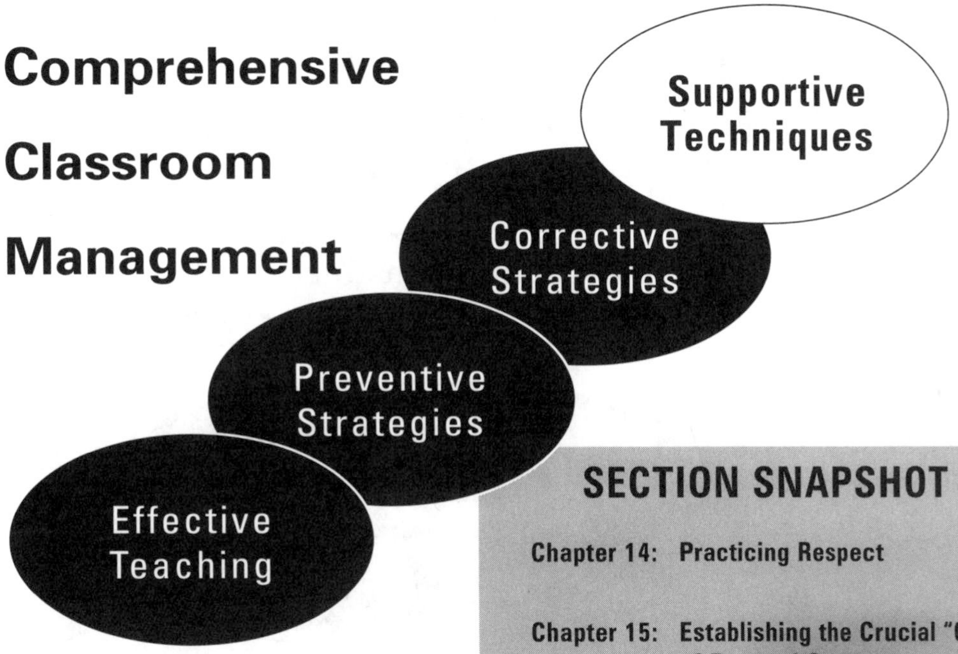

## Comprehensive Classroom Management

Effective Teaching

Preventive Strategies

Corrective Strategies

Supportive Techniques

# Practicing RESPECT

**R**esponsible behaviors taught

**E**stablish classroom harmony

**S**tudent involvement

**P**arent/staff involvement

**E**ncouragement

**C**apable strategies

**T**eacher/student relationship

R
E
S
P
E
C
T

## OBJECTIVES

Learners will be able to practice strategies for developing RESPECT in their classrooms.

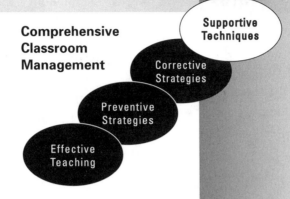

Comprehensive Classroom Management

Supportive Techniques

Corrective Strategies

Preventive Strategies

Effective Teaching

**CHAPTER SNAPSHOT**

- <u>R</u>esponsible Behaviors Intentionally Taught
- <u>E</u>stablishing Classroom Harmony
- <u>S</u>tudent Involvement
- *Nelsen, Lott, and Glenn's Approach*
- *Kohn's Approach*
- <u>P</u>arent and Staff Involvement
- <u>E</u>ncouragement and Effective Praise
- <u>C</u>apable Strategies
- <u>T</u>eacher-Student Relationship
- RESPECT School-Wide

# <u>R</u>esponsible Behaviors Intentionally Taught

You want your entire discipline and management program to be part of the process of intentionally teaching responsible behavior. Some of the aspects we have previously discussed are:

> ➤ Creating rules and consequences will teach decision-making and responsibility for your own actions.
> ➤ Your modeling of self-control will teach self-control.
> ➤ Your effective teaching strategies will exemplify how to communicate successfully with others.
> ➤ Your use of "button pusher escapes" and brief choice language will demonstrate how to deal verbally with a conflict.
> ➤ Your use of body language and voice tone to project firmness and purpose, but not aggression, will display how to defuse a conflict.
> ➤ Your use of chat time will exhibit how to listen to another to solve problems.
> ➤ Your use of chill out time will make evident the importance of calming down before problem solving.

There will be much that your students will learn from what you "do" and how you interact with them. That is the way a discipline program works most effectively. The more you share with your students the strategies you are using and their purpose and rationale, the more the students will learn responsible behaviors through what happens intentionally in your class. There will be times, though, when teaching responsible behavior directly will be necessary. Teaching content is your primary focus whether your content is tenth grade science or third grade math, but in order for students to be able to go out in the world and work and live with others, they also need to know how to apply what they have learned in school in their interactions with others. As an augmentation to your academic content, your students need to know:

## <u>Responsible Behaviors Intentionally Taught</u>

| STUDENTS NEED TO KNOW | FOCUS |
|---|---|
| Character development | Focuses on instilling character virtues that are basic to the development of good character. There are many virtues connected with character education that are integral to helping students cultivate positive character. These virtues include: accountability, caring, charity, citizenship, compassion, consideration, cooperativeness, courage, courtesy, diligence, fairness, good judgment, impulse control, helpfulness, honesty, integrity, kindness, leadership, loyalty, perseverance, promise keeping, self-discipline, self-motivation, trustworthiness, reliability, respect for self and others, responsibility, understanding, and unselfishness. |
| Communication skills | Encompasses listening skills, paraphrasing another's ideas, clarifying information, and summarizing what was said. |
| Social skills | Incorporates the skills students need to be able to interact effectively with one another, such as greeting each other, taking turns, disagreeing without fighting, and sharing materials. |
| Anger management | Consists of students recognizing their anger and its sources, identifying its triggers, developing strategies to get it under control and actually using those strategies to deal with anger in a constructive manner. |
| Conflict resolution | Includes knowing what the steps are for resolving conflicts, getting to practice those steps, and having opportunities to put them to use when conflicts arise. |
| Responsibility for ones' actions | Emphasizes students developing the ability to take responsibility for their own actions, even if that means accepting the logical consequence of their choices. Learning from their mistakes is an important aspect. |
| Self-control skills | Involves learning to recognize when they are losing control of their emotional reactions and having coping strategies that allow them to calm themselves down before they lose control and choose inappropriate behavior. |
| Decision-making skills | Extends to students having the opportunity to make decisions within structured choices, so they can learn effective decision-making from doing it and can learn from poor decisions they make as well. |
| Emotional intelligence development | Emphasizes the emotional development of students—their awareness and control of their own emotions, their empathy, and relationships with others. |

Your students will not be able to put your academic content to good use in their lives, unless they combine their academic knowledge with the responsible behavior skills. Sometimes we hear teachers say things like, "I am just here to teach ___ (content); it is not my job to teach behavior." But unless the knowledge gained from your content instruction works in concert with the responsible behavior skills identified above, it will be hard for your students to get the most out of using that content in their work and personal life.

Please note that we are not suggesting that you neglect content to teach responsible behavior. We want most of the learning of responsible behavior to come intentionally from what happens in your class in your effective teaching component, your preventive component and your corrective component, but there will be a need at times to intentionally teach responsible behavior as the content itself. Your options are:

> Whole class instruction and practice from you or the school counselor
> Cooperative learning activities
> Small group instruction and practice from you or the school counselor or school psychologist
> Individual instruction and practice during chat time or with the school counselor or school psychologist
> Partnerships for teaching responsible behavior

## Whole Class Instruction

There are many teacher and counselor materials available in teacher stores or through catalogs that include developed lessons to teach all of the responsible behavior skills: communication skills, character development, social skills, anger management, conflict resolution, responsibility for one's actions, self-control, decision-making, and emotional development. You and/or your school counselor can teach the ones that are relevant for your class. Active participation by the students and a focus on practicing the skills is integral. *Character Education in America's Schools* (Akin, Dunne, Palomares, and Schilling, 1995) offers classroom lessons that can be adapted to suit various grade levels, ability levels, and cultural backgrounds, along with connections to appropriate literature.

**FROM RESEARCH**
If you want students to actually apply what they learn in character education, it is important that the classroom provide an opportunity for them to see examples and experience cooperation and the democratic process.
—*Black (1996)*

**FROM RESEARCH**
Multifaceted character education programs reduced discipline referrals and positively impacted academic achievement.
—*Brooks and Kann (1993)*

You want to make sure that you watch for, comment on, and encourage implementation of the responsible skills in the day-to-day running of the class. If the counselor is conducting the instruction, it is important for you to be there, so you can follow through with skill application and emphasize implementation. The counselor's lessons are designed with teacher implementation in mind, so the more it can be a counselor-teacher partnership, the better. You need to use the responsible behavior terminology the students are learning in your interactions with them and intentionally model the learned skills. You are furthering the goal of the students actually using the responsible behavior skills. Help link the terminology to specific actions as well. Projecting positive expectations is also important.

Point out and encourage responsible behavior choices that students make, whether it is individual, small group, or whole group examples that you highlight. At the secondary level this needs to be much more low key than at the elementary level. Older students tend to prefer a more private focus on responsible behavior. With young children you can be as public as you want in putting the spotlight on responsible behavior, but from about fifth grade on up, a less public focus is more desired by the students. The older students still like it when their responsible choices are highlighted, even if they don't act like they do, but they do not care for being singled out in a public arena.

# Responsible Behavior Connections with Content

You can also find ways to integrate the responsible skills instruction into your other content. Choose stories to read that exemplify responsible skills, have students write stories or journal entries related to the skills, have them act it out as it relates to content you are studying. Explore historical characters or historical events that epitomize responsible behavior. You can even draw connections to the cooperation and interdependence of nature and humanity in your science instruction. Some content areas lend themselves more to connections with responsible behavior, but no matter what you are teaching, look for connections and integrate responsible behavior into your content as much as possible. Point out responsible behavior connections with your content to your students. Find all the literature links you can with responsible behavior examples.

> **FROM RESEARCH**
> Teachers need to model the beliefs that they want to instill in their students. If teachers believe in cooperation and appreciation of differences, they need to practice that in the classroom.
>
> —*Vasconcellos, J., and Murphy, M. (1987)*

# Cooperative Learning Activities

Cooperative learning activities are particularly effective for accomplishing responsible behavior instructional goals embedded in the teaching process rather than as a separate content in itself. Spencer Kagan (1994) has developed dozens of cooperative learning structures that structure the interaction between the students in such a way that responsible behaviors are learned from the process of how the students interact with the content. Kagan and Kagan (1998) extended this to include the connection between cooperative learning structures and multiple intelligences.

The research conducted to illustrate that the goals of character education are accomplished through students interacting together in cooperative learning structures was depicted in a video entitled *Cooperative Learning and Character Development* (Kagan, 1999). Utilizing cooperative learning structures develops all of the responsible behavior skills we have been focusing on: character development, communication skills, social skills, anger management, conflict resolution, taking responsibility for one's actions, self-control, decision-making, and emotional development. Responsible behaviors are better learned through being embedded in the instruction rather than as separate entities, since the students are then practicing responsible behavior skills as they learn them.

That is an especially powerful combination. There are many options for you to create opportunities for students to learn responsible behavior at the same time that they are learning your academic content.

# Small Group Instruction

Sometimes small group instruction or even small group counseling (counseling conducted by the school counselor or psychologist) can be an effective way to help individuals who are having particular problems with responsibility skills. Anger management and social skills groups are common. The students have an opportunity to also practice communication skills within the group. Students are typically given a choice about participating, and parental permission is obtained.

Students can also get training as peer mediators and help their fellow students resolve conflicts. It has the nice side effect of being a great way for students needing control to get that need met through responsible behavior as they mediate for others.

# Individual Instruction

Teacher-student chat time is a great venue for individual instruction of responsibility skills. Providing an opportunity to practice the skills first with you and then encouragement as they practice the skills in reality is important.

Sometimes your school counselor or school psychologist can also meet individually with students who are having more severe problems with exhibiting responsible behaviors. This may be an option for violent students in particular.

# Partnerships for Teaching Responsible Behavior

Parents, of course, have the primary responsibility for teaching responsible behavior to their children. Parents, though, don't have the same opportunities you do to have the students practicing and applying those skills in the context of interacting in a large group. Being able to put responsibility skills into action in your interactions with others is a valuable skill to be able to take off to the work world later. Forming partnerships with parents to assist, support, and follow through with the learning and implementation of responsible behavior skills makes good sense. Our goal is to help the students to meet their needs through responsible behavior choices rather than through misbehavior.

Be expansive in your view of partnerships to encourage and teach responsible behavior. We could have teacher-teacher partnerships within the school. We could also have classroom teacher partnerships with special educators and school counselors and psychologists. We can have community partnerships as well. Get businesses involved. Consider a foster grandparents program that would tap into the older expertise in your community. The more we all work together to foster and teach responsible behavior, the better.

# Responsible Behavior and Students with ADHD and Emotional Challenges

Students who have ADHD (Attention Deficit Hyperactivity Disorder) or exhibit behaviors like ADHD have some challenges that make it more difficult to learn responsible behavior. Their tendencies toward inattention, distractibility and impulsivity have them making some poor behavior choices at times. They have the ability to learn responsible behavior, but it will usually take more structure, more follow-through, and more support. Meeting with the school counselor, school psychologist, and even the child study team (the team in the school that meets to help meet the needs of all students) can help in developing a plan to give these students the extra support they need. Also, approaching them from a positive perspective is crucial.

Students who have emotional problems, either diagnosed or not, also need planning to provide them with the extra structure, support, and follow-through to help them in gradually learning responsible behavior. They also can learn responsible behavior. It just takes longer and more adults working together to support them in this endeavor. Do tap into the support resources available in your school and community.

Students with ADHD and students with emotional problems can be exhibiting behaviors from any of the levels of seriousness of misbehavior. They could be enacting the low-level distracting behaviors or the middle level challenging behaviors or the more serious level angry and violent behaviors. Use the corrective strategies in section IV that connect with the appropriate level of seriousness as starting places with these more challenging students, but be sure to also focus on effective teaching options and supportive options that will help to go beyond the immediate situation with these challenging students.

> **FROM RESEARCH**
> ADHD is probably over-diagnosed.
> —*Taylor (2001b)*

## Supporting Students with ADHD and Emotional Problems

First look back to the strategies in the effective teaching CLEAR Model for solutions when working with students with ADHD and emotional problems. The more CLEAR your instruction is, the better for students with these challenges. You also need to use supportive strategies from this section liberally. Choose ones that seem most relevant for each challenging student you are working with, but do consciously choose. Corrective strategies deal with the immediate situation, but must be used in combination with effective teaching strategies and supportive strategies. Effective teaching strategies help engage the student in the learning process. The supportive strategies covered in this section lead to more sustained results.

## Meeting the Needs of Students with ADHD Challenges

Following are a variety of effective teaching strategies and supportive strategies that are particularly relevant with students with ADHD challenges:

> ➢ Focusing their attention
> ➢ Alerting them to transitions

- Clear directions given both orally and visually
- Using lots of visual back-up during presentations
- Monitoring progress in small increments
- Using encouragement and effective praise (See the Second "E" in RESPECT)
- Focusing on their strengths (See the "C" in RESPECT)
- Breaking tasks into smaller bits and smaller time segments
- Off-task reminders and signals
- Emphasizing accuracy over speed
- Screens and cutouts that focus attention on a page
- Colored overlays to focus letters
- Assignment organizing support
- Emphasizing usefulness and relevance of the learning
- Energy breaks
- Distraction-free environments in which to work
- Using study carrels
- Using a study buddy (See the "S" in RESPECT)
- Allowing different seating
- Encouraging self-monitoring
- Monitor medication, if applicable
- Teaching social skills (See the "R" in RESPECT)
- Looking for improvement, not perfection (See the "C" in RESPECT)
- Commenting on improvement (See the "C" in RESPECT)
- Eliciting parent support and follow-through (See the "P" in RESPECT)
- Reducing distraction where possible
- Creating individual contracts (See chapter 13)
- Utilizing high interest curriculum

# Meeting the Needs of Students with Emotional Challenges

Following are a variety of effective teaching strategies and supportive strategies that are particularly relevant with students with emotional challenges:

- Teaching responsible behaviors (See the "R" in RESPECT)
- Teaching students to recognize the triggers that cause them to lose control
- Teaching self-control strategies (See the "R" in RESPECT)

- ➤ Modeling self-control (see chapter 10)
- ➤ Providing chill out time when needed (see chapter 13)
- ➤ Providing high structure and predictability for the day or period
- ➤ Working on teacher-student relationships (see the "T" in RESPECT)
- ➤ Incorporating logical consequences—the 5 R's are crucial (see chapter 12)
- ➤ Using structured choices
- ➤ Having a plan of action with other school personnel for volatile episodes
- ➤ Assignment or homework buddy (see the "S" in RESPECT)
- ➤ Using lots of encouragement and effective praise (see the second "E" in RESPECT)
- ➤ Eliciting parent support and follow-through (see the "P" in RESPECT)
- ➤ Focusing on their strengths (see the "C" in RESPECT)

# **E̲stablishing Classroom Harmony**

Establishing the environment was addressed in chapter 9, focusing on you and the students developing rules or code of conduct and procedures together to create a classroom climate conducive to learning. In the first day and week it is also critical that you establish a warm, supportive environment that has everyone feeling as if they are an important part of the class. Students of every culture and every learning challenge need to feel as if they are an integral part of the class. Together with the students you are creating the feeling of "our class" and the "learning community" that impacts everyone, all working together to have a positive classroom climate.

This doesn't just happen. You need to make it happen. E̲stablishing classroom harmony starts on day one, develops throughout the first week and then requires on-going maintenance throughout the school year. If you are in a secondary classroom, you need to establish that "our class" and "learning community" in each period. Even though that might sound as if you would be wasting valuable content time if you were to do it for each period, in the long run, it will save you time by preventing problems that you would be dealing with if you do not establish classroom harmony.

It is recommended that you spend about one-third of your time in the first week (and in each period for secondary classes) building the management foundation that will support your class throughout the school year. That

Valued
Included
Accepted
Belonging
Listened to
Encouraged

management foundation consists of establishing the environment (from section III) and establishing classroom harmony. The goals of Establishing classroom harmony are for everyone to feel Valued, Included, Accepted, Belonging, Listened to, and Encouraged, so we have a class capable of growth. Some of your tools to accomplish this are class building activities, team building activities, and class meetings.

## Class Building Activities

Class building is designed to pull the whole class together into a learning community. The idea is that if everyone gets to know each other on a human-to-human level, we can figure out how to work together. I tell my students that this does not mean that everyone in class will be best friends, but it does mean that we can all sort out how to work in the same room with each other in a manner that everyone feels as if they belong there. You want everyone to know they have an important place in the class. You want everyone to get along with one another. We can all accept each other's diversities and realize that the differences we all bring to the class are actually enriching.

Since we are talking about Establishing classroom harmony, think of it as creating a class orchestra. You have all of these different instruments in your room all having their own unique sound. The job of the orchestra conductor is to pull the unique and varied performers together into something that can harmonize with one another. Each retains its own sound, but all learn to come together into a harmony that pleases the ear. Discordant notes are worked out and tuned up. I use this analogy with my students. Use it, if it works for you.

Depending on what fits for your grade level and what you think is appropriate, you can have a class motto, a class name, a class banner, a class symbol, a class song, a class cheer, a class bulletin board, class incentives, class goal setting, class energy breaks, class cooperative games, class pets, a class suggestion box, a class appreciation box, or a class mural. Any and all of these will help to pull students together as a learning community.

Class building activities get all students in the class up, moving around, interacting with one another, getting to know one another better, and working together in an energizing manner. Without class building activities, you would be surprised how many students do not know other students in the class even after well into the school year. In the first week of school class builders are usually geared to getting acquainted, but after the initial introductions, they focus on having the students all interacting with one another in positive ways about the content in your class. The book *Classbuilding* by Kagan, Robertson, and Kagan (1998) is a great resource for implementing active class building activities. The purposes of "conducting" class building activities are:

> Creating a positive classroom climate
> Building positive student to student relationships
> Having everyone working together and feeling they are an important member of the group
> Fostering motivation to learn
> Solving classroom problems through knowing each other better
> Valuing and celebrating diversity

Some examples of class building activities are listed in the table:

**FROM RESEARCH**
Teacher behaviors that create a positive classroom climate also promote increased learning.
—*Greenblatt, Cooper, and Muth (1984)*

## Class Building Activities

| Getting Acquainted | The students participate in activities that give them an opportunity to get to know one another. |
|---|---|
| Community Circle | The students communicate with one another about topics designed to bring the class together as a community of learners. |
| Class Goals | The class establishes goals together to foster the students working together from common aims. |
| Class Bulletin Board | The class works together on a bulletin board that represents the class. |
| People Search | Students search to find others with certain experiences or qualities. Find a person who has _____ . |
| Corners | There is a different topic to be discussed in each corner of the room. Students choose the topic they want to explore with colleagues. |
| Similarity Groups | Groups are formed based on similarities of various students. Discussions and paraphrasing take place about the topics that are generated to form the groups. |
| Creating Class Themes | Students choose a class motto, a class banner, or a class flag that represents the spirit of the class. |
| Conflict Resolution | The students learn a process for resolving conflicts with one another. |
| Class Projects | The class decides on a project to work on collaboratively. |

# Team Building Activities

Team building activities are designed to get students to know each other in small groups, to work more effectively together, and to create a positive climate in the class. Team building activities help to build positive relationships in the class. Team building activities involve interviewing members of the team, taking turns discussing a topic, working on a team project together, developing a team statement, or engaging in lively brainstorming together. The time invested in getting teams to work well together will be well spent in terms of fewer classroom problems and increased positive feelings towards diversity. In the initial week the team building would focus on getting acquainted with team members, but then would become content oriented. The book *Teambuilding* (Kagan, Kagan, and Kagan, 1998) is a valuable resource for utilizing team building to establish classroom harmony.

Learning to work well on a team is another valuable skill to take into the work world later in life. Teamwork skills are invaluable in today's world.

> **FROM RESEARCH**
> Positive classroom climate has a significant effect upon the behavior choices of secondary students.
> —*Short and Short (1988)*

# Class Meetings

"Conducting" class meetings is another way to get the class orchestra in tune with one another. Class meetings are designed to involve students in problem-solving and class decision-making. They help to empower students and act as a laboratory for the democratic process. We would encourage you to have some type of class meeting to help all students feel as if they are integral parts of the classroom. It gives students a venue to have their say and to give input into decisions about problems and about classroom events and activities. Again the time invested in class meetings is time well spent in terms of the communication skills, negotiation skills, problem-solving skills, conflict resolution skills and social skills, like taking turns and considering different points of view, which students learn from the process. Academic skills are also learned from class meeting participation: better developed critical thinking skills, decision-making skills, and problem-solving skills. You can conduct informal class discussions, or you can have regularly scheduled class meetings. Class meetings usually incorporate the activities in the following box.

## Conducting a Class Meeting

| | |
|---|---|
| Forming a circle | This allows everyone access to speaking and listening. |
| Beginning with compliments or appreciations | This sets a positive tone for the meeting. You need to teach students what are appropriate compliments and appreciations. Older students (about fifth grade and up) usually prefer the appreciations. |
| Creating an agenda | Throughout the week, problems are written on the agenda as they come up. Solutions to the problems on the agenda are the focus of the meeting. During the meeting, if a problem is already solved, you move on to the next item on the agenda. |
| Seeking win-win solutions | The teacher guides the process of seeking solutions to classroom problems together. You seek to find solutions that will be workable for all involved. It is the teacher's responsibility to make sure a helpful tone is maintained throughout. |
| Planning classroom activities | The students help make decisions about classroom events, assignments, field trips, etc. |
| Closure | The meeting ends with a review of the decisions, action plans, and who is responsible for carrying out the actions. |

Nelsen, Lott, and Glenn (1993) offer practical details on how to conduct regular class meetings in their book *Positive Discipline in the Classroom*.

Some schools have incorporated a teacher advisor concept as an adaptation of class meetings. They create an extra period during the school day by borrowing five minutes from each period. Every professional in the school (administrators, classroom teachers, specialists of all kinds, counselors, psychologists) has the responsibility of meeting with and providing guidance to a small group of students throughout their schooling. This is **E**stablishing classroom harmony on a school-wide level.

> **FROM RESEARCH**
> Respect for the individ-ual, self-esteem building, and promoting self-effi-cacy have a positive im-pact upon school climate and student discipline.
> —*Sweeney (1992)*

# Positive Classroom Atmosphere

The purpose of **E**stablishing classroom harmony is to create a classroom where everyone wants to be, including you. The atmosphere says to all, "You are valued here, you are listened to here, your opinions count, your views are important here, you belong and are accepted here, and our diversity is our strength." All feel **V**alued, **I**ncluded, **A**ccepted, **B**elonging, **L**istened to, and **E**ncouraged, so we can have a **VIABLE** class capable of growth.

# <u>S</u>tudent Involvement

Actively involving students in the learning process is emphasized in the effective teaching component. It is equally important to actively involve students in the discipline process. Active involvement gives the students a sense

## NELSEN, LOTT, AND GLENN'S APPROACH

### Assumptions
➤ Looking for solutions rather than punishment is important.
➤ Creating an encouraging learning environment is key.
➤ When you have a climate of acceptance, respect, and encouragement, discipline problems are fewer and fewer.

### Main Points
➤ You need to help students to perceive themselves as capable, significant, and in control of their lives.
➤ Showing students that you care about them is paramount.
➤ Class meetings are one of your best tools to have everyone participate and learn how to solve problems.
➤ Make sure that your consequences are logical and follow the three R's of Consequences: Related, Reasonable, and Respectful.
➤ Look beyond consequences, as well, to seek solutions.
➤ Student involvement in solutions is integral.
➤ Look to the future with students rather than focusing on the past.

### Implementation
➤ Start with teaching students to participate responsibly in class meetings during the first week of school and continue them throughout the year. Class meetings teach students the democratic process, problem solving, decision-making, conflict resolution, and critical thinking skills.

### Limitation
➤ It can take time to get the results you want.

of ownership of the class. It helps them to buy in to being part of the solution rather than part of the problem. Think about a time when someone made a suggestion to you that sounded all right when the other person offered the idea, but you never followed through with it. What was the reason that you did not follow through? Was it that you really didn't want to do it or didn't know how to do it? Or was it that the suggestion did not really fit your way of doing things or it didn't seem doable to you? When students are not part of the decision-making process, they don't follow through for similar reasons. Student buy-in is integral for long-lasting results.

Again this does not mean that students are not held responsible for poor choices that they make—they are. What it does mean is that when they help to create the solutions, it is more likely that it will be doable or understandable or palatable for them. It is more likely that they will actually follow through and make some positive changes in their lives.

Alfie Kohn (1996b) advocates for student involvement in the discipline process. He emphasizes that when you meet with a student, you should say, "What do you think we can do to solve this problem?" Involving students, Kohn maintains, is the only way to have lasting solutions. How can students learn to be effective decision-makers, he says, if you don't give them an opportunity to learn through making decisions? Let's reiterate all the ways that have been discussed so far that students can be actively involved in the discipline process.

> **FROM RESEARCH**
> Positive approaches to discipline that promote students to take responsibility for the classroom academic and social environment help to improve discipline in urban schools.
>
> —*Sudzina (1997)*

> **FROM RESEARCH**
> Students need an engaging curriculum and a caring classroom in order to be able to tap into their natural desire to learn. Choice is integral. Students learn to make good choices by making choices.
>
> —*Kohn (1996b)*

## Student Involvement in the Discipline/Management Process

| | |
|---|---|
| Creating rules/code of conduct | Creating a contract |
| Creating activity procedures | Involvement in appropriate curriculum decisions |
| Creating accountability procedures | Assignment mode choices |
| Creating consequences | Class building activities |
| Chill out refocus form | Team building activities |
| Chat time involvement | Class meetings |
| Students develop plan of action with the teacher | Students set their own goals with the teacher |

Active involvement in the discipline process also gives students a legitimate avenue for feeling a sense of control in the classroom. The more you involve students, the better. That is why taking the time to teach them to participate responsibly is vital. Anytime students are not participating responsibly, you should use the brief choice language and say something like:

"It would be valuable for you to be part of this decision-making process, but I need you to take it seriously and give me some responsible suggestions or I will need to decide for this week," or "I would like you to be able to contribute to class by _____ , but I need you to behave responsibly or I will need to assign that job to someone else for now."

Keep in mind that how you deliver this message is integral to students learning to participate responsibly. A controlled business-like demeanor is essential.

Some other ideas for student involvement in the discipline process include: classroom responsibilities, study buddies, homework buddies, peer tutors, peer mediators, peer counselors, peer recognition, and student led conferences.

---

Remember that if you offer to share the power with students (involve them in the decision-making process) and they do not participate responsibly, you take the power back and fulfill your teacher responsibilities and decide for the students. But you first need to really listen to students and encourage them to participate responsibly. If you do need to decide for now, you continue to invite students to be a viable and authentic part of the process.

---

## Classroom Responsibilities

**FROM RESEARCH**
Students need to have classroom responsibilities, so they can feel like citizens in their classes rather than like tourists. You want them to be partners in the classroom.

—*Freiburg (1996)*

Having students take care of classroom responsibilities or jobs is a great way to have them make a contribution to class, have a positive sense of power, and also to free you up so you have more time to help students. Don't do anything for students that they can do for themselves. You want students to have as many opportunities to act responsibly as possible.

Classroom responsibilities will vary by grade level. They need to rotate so that all are involved. Some possibilities are: materials monitor, lunch count monitor, role taking monitor, class messengers, line monitor, equipment monitor, computer monitor, librarian, visitor monitor, classroom meeting facilitator, class newsletter

# KOHN'S APPROACH

## Assumptions

➤ Your classroom needs to focus on critical thinking, decision-making, and caring about others.

➤ Creating a classroom community is essential.

➤ Involving students in the decision-making process teaches them to make effective decisions. You cannot learn to make good decisions unless you get to practice making decisions.

## Main Points

➤ You need to trust your students and help them to learn self-control and self-discipline. Complaint behavior is not what we are after.

➤ Constructivist teaching is necessary to actively involve students in the learning process.

➤ Use collaboration and a participative management style with your students rather than coercion.

➤ Class meetings are one of your most effective tools for students to learn problem solving and to deal with class issues.

➤ Class meetings need to focus on sharing, deciding, planning, and reflecting.

➤ Providing an engaging curriculum that connects with students' interests is essential.

➤ If students are off-task, you should ask yourself, "What is the task?" "Is the task irrelevant and non-engaging?"

➤ In addition to focusing on student-teacher relationships, you want to encourage and foster student-to-student connections.

## Implementation

➤ You want to make sure that you start out in the very beginning establishing a caring community in the classroom, providing choices for students and opportunities to make decisions. Look at your curriculum and instruction choices. Reflect upon whether or not they are engaging and relevant for your students.

## Limitation

➤ Main focus is on supportive strategies.

> **"** Anytime you do something for someone else that they can do for themselves, you are retarding their growth. **"**
>
> —Lou Brown

> **"** All too often we are giving our children cut flowers when we should be teaching them to grow their own gardens. **"**
>
> —Author Unknown

editor, class news reporters, and substitute monitor. Be creative and put your students to work making contributions to class.

Sometimes teachers hold back from turning classroom tasks over to students because the students wouldn't perform the tasks as "perfectly" as the teacher would. Please don't slip into that type of thinking in your pursuit of perfection. If you do, you are robbing students of a valuable opportunity to contribute to the class and feel as if they are an integral part of the class. You are also robbing them of the opportunity to hone their responsibility skills through carrying out responsibilities. Remember, "Don't do anything for students that they can do for themselves."

## Study Buddies

Having everyone in class assigned a study buddy can help with students assuming responsibility for their own assignments in class. It can also help with developing study skills, needed more and more the older the students get. You want to teach students how to be effective study buddies for one another and emphasize effective study habits, like recording assignments, note taking, and outlining. Then they can support each other in following through.

## Homework Buddy

Homework buddies fulfill a similar function as that of study buddy. Everyone having a homework buddy can not only keep everyone on track with what the homework assignments are on a day to day basis, but each student's homework buddy can also be in charge of letting an absent homework buddy know what she missed. You will need to prepare a list of responsibilities for both study and homework buddies to be made available on file or posted in the classroom.

## Peer Tutors

Some students finish their work rather quickly and need extra stimulation. Utilizing them as tutors on a choice basis is actually beneficial for both the tutor and the student being tutored. Having a choice about whether or not to serve as a tutor is critical. We don't want tutoring to be a chore, but rather a contribution that is enhancing for both. It is beneficial for the tutor, because many students as well as teachers actually learn more from the teaching process than they do from the learning process. When we are preparing to teach to someone else, we focus on the content in-depth. So tutoring helps the tutor to learn content more deeply. The tutoring is beneficial for the student being tutored because often a peer can explain the material on their level more effectively than the teacher can.

We also encourage you to find ways for less able students to be tutors. It can be a great way to build up their capability level (discussed more in Capable Strategies in this chapter). Even though less able students may be struggling with their current content, they may have special skills that they can share with their peers or they may be able to tutor younger students in areas they have since mastered. The process of tutoring younger students can help them develop the confidence to tackle difficult content at their level with more assurance.

> **FROM RESEARCH**
> Student participation in class decision-making resulted in improvements in behavior.
>
> —Sorsdahl and Sanche (1985)

## Peer Mediators

Involving students as mediators helps students in general to learn to solve problems and helps the mediators to have a legitimate sense of power and control in the school. Sometimes it can be amazing how being a peer mediator can turn a student heading for trouble into being part of the solution.

Conducting training with the students and adult supervision is integral for peer mediation to work effectively. Johnson and Johnson (1991, 1995) have created useful resources for implementing peer mediation and peer mediation training. There are many programs that actively involve students in preventing and dealing with bullying.

## Peer Counselors

With training and guidance students can be very effective at counseling one another. The value of peers being able to relate on the same level can be very powerful.

## Peer Recognition

Have students give recognition to one another for their accomplishments and contributions to the class. It doesn't all have to come from you, the teacher. This contributes to a sense of a learning community as well.

## Student Led Conferences

One strategy that is becoming more common is that of having the students in charge of conducting the conference between the students, their parents, and the teachers. This puts the responsibility for the choices made, both behaviorally and academically, on the student's shoulders. The teacher would, of course, guide this process and hold students accountable for accuracy in the conference, but it can be very empowering for students to assume the responsibility of student led conferences.

# Parent and Staff Involvement

Parents are the central element or the keystone in the supportive arch of this RESPECT chapter. The keystone is the stone that holds the other stones in place or the central supporting element. We need to view parents from that perspective.

Parents can be an invaluable support, only if we implement an inviting approach that creates a feeling of being allies rather than adversaries. How we interact with parents—what we project to them—does make a difference in what we get back from them. We want our interaction to be giving the message, "Let's work together to meet the needs of your child." The tools you have to accomplish this are the **Crucial C's of Parental Support:**

> ➤ Parent/Teacher **C**ommunication
> ➤ Parent/Teacher **C**onnection
> ➤ Parent/Teacher **C**ollaboration

Since this is such a vital issue, the "P" in RESPECT will be expanded into its own chapter. We will explore in chapter 15 how to create a situation where parents do feel that they are the central supporting element, or the keystone to meeting the needs of our students.

## Staff Involvement

Staff involvement in your classroom is also important if you are going to be able to meet the needs of your students. We as teachers no longer operate in isolation from one another. You need to collaborate with many other educators in solving both learning and discipline problems. The special education teacher, the school nurse, the music and PE teachers, the school social worker, the occupational therapist, the speech and language pathologist, the ESL (English as a second language) and the bilingual teacher, the administrators, the school counselor and the school psychologist are all support people in meeting your students' needs. The more these individuals work together, the better we can serve students.

The multi-disciplinary team (MDT) is the most common venue for inter-action among various members of the staff in order to help students. This team has different names in different locales, but it is the team of educators that meets on a regular basis to make recommendations about students' needs. It is most effective, though, to collaborate with other staff as needed and not necessarily wait for the more formalized meeting time. As a matter of practice, the emphasis should be on prevention and early intervention, which comes long before an MDT meeting. Many MDT's would also like specific informa-tion about what was tried previously, so reach out and tap into the expertise in your school. Staff involvement leads to solutions.

# <u>E</u>ncouragement and Effective Praise

Focusing your attention on responsible behavior is one of the most effective ways to bring about responsible behavior in your class. Sounds simple doesn't it, but it is not something that we seem to do naturally in our society. The old adage "accentuate the positive, eliminate the negative" shows up in song, but not as often in our classrooms. I have gone into many classrooms along with other teachers helping me and we have clocked how much time teachers give attention to responsible behavior versus how much time attention is given to misbehavior. The ratio is strongly towards attention to the negative (Kyle, 1991b).

I have then taught those teachers about the power of encour-agement and effective praise, or in others words, the power of giving attention and focus to responsible behavior. The result was that many teachers focused more on giving attention to positive behavior. This had a significant positive impact on student behav-iors. I want to be very clear that I am not implying that we should not give any attention to negative behavior. It is critical that we deal with misbehavior when it occurs, but as previously stated, we need to be as short and succinct as possible giving the negative as little attention as possible. All of the strategies in the corrective component are designed to help you accomplish that.

We need to emphasize, notice, and comment on responsible choices that students make and to give more attention to respon-sible behavior. As previously noted, that positive attention needs to be more low key and more private from fifth grade on, but focusing on responsible behavior needs to permeate throughout our educational system, even at the university level. We somehow think that if we go around telling students what not to do, that

> **FROM RESEARCH**
> Problem students are even more affected by the teacher using encour-agement versus negative interaction than non-problem students. They exhibit more disruptive behavior and demon-strate even shorter attention spans when teachers use negative interaction rather than encouragement.
>
> *—Fry (1983)*

they will automatically be able to fill in what to do, but it doesn't work that way. We need to be very concrete about what behavior choices contribute to the class being able to enjoy teaching and learning together, so we have a **VIABLE** class, where learning takes place.

Whatever you give your attention to is strengthened, or in behavioral terms, is reinforced. What type of behavior do you want strengthened in your classroom?

I also want to be clear that we are not talking about using a positive focus as a manipulation. We are not talking about saying, "I like the way Ernesto is sitting in his chair" because what we really want is for Sally, who is sitting next to Ernesto, to shape up and sit responsibly in her chair. You need to deal with Sally's situation directly and use the positive focus in your class as a genuine and authentic attempt to focus appreciation and attention on the responsible choices that your students make.

What we all need to do is to utilize **E**ncouragement and effective praise to accentuate the positive and eliminate the negative and to make it clear, whether the students are five or fifteen, what behavior choices will contribute to the class and which will detract. We need to emphasize responsible behavior in order to strengthen that.

Encouragement is a more global tool that allows for a more pervasive focus on responsible behavior. You can encourage responsible behavior at any point in a student's growth. You do not have to wait for a finished product, as with praise. You can encourage positive steps, movement, improvement, and progress of the student. You can encourage students' efforts and strengths. Encouragement also focuses on getting the student to look within for validation. You want your students to examine their own reactions to their accomplishments and their strengths.

Praise has been criticized as being your evaluative opinion of a student and for needing something accomplished before you can utilize praise. But praise does have a place, when it is reframed into effective praise, and when it is balanced with the use of encouragement as well. Praise is giving feedback to the students about how they are doing. Brophy (1998) defines effective praise as encompassing the following qualities:

> Appreciative rather than controlling
> Informative feedback rather than evaluative
> Genuine

**FROM RESEARCH**
Teachers using specific praise created positive changes in the students' behavior. Disruptive behavior decreased and work completion increased.

—Armstrong, McNeil, and Houten (1988)

" Without recognizing the good in each child, one cannot hope to encourage him. "
—Dinkmeyer and Dreikurs (2000)

➤ Specific
➤ Non-verbals congruent with the praise message
➤ Using a variety of phrases—"good job" is not sufficient

An example of the difference between effective praise and encouragement for a student drawing is:

➤ Effective Praise (external focus): "I admire the unusual way that you used colors in this picture. It creates a very pleasing effect."
➤ Encouragement (internal focus): "It looks as if you put a lot of effort into this picture. I'll bet you are proud of it."

# Affirmations

Affirmations are a type of encouragement that highlight students' positive qualities—their strengths and character virtues. Affirming words include hard-working, honest, helpful, lively, involved, determined, open-minded, sharing, cooperative, persevering, perceptive, creative, detailed, responsible, trustworthy, loyal, dependable, courageous, sincere, candid, principled, reliable, supportive, accepting, diligent, self-disciplined, kind, and considerate.

Use affirmations liberally, but remember to seek out and comment on the strengths and positive qualities of ALL of your students. They all have positive qualities! Some are easier to find than others, but you need to exercise persistence in finding the positive aspects of every student that you work with. It is harder to find positives with your students who choose angry or violent behaviors, but even more critical to do so, if you want to find lasting solutions to the problems.

# Express Appreciation

Expressing appreciation is a particular type of praise that emphasizes the positive impact that students' actions have on others. It is one of the most effective uses of praise. You are having students concentrate on their responsible behaviors, thereby making responsible behavior choices more likely in the future.

Sometimes teachers will say something like, "Why should I express appreciation to my students? They are supposed to do that." Even when we are doing something we are supposed to be doing, it feels good to have someone express appreciation for our actions. It motivates us to continue the responsible behavior mentioned. Think of a time when you were doing something you were supposed to be doing and someone expressed his or her appreciation. It feels good, doesn't it?

Appreciations can be expressed verbally or they can be delivered in written form. When we were discussing using refocus notes as an attention-focusing strategy with distracting behaviors, I mentioned that some teachers also use notes for responsible behaviors. You can have notes made up ahead of time that say, "I appreciate _____ " and then fill in what the responsible behavior is that the student is enacting. You can also use the strategy that is more popular with older students, that of using post-it notes to write your appreciations. You just quietly put the post-it note on the students' desk, drawing their attention to the responsible behavior you appreciate. Whatever method you use, watch for and express appreciation to ALL of your students for responsible behaviors that contribute to the class or to their own learning.

> It is crucial that praise and encouragement be used with all students, not just the high achievers. Look for ways to focus on the positives of your students who are struggling academically and your students who are misbehaving. Pointing out their positives, even if they are harder to find, is integral to finding solutions.

## Incentives

An incentive is defined as something that encourages and motivates someone to action. They can help to spur on students in accomplishing academic tasks and in following through with responsible behavior commitments. Different teachers feel differently about the use of incentives. Usually those with a negative reaction toward incentives want students to be more intrinsically (internally) motivated rather than extrinsically (externally) motivated. Each teacher needs to decide for him- or herself what he or she feels comfortable with in the use of incentives.

My own personal decision is that I like to meet students where they are and use incentives to help them to move towards being more intrinsically motivated. Intrinsic motivation is definitely the goal, but I find that many students need help and support getting to the point where they are intrinsically motivated. Feeling capable of performing the tasks (coming up next) is essential. Feeling as if they are an integral part of the learning community is also necessary for intrinsic motivation to flourish. Being engaged in a variety of relevant learning tasks is also critical. A positive learning environment in which problems are dealt with in a controlled manner is also foundational to intrinsic

motivation. Everything that we have been talking about in this book helps students to move closer and closer to intrinsic motivation. Make your own choices about using incentives, but realize that intrinsic motivation is tied up with the integration of all four components of effective teaching, management, and discipline.

Involving the students in creating what the incentives will be helps. Here are some examples of what students have come up with:

**Student Created Incentives**

| | |
|---|---|
| Choice time | Homework time—5 minutes during class |
| Good choice points | Free time |
| Interaction time with one another for 5 minutes | Tell stories or jokes for 5 minutes |
| Extra library time | Go to lunch early |
| Extra time between classes | Cut passes (to take cuts in line legitimately) |
| Educational games | Draw |
| Upper grade students listen to their reading | Make something for the bulletin board |
| Visit another class for one subject | Make a sculpture |
| Listen to a tape recorder | High-five from teacher |
| Write a creative story | Choice as to where to work |
| Use a stop watch | Work with clay |
| Teacher time | Walk with the teacher |
| Positive teacher note to take home | Eat lunch in the classroom |
| Read a story to a younger student | Daydream time |
| Create a puppet show for the young students | Personal activity time and personal interest time |

# Choice Time

I like to set aside time that the students can use in any way they choose as an incentive for responsible choices. Even though this choice time takes away from the schedule, it can actually save you time in the long run in terms of fewer problem situations that need to be dealt with. It motivates students to make responsible choices so they can participate in choice time. With elementary students it has usually been ten minutes a day, and with secondary students, five minutes a period. You can create opportunities for students to add seconds and minutes to choice time. Be careful to keep the activities within the boundaries of school rules and common courtesy (noise for other classrooms, in particular).

The students should know all about choice time in the first week of school. They also need to know that they can lose part or all of choice time from irresponsible choices.

# <u>C</u>apable Strategies

Building up the capability level of your students is something that all students need, but students who have "I Can't" messages in their head especially need these strategies. Lew and Bettner (1995) emphasize the importance of helping students to feel capable. They suggest:

➢ Making mistakes a learning opportunity
➢ Focusing on improvement, not perfection
➢ Building on student strengths
➢ Allowing students to struggle and succeed within their ability level
➢ Acknowledging the difficulty of the task
➢ Analyzing past successes, and then focusing on the present
➢ Breaking the task into bite-sized instructional pieces
➢ Working on positive self-talk
➢ Celebrating accomplishments

## Making Mistakes a Learning Opportunity

Making mistakes a learning opportunity is critical for all students. When you learn new information, making mistakes is a natural part of the process. Mistakes are in actuality a feedback system letting you know what you know and what you still need to learn. Have you as an adult learned a new language or a new sport? Did you make any mistakes while you were doing that? Most teachers answer yes to both of those questions. Whenever we are learning new material, no matter what our age, we will make some mistakes. Whenever you put out an effort to learn, you will make some mistakes. Instead of fearing or dreading mistakes, the emphasis needs to be on learning from our mistakes.

Creating a class based on the idea that mistakes are part of the learning process helps to create an environment where mistakes and risks are okay. The emphasis becomes correcting and learning from our mistakes, and not fearing making mistakes. There is more of an opportunity to learn when the risk of making a mistake is not dreaded. Some students are afraid that mistakes will humiliate them. This impedes learning.

**FROM RESEARCH**
Discipline that focuses on students feeling more capable results in higher academic achievement.

—*Burden (1995)*

A recommendation was made in the preventive component that you wait until the later stages of new learning before you record scores to be averaged into students' grades. The suggestion was that in the initial stages of new learning, the focus is on points for a completed and corrected assignment. This is so students can make mistakes in those initial learning activities, correct their mistakes, and learn from them without the tension that it is somehow going to mess up their grade in the class. Whenever we learn new material, a natural part of the process is to make mistakes. With older students you need to make sure the earlier activities "count" or they won't want to do them, but they can count as so many points for a completed and corrected assignment.

## Teacher Perfectionism

One thing that at times gets in the way of creating a class that makes mistakes a learning opportunity is that teachers sometimes have a tendency towards perfectionism. You can decide if this fits for you or not. But if a teacher does have a propensity towards perfectionism, what happens is that teacher verbalizes to the class one perspective: "Mistakes are a natural part of the learning process and that we all make mistakes in the initial stages of learning. What is important is to correct your mistakes and learn from them." But then the teacher reveals through his/her reactions that mistakes really aren't okay and the students get a mixed message. Remember that students learn more from what you do than what you say.

If you are going to help all of your students to build up their capability level through creating a class based on the idea that mistakes are a learning opportunity, and what we need to do is correct and learn from our mistakes, then you need to examine what you are modeling to your students in this area.

## Unmotivated Behaviors Stemming from "I Can't" Messages

In the chapter on corrective strategies with controlling behaviors, we discussed that some unmotivated behaviors come from the attitude "I don't want to be bothered doing this—it is too much trouble." Unmotivated behaviors of students can also come from their having a very loud "I can't" message in their head. Their "I can't" message is so loud

> The race goes not always to the swift . . . but to those who keep on running.

> Study and dissect your mistakes so you can avoid repeating them. Study and analyze your successes so you can re-peat the behavior that has brought you positive results.

**FROM RESEARCH**
A teacher attitude that "students could and would master their les-sons" reaped benefits. Test scores were raised and discipline improved.
—*Lutz (1983)*

> Make your class-room safe for the students to risk failure. Create a safe-**to**-fail environment, not a safe-**from**-failure environment.

that when you say, "You can do it," your message doesn't really penetrate their "I can't" message. The unmotivated behaviors of these students are coming from a very different place than the "I really don't want to be bothered" unmotivated behaviors.

Building up their capability level is the main path to long-term solutions with students who are operating from an "I can't" frame of reference. Use the "capable" strategies highlighted previously. Changing students' "I can't" messages into "I can" messages does not happen easily, but will happen gradually over a period of time.

---

**FROM RESEARCH**

Learning disabled students were more apt to view their academic success as controlled by powerful others, whereas more academically successful students were able to perceive that they had some control.

*—Grolnick and Ryan (1990)*

---

For students who are unmotivated due to "I can't" messages we:

➤ Create an environment in which it is safe to make mistakes and learn from our mistakes.
➤ Focus on their improvement and use encouragement to emphasize even small steps.
➤ Use encouragement to help them to see what their strengths are.
➤ Gear the learning tasks to their needs.
➤ Make sure we break the tasks into manageable pieces and emphasize their successes on each piece.
➤ Acknowledge the fact that some learning tasks are difficult, but express our faith that they can do it eventually if they keep working at it.
➤ Help them to see where they have been successful in the past and how that relates to what they are doing now.
➤ Foster gradually the development of positive self-talk rather than the current defeating messages.
➤ Encourage them to give themselves put-ups in place of put-downs.
➤ Give them positive, but realistic phrases to encourage themselves.

All of these strategies help over time. Lots of encouragement, which focuses on improvement, growth, and effort, is integral.

# Teacher/Student Relationship

The teacher-student relationship is the glue that holds the whole class together. Building positive relationships with your students is the last of the RESPECT supportive strategies, but foremost in terms of its effect upon the whole class and the decisions that students make about their behaviors. Positive teacher-student relationships are one of the primary motivators toward responsible behavior choices. Start building positive relationships on day one, add to that in the first week, and continue to focus on that throughout the entire school year. Believing that all students can succeed and can learn responsible behavior is foundational to solid teacher-student relationships. Relating to your students on a person-to-person level is also paramount. Not only caring about them, but also projecting that caring and demonstrating it in your interactions with them is vital. Keep in mind that does not mean to ignore their misbehavior, but rather deal with it in the controlled, business-like manner we have been discussing throughout the book. Then add the supportive strategies in this chapter to the equation on an on-going basis. Create a trusting atmosphere through extensive use of supportive strategies highlighted in this chapter.

Sometimes teachers think that the supportive strategies are icing on the cake, something to get around to when you have time, but actually they are essential ingredients in any discipline program. Remember corrective strategies are short-term solutions only, designed to deal with the immediate situation. Without the supportive strategies, you will not get the sustained results that create a classroom where you want to be and your students want to be. You will not create a classroom conducive to learning. Combining many supportive strategies in this chapter with specific strategies to build positive, trustful relationships with your students is critical to your enjoyment of teaching and your students' enjoyment of learning.

We are going to list many options that you have to connect with your students and form quality teacher/student relationships that motivate students to help create a positive learning environment. No teacher does them all. Choose the ones that will work for you.

> **"** Teachers need to help students accept responsibility for their actions and the well-being of the class. **"**
> —*Charles (2002)*

**FROM RESEARCH**
Positive teacher-student relationships promote favorable student attitudes towards school.
—*Murphy (1995)*

**FROM RESEARCH**
Positive teacher-student relationships are integral to problem prevention.
—*Shockley and Sevier (1991)*

### Building Positive Teacher-Student Relationships

| | |
|---|---|
| Give respect to get respect. | Keep lines of communication open. |
| Listen to your students. | Use a collaborative discipline style. |
| Involve them in class decision-making—give voice and choice. | Look for and comment on students' strengths—use affirmations. |
| Prize the unique gifts of each student. | Focus on positive behavior. |
| Communicate positive expectations. | Send positive messages to your students. |
| Let your enthusiasm for teaching shine through. | Model kind behavior. |
| Elicit student input. | Be helpful. |
| Greet students by name. | Send a morning message for each student. |
| Show interest in their interests. | Attend events of your students. |
| Remember information about their lives outside of school. | Have one-on-one time with your students. |
| Chat with your students outside of class. | Focus on successes of all. |
| Celebrate accomplishments. | Have a class suggestion box. |
| Eat lunch with your students. | Invite students to eat in the classroom. |
| Recognize their birthdays. | Display their work—let them choose. |
| Accept individual differences. | Value your students' diversity. |

# RESPECT School-Wide

It is most powerful when the entire school is committed to practicing **RESPECT.** We encourage you to initiate a school-wide discipline program, if it does not currently exist. Having all adults in the school working together toward the same goals accomplishes a lot. Your school can adapt each aspect of **RESPECT** to a school-wide focus.

**R**esponsible behaviors can be intentionally taught throughout the school. There could be a different responsible behavior highlighted each week with everybody in the school on the lookout for those behaviors. Assemblies could be held to showcase examples of responsible behaviors. Outside speakers could have responsible behavior as their focus.

**E**stablishing school-wide harmony would be achieved through working on creating a "learning community" throughout the school accompanied by a "This is Our School" message. We have a VIABLE school where everyone is **V**alued, **I**ncluded, **A**ccepted, **B**elongs, **L**istened to, and **E**ncouraged."

<u>S</u>tudent involvement would be geared to students having voice and choice school-wide. Voice and choice do not mean that students get to do whatever they want. The adults in the school have the ultimate responsibility to create a school environment conducive to learning. Students would be invited to participate responsibly in that process. A student council or student court could be part of the decision-making process where student views about school-wide issues would be heard.

<u>P</u>arents would be a viable part of the whole school process. This could be accomplished through PTA's and PTO's or parent focus groups. Parents would feel that they were a real part of the decision-making process. Staff would also be involved in the school decision-making process and feel empowered to help create a school where RESPECT was the foundation.

<u>E</u>ncouragement and effective praise would be frequent tools used school-wide. Students would not be the only ones encouraged, but also educators, staff, and even principals. The emphasis would be on the positive aspects of the school and its members.

<u>C</u>apable strategies would be implemented to help everyone feel that they were capable of succeeding in their contribution to the school, whatever that was.

<u>T</u>eacher/student relationships would be the focus throughout the school, but the interpretation of "teacher" would be any adult that impacts the learning and growth of the students.

Purkey and Stanley's (1991) book *Invitational Teaching, Learning, and Living* espouses the importance of creating schools that are invitational. They encourage schools to establish welcoming, respectful climates in which all feel invited—students, parents, educators, and the community. Faculty and staff valuing each other and working together are important along with fair policies that have students' best interests at heart. Inclusiveness and acceptance of individual differences are critical in an invitational school. Please join with the other adults in your school and use the RESPECT strategies to create a school where all feel welcomed and valued.

| In This School Everyone Is: |
| --- |
| <u>V</u>alued |
| <u>I</u>ncluded |
| <u>A</u>ccepted |
| <u>B</u>elonging |
| <u>L</u>istened to |
| <u>E</u>ncouraged |

# Summary

Supportive strategies are integral aspects of creating classrooms conducive to learning and positive classroom climates. *Responsible behaviors* need to be intentionally taught. *Establishing classroom harmony* is essential. *Student involvement* empowers students and helps them to feel ownership of the class. *Parent involvement* is the keystone, or central support, of the RESPECT arch. You need to reach out to various staff members for problem-solving help. A *team approach* works best. *Encouragement and effective praise* are vital tools in your classroom. All students need to have their capability level built up through *Capable strategies.* Students with "I Can't" messages need lots of capable strategies. Positive *teacher-student relationships* are the underpinnings of your entire discipline program. Use RESPECT strategies to create *school-wide discipline programs* that help all to feel included in the process.

# Reflection Questions

1. What responsible behavior skills will you teach intentionally in your class?
2. Describe the strategies for establishing classroom harmony.
3. Brainstorm ways in which you will actively involve students in the discipline and management processes.
4. Discuss the aspects of parents as the keystone in the supportive arch of RESPECT.
5. Demonstrate the use of encouragement and effective praise through role-playing.
6. Explain how you will approach mistakes as learning opportunities in your classroom.
7. Choose the teacher-student relationship building strategies that you believe will be most effective for you.
8. How can a school develop a school-wide discipline program?

9.  Discuss the following scenarios.

**Elementary: Art**

Kent, Kari, and Krista are working together on an art project. Kent needs the tangerine crayon to finish the trim on an Indian blanket. Kari really needs the tangerine crayon to touch up the sunset. Krista really, REALLY needs the tangerine crayon to do the tree leaves. A major conflict is about to erupt! How will you use this as a learning opportunity to teach the concept of sharing?

**Elementary: I Can't**

Joshua spends a great deal of his time with his head on his desk. When you try to get him to participate in class activities or to work independently on his schoolwork, all he says is, "I can't." What can you do to help Joshua?

**Secondary: Class Clown**

Danny has made his mark in the school as class clown. His grades are consistently low, which contrasts with his bright eyes and quick wit. He appears to be well-read in everything, but required subjects. You are aware that he comes from a dysfunctional family. At semester break he changes his schedule and is assigned to one of the courses you teach. You have a chance to plan ahead! What strategies will you use with Danny?

**Secondary: Not Doing Assignments**

Adam is a bright kid. You can tell by his intelligent conversation and use of sophisticated vocabulary. He has a reputation for being ready, willing, and able to help anyone with their homework. He is very athletic, large for his age, handsome, polite, everything you could want in a junior high male student except for one thing. Adam almost never gets his assignments done and handed in. Now, that seems to be a bit of a paradox. Why, do you suppose, doesn't Adam do his own work? What will you do to remedy the situation?

# References

Akin, T., Dunne, G., Palomares, S., & Schilling, D. (1995). *Character education in America's schools.* Spring Valley, CA: Innerchoice Publishing.

Armstrong, S. B., McNeil, M. E., & Houten, R. V. (1988). A principal's in-service training package for increasing teacher praise. *Teachers Education and Special Education* 11 (3): 79–94.

Black, S. (1996). The character conundrum. *American School Board Journal* 183 (12): 29–31.

Brophy, J. (1998). *Motivating students to learn.* Boston: McGraw-Hill.

Burden, P. (1995). *Classroom management and discipline.* New York: Longman.

Curwin, R., & Mendler, A. (1997). *As tough as necessary.* Alexandria, VA: Association for Supervision and Curriculum Development.

Dinkmeyer, D., & Dreikurs, R. (2000). *Encouraging children to learn.* Philadelphia: Brunner-Routledge.

Freiburg, H. (1996). From tourist to citizens in the classroom. *Educational Leadership* 54 (1): 32–36.

Fry, P. (1983). Process measures of problem and non-problem children's classroom behavior: The influence of teacher behavior variables. *British Journal of Educational Psychology* 53 (1): 79–88.

Greenblatt, R., Cooper, B., & Muth, R. (1984). Managing for effective teaching. *Educational Leadership* 41 (5): 57–59.

Grolnick, W., & Ryan, R. (1990). Self-perceptions, motivation, and adjustment in children with learning disabilities: A multiple group comparison study. *Journal of Learning Disabilities* 23 (3): 177–184.

Johnson, D., & Johnson, R. (1991). *Teaching students to be peacemakers.* Edina, MN: Interaction Book Company.

——. (1995). *Reducing school violence through conflict resolution.* Alexandria, VA: Association for Supervision and Curriculum Development.

Kagan, S. (1994). *Cooperative learning.* San Clemente, CA: Kagan Cooperative Learning.

——. (1999). *Cooperative learning and character development* video. National Video Resources.

Kagan, S., & Kagan, M. (1998). *Multiple intelligences.* San Clemente, CA: Kagan Publishing.

Kagan, L., Kagan, M., & Kagan, S. (1998). *Teambuilding.* San Clemente, CA: Kagan Publishing.

Kagan, M., Robertson, L., & Kagan, S. (1998). *Classbuilding.* San Clemente, CA: Kagan Publishing.

Kohn, A. (1996a). What to look for in a classroom. *Educational Leadership* 54 (1): 54–55.

——. (1996b). *Beyond discipline: From compliance to community.* Alexandria, VA: Association for Supervision and Curriculum Development.

Kyle, P. (1991b). *The effects of positive discipline strategies and active student involvement in the discipline process on selected elements of classroom climate.* Dissertation: University of Idaho.

Lew, A., & Bettner, B. (1995). *Responsibility in the classroom: A teacher's guide to understanding and motivating students.* Boston: Connexions Press.

Lewis, C., Schaps, E., & Watson, M. (1996). The caring classroom's academic edge. *Educational Leadership* 54 (1): 16–21.

Lutz, J. (1983). Attitudes key to school success. *Executive Educator* 5 (11): 26–30.

Murphy, C. (1995). Managing students: Building positive attitudes in the classroom. *Schools in the Middle* 4 (4): 31–33.

Nelsen, J. (1987). *Positive discipline.* New York: Ballantine Books.

Nelsen, J., Lott, L., & Glenn, S. H. (1993). *Positive discipline in the classroom.* Rocklin, CA: Prima Publishing.

Purkey, W., & Stanley, P. (1991). *Invitational teaching, learning, and living.* Washington, DC: DEA Professional Library, National Education Association.

Shockley, R., & Sevier, L. (1991). Behavior management in the classroom: Guidelines for maintaining control. *Schools in the Middle* 1 (12): 14–18.

Short, P., & Short, R. (1988). Perceived classroom environment and student behavior in secondary schools. *Research Quarterly* 12 (3): 35–39.

Sorsdahl, S., & Sanche, R. (1985). The effects of classroom meetings on self-concept and behavior. *Elementary School Guidance and Counseling* 20 (1): 49–56.

Sternberg, R., Okagaki, L., & Jackson, A. (1990). Practical intelligence for success in school. *Educational Leadership* 48 (1): 35–39.

Sudzina, M. (1997). From tourist to citizens in the classroom: An interview with H. Jerome Freiberg. *Mid-Western Educational Researcher* 10 (2): 35–38.

Sweeney, J. (1992). School climate: The key to excellence. *NASSP Bulletin* 76 (547): 69–73.

Taylor, J. (2001b). *Helping your ADD child.* Roseville, CA: Prima Publishing.

Vasconcellos, J., & Murphy, M. (1987). Education in the experience of being citizens. *Educational Leadership* 45 (2): 70–73.

# Establishing the Crucial C's
# of Parental Support

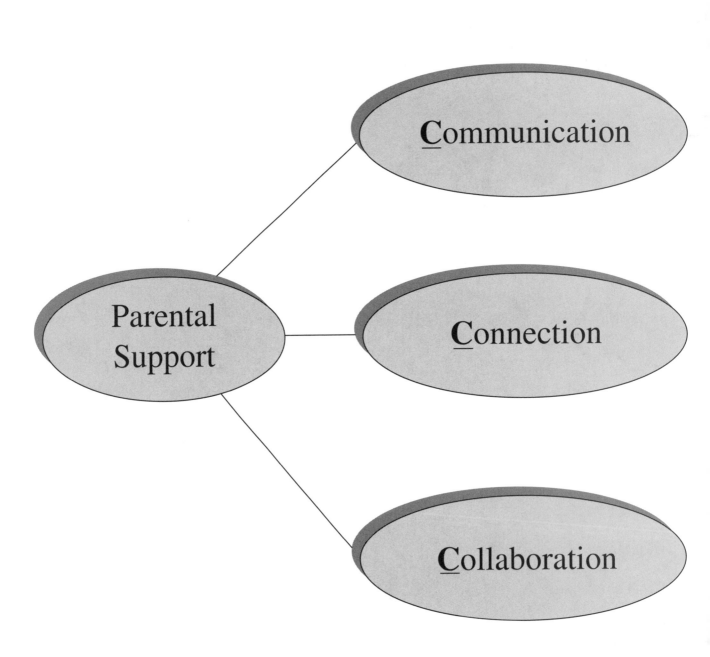

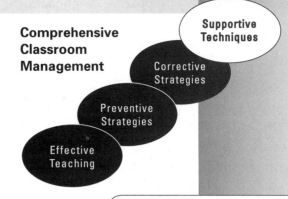

**OBJECTIVES**

The learner will be able to imple-
ment the Crucial C's of Parental
Support: Communication,
Connection, and Collaboration.

# Communication, Connection, and Collaboration

Communicating with, Connecting with, and Collaborating with parents are essential elements in a comprehensive management program. As stated in the last chapter, parents are a very central element or the keystone in the supportive arch of RESPECT. The keystone is the stone that holds the other stones in place or the central supporting element. Eliciting parental support is not only a professional responsibility, but also a valuable tool to lead toward solutions. We need to view parents as central in the lives of our students and, therefore, central to truly meeting the needs of all students. The more that teachers and parents can Communicate, Connect, and Collaborate, the more success we will have. Keep in mind that some students will be living with grandparents or guardians. When we say parents, we are using it broadly to include adults in a parenting role.

Including parents as partners in the discipline process is key. Not all parents will necessarily respond to that, but continued invitations to Communicate, Connect, and Collaborate bring about more and more positive parent responses. We do want to have an inviting attitude in our interactions with parents. Parents can be an invaluable support, when an inviting approach creates a feeling of being allies rather than adversaries.

Parent involvement needs to be pivotal to the supportive component in our classrooms. You need to think of parent involvement

**FROM RESEARCH**

Effectively engaging parents and families in the education of their children has the potential to be far more transformational than any other type of education reform.

—*Sullivan (1998)*

**FROM RESEARCH**

Parent involvement models that emphasize teacher/parent communication have a positive impact on student achievement.

—*Watkins (1997)*

**FROM RESEARCH**

School-home communication was an important factor in significantly improving adolescent conduct in school.

—*Gottfredson (1993)*

➢ Parent/Teacher **C**ommunication
➢ Parent/Teacher **C**onnection
➢ Parent/Teacher **C**ollaboration

in its broadest sense, though. Sometimes teachers only think of parent involvement in terms of parents coming into the school and performing tasks. That is a helpful and supportive aspect of parent involvement, but parent involvement is even more critical at home without the parents even coming into school. The most crucial element of parent involvement is what parents say to their children about school . . . about you, their teacher, and about the importance of education.

Having parents on our side to the extent that they say positive things to their children about teachers, and about the school community and about education, in general, is one of the most powerful tools that we can have. Communicating, connecting and collaborating with parents helps to bring that essential, positive, supportive message into our students' homes. Yes, it is great when parents come to school and interact and support in positive ways, but imagine parents saying to their children, "Education is important. Your teacher is there to help you learn. Your school wants you to succeed in life and will equip you with the skills to do that." Of course, it doesn't need to be exactly those words. Most parents don't speak to their children quite like that, but the message behind those words is a powerful motivator for children and their attitude toward school.

For those of you in secondary, the parents of your students are less likely to come to school and actually contribute to your classroom activities. This is also compounded by the fact that you might have 150 sets of parents to interact with. As you read this chapter, please choose strategies from the options provided that will be managable for you at the secondary level, remembering that positive communication, connection and collaboration from you will likely translate into positive messages at home. That is the best support you can get from parents. Parents of secondary students can still be the important keystone that holds up the RESPECT support arch.

How we interact with parents—whether or not we create a welcoming atmosphere for them—does impact their response to the school and to us. We want our interaction to be giving the message, "Let's work together to meet the needs of your child." The tools you have to accomplish this are the **3 Crucial C's of Parental Support:** **C**ommunication, **C**onnection, and **C**ollaboration between teachers and parents.

# Parent/Teacher <u>C</u>ommunication

On-going communication with parents starting in the first week of school and continuing throughout the year is key to positive messages at home. The table below illustrates many options for communicating with parents on a regular basis. Choose whatever options work for you, but do choose. Nothing brings about parent support better than on-going communication.

> **FROM RESEARCH**
> High parent involvement is brought about through newsletters, phone calls, parent/teacher conferences, surveys, and parent education classes.
> —*Kirschenbaum (1999)*

## Options for Communicating with Parents

- ☐ Achievement and improvement letters
- ☐ Anecdotal logs
- ☐ Assignment books
- ☐ Brag notes for responsible good behavior
- ☐ Class website
- ☐ Comment boxes and cards
- ☐ Communication with all parents and guardians
- ☐ Communication to circumvent problems
- ☐ Conferences on a regular basis
- ☐ Dialogue journals
- ☐ E-mails: All parents or personal
- ☐ Evening meetings to inform parents of plans
- ☐ Event letters
- ☐ Facilitate parent/student communication
- ☐ Faxes
- ☐ Friday folders
- ☐ Good day notes
- ☐ Inform parents about curriculum
- ☐ Inform parents of upcoming events, projects, parties
- ☐ Introduction to school year letter
- ☐ Inviting parents into classroom to observe
- ☐ Mailing letters to home
- ☐ Miss you notes to student when absent
- ☐ Newsletter

- ☐ Notes from home for meeting time
- ☐ Notes: Thank you and appreciations
- ☐ Parent initials homework
- ☐ Phone calls
- ☐ Phone or voice mail system
- ☐ Planners and assignment notebook
- ☐ Portfolios
- ☐ Positive calls, e-mails, or notes to parents
- ☐ Positive feedback conferences
- ☐ Pre-year meeting
- ☐ Progress reports
- ☐ Report cards
- ☐ Sending a letter or note
- ☐ Sending happy-grams
- ☐ Sending thank you notes for help
- ☐ Strategies for better day notes
- ☐ Student generated letters to parents
- ☐ Student-led conferences
- ☐ Student work samples
- ☐ Take-home folder comments
- ☐ Thank you and appreciation notes
- ☐ Voice mail: Teacher's recording
- ☐ Web page
- ☐ Website
- ☐ Weekend journals

# Parent/Teacher Conferences: An Integral Communication Tool

In conjunction with the various communication choices you make, conferences with parents on a regular basis are critical. You can implement formalized conferences, when the whole school is participating in them simultaneously or you can enact informal ones as needed. There is nothing parents dislike more than to hear about a problem after it is already a big, long-term problem. Communication early on is important. You can certainly start with trying to solve the problem with the student first before communicating with the parents—just don't wait until too far into the problem situation. Waiting until the problem is big tends to trigger parent frustration rather than parent support.

Planning and preparing for conferences is important for success. The following can help you to prepare before, during, and after for effective and efficient parent/teacher conferences:

### Planning and Preparing for Parent/Teacher Conferences

**Before the conference:**
- ☐ Keep careful records on student progress and improvement
- ☐ Plan ahead—write down what you will do
- ☐ Be prepared with examples/samples
- ☐ Review your student records

**During the conference:**
- ☐ Start with a positive about the student
- ☐ Use active listening to understand the parents' perspectives
- ☐ Establish a partnership with the parent
- ☐ Seek/affirm parental backup and support at home
- ☐ Emphasize contributions that parents can and do make
- ☐ Consult parents as resources
- ☐ Involve the student in the conference
- ☐ Emphasize student's strengths as well as challenges
- ☐ Tell the truth supported with examples/samples
- ☐ End on a positive note

**After the conference:**
- ☐ Plan a follow-up
- ☐ Write follow-up activities in your plan book
- ☐ Keep communication ongoing

# Communication with Upset/Angry Parents

Utilizing the Crucial C's of Parental Support strategies minimizes the possibility of upset or angry parents. But parents have a lot of emotion invested in the success or failure of their children, so despite communicating, connecting, and collaborating with them, sometimes you will have parents to deal with who feel negative about the school or your classroom. Your first step is to mentally step back from the situation and not take their defensive reactions personally.

> *Keep cool; anger is not an argument.*
> —Daniel Webster

Most of the time that you inadvertently push parents' defensive buttons, it really doesn't have anything to do with you personally. It might be the parents' fear for their child coming through or bad memories from their own schooling they are still carrying around with them. It also could be that they are struggling with things in their own life, and one more thing—their child having problems in school—is more than they can handle. The defensive reaction could also be coming from their interpreting what you are saying as they are lousy parents—even when that is not what you are intending at all. Realizing that the parents' upset or angry reaction usually has nothing to do with you personally can help you to get your reaction under control and respond professionally. Getting your response under control is key.

Your next step is to use active listening skills until the parents have calmed down. Utilizing paraphrasing, and reflecting give the upset/angry parent an opportunity to feel heard and understood. That does not imply that you are agreeing with them, but that you are giving them the respect to really listen and hear their concerns. That process itself usually calms things down, so you can then pursue solutions to the problem. It is not a good idea to rush into solutions when the parent rationally is still upset or angry.

> Teachers who communicate well with parents find that they enjoy, in return, increased parental support in matters of discipline and curriculum.
> —Senter and Charles (2002)

A few years ago I was the counselor in a school where the principal would send all of the upset or angry parents to my office for solutions to problems. This got to be usual practice because the parents rarely came back to the principal since a solution to their problem was found. I ended up with quite a reputation for working effectively with upset and angry parents. My secret was just what I have shared with you:

> ➤ I did not take their defensive reactions personally.
> ➤ I utilized active listening skills until they felt heard and understood and had calmed down.
> ➤ Then we collaboratively sought solutions.

We encourage you to try this process and see the benefits.

# Communication with Hostile or Violent Parents

You have **NO** obligation to remain in a conference, or in a room for that matter, if the angry parent is hostile or violent. Seeking immediate safety and meeting that parent in the future with others present would be advised. Also if a parent is bordering on hostility, but not actually hostile at this point, and your best judgment says that this is not a good time and that active listening is not going to calm things down soon enough, then you need to say to the parent something like, "It seems as if you are a little too upset for us to work on solving this problem today. Let's schedule a time to meet when we can both approach this from a reasoned position."

# Communication at Inappropriate Times

Even though being available and open to communication with parents is an integral professional responsibility for teachers, it is not appropriate to stop in the middle of teaching to address parent interaction or concerns. Sometimes parents will initiate communication at inappropriate times, such as when you are right in the middle of a lesson teaching your class. You want to be welcoming at such times, but indicate that they will need to wait until a break at which time you would be happy to talk with them or that you can reschedule at a time when you are not teaching. As important as parent/teacher communication is, during class time your students are your first priority.

---

**FROM RESEARCH**
Schools need to do more to make parents feel welcome in the school and to make parent involvement fun.

—*Barber and Patin (1997)*

---

**FROM RESEARCH**
Educators reaching out to parents is essential. Our most pressing need in education is reestablishing parent support.

—*Brandt (1998)*

# Parent/Teacher <u>C</u>onnection

Options that create a connection between you and the parents of your students further the goal of establishing parent/teacher partnerships. Following is a list of options for creating Parent/Teacher <u>C</u>onnections. Choose the options that will work for you and incorporate them into your management plan. Strategies that help you to form relationships with the parents of your students will reap many benefits.

> **FROM RESEARCH**
> On-going parent/teacher communication is crucial and needed.
>
> —*Gettinger and Guetschow (1998)*

## Options for Creating Parent/Teacher <u>C</u>onnections

- ☐ Acknowledging their role as parent
- ☐ Assemblies to celebrate responsible behavior
- ☐ Attending extracurricular activities
- ☐ Banquets
- ☐ Being available
- ☐ Being sensitive and accommodating to language barriers
- ☐ Biography bulletin boards
- ☐ Catch them in the act of being responsible—digital camera
- ☐ Connections for multicultural students
- ☐ Exhibits that parents are invited to
- ☐ Family night
- ☐ Family reading nights (library)
- ☐ Going to the school fair
- ☐ Highlighting whole family for V.I.P. student
- ☐ Home visits
- ☐ Ice cream social
- ☐ Involving parent volunteers in the planning
- ☐ Lunch guest
- ☐ Making a school video for parents to watch
- ☐ Math or science night
- ☐ Open house
- ☐ Parent event: Donuts with Mom and Dad
- ☐ Parent luncheons
- ☐ Parent night to talk about projects and project tours
- ☐ Parent/Family lunch day
- ☐ Parents' Day—parents drop in
- ☐ Personal information surveys filled out by parents
- ☐ Project presentations
- ☐ Projecting sincere enthusiasm about their child
- ☐ Return phone calls promptly
- ☐ School functions
- ☐ School programs
- ☐ Social activities: Lunch or dinner
- ☐ Student led reception
- ☐ Teacher attending extracurricular activities
- ☐ Teacher attending school sponsored activities
- ☐ Teacher attending community events
- ☐ Teacher has positive attitude and open-mindedness
- ☐ Teacher is nonjudgmental of parenting styles
- ☐ Teacher is open to suggestions
- ☐ Teacher is supportive of parents' views
- ☐ Tours of class or school
- ☐ Weekly bulletin board that parents and students put together
- ☐ Welcome signs for parents

# Parent/Teacher Collaboration

Actively involving parents in the classroom entails a variety of options. Involving parents creates alliances and they feel as if they are partners in the process of their children's education. Following is an extensive list of Parent/Teacher Collaboration activities. Put in your management plan the options that are most relevant for your teaching situation realizing that having parents contribute to the class not only lightens your load, but increases the likelihood that parents will be supportive.

## Parent/Teacher Collaboration Activities

- [ ] Asking parents their input on what would help their child
- [ ] Asking parents to share which strategies work at home that might work at school as well
- [ ] Book-It programs run by parents
- [ ] Class volunteering by parents
- [ ] Encouraging parent volunteer time
- [ ] Field trip involvement by parents
- [ ] Fundraisers organized by parents
- [ ] Interest inventories—asking parents what they'd like to share with school
- [ ] Inventory for parents to fill out about child's academic needs
- [ ] Parental input about discipline
- [ ] Parent chaperones
- [ ] Parent experts
- [ ] Parent focus groups
- [ ] Parent guest speakers
- [ ] Parents helping with field trips and activities
- [ ] Parent input into school mission statement
- [ ] Parent involvement in developing code of conduct
- [ ] Parent involvement in lessons and presentations
- [ ] Parent library
- [ ] Parent mentors and tutors
- [ ] Parents teaching a topic
- [ ] Parent volunteer handbook
- [ ] Parent/student homework
- [ ] Parent/Teacher Association or Organization
- [ ] Parent suggestion box
- [ ] Parent education classes and/or materials

- [ ] Parents assisting with after-school activities and programs
- [ ] Parents assisting with computer programs
- [ ] Parents conducting conferences about student writing
- [ ] Parents cooking with groups of students
- [ ] Parents explaining directions of work or educational games
- [ ] Parents gathering materials for projects
- [ ] Parents helping with math manipulations
- [ ] Parents helping students to research information
- [ ] Parents leading games or songs
- [ ] Parents making books
- [ ] Parents offering solutions
- [ ] Parents presenting crafts in class
- [ ] Parents reading to small groups
- [ ] Parents sharing on career day
- [ ] Parents supervising at centers
- [ ] Parents supervising science experiments
- [ ] Parents supervising small groups in the library
- [ ] Parents taping students' stories or books for listening center
- [ ] Parents viewing class exhibits
- [ ] Parents working in classroom
- [ ] Parents working on bulletin boards
- [ ] Profiling parent volunteers: newsletter or website
- [ ] Show and tell with parents' occupations
- [ ] Soliciting parents' point of view
- [ ] Team effort between parent and teachers

# Parent Education Programs

Many schools conduct parent education classes or have parenting materials on hand as important tools to collaborate with parents. The following two boxes give a synopsis of two parent education programs that your schools could schedule or you could have on hand as a resource when parents ask you for help:

## POPKIN'S ACTIVE PARENTING APPROACH

**Assumptions**

➤ Parenting well is extremely important, but it is also extremely difficult.
➤ Successful parenting needs to emphasize character development, particularly developing courage, responsibility, cooperation, respect, and self-esteem.
➤ Democracy requires that its citizens make decisions and accept responsibility for those decisions. Parents need to teach their children the skills to do that.

**Main Points**

➤ It is the job of the parents, not the children, to establish a leadership role in the family. Active involvement of children in that process is crucial.
➤ Parents not only influence their child's development, they can do the most about it.
➤ Logical consequences teach children about the effectiveness of their choices and behavior.
➤ Children are goal driven. Their behavior choices are to estabilsh contact, belonging, power, protection, withdrawal, or challenge.
➤ Parents can use the FLAC method to deal with power struggles: Feeling Limits, Alternatives, and Consequences.
➤ Parents need to encourage their children.
➤ Effective parenting while the children are young will help to avoid problems later, like teen drug abuse, pregnancy, abortion, crime, AIDS, and suicide.

**Implementation**

➤ Implementing family meetings that focus on both problem solving talks and also that apply a problem solving model are parents' best tools.

**Limitation**

➤ Implementing can take time.

# DINKMEYERS' AND MCKAYS' STEP APPROACH

## Assumptions

➤ Expectations that parents have of their children have a powerful influence upon them. Expecting responsible behavior will help to bring it about.

➤ Parents should treat their children as they would their best friend.

➤ Parents need to act toward and around their children as they would like them to act.

## Main Points

➤ Children with no limits may have trouble learning to interact with other people.

➤ Children have goals for their misbehavior. They can be vying for attention, power, or revenge or they can be displaying inadequacy.

➤ Parents need to do two main things to teach responsible behavior to their children: (1) They need to give choices and set limits and (2) they need to utilize logical consequences.

➤ Parents must use encouragement with their children and truly listen to them.

➤ Reflective listening and I-Messages are important techniques for parents to use with their children.

➤ Parents teach values to their children by a combination of saying and doing.

➤ Parents need to look at their parenting styles. An authoritarian or a permissive parenting style does not teach children self-discipline. A democratic parenting style that involves children in the decision-making process is needed.

## Implementation

➤ Family meetings are an invaluable way for parents to cooperate with their children and to teach them responsible behavior. Scheduling regular meetings is critical.

## Limitation

➤ It is not a quick fix.

# Ways That Parents Can Collaborate with Teachers from Home

Parents will often ask teachers about what they can do at home to help and support the teachers' efforts. There are many ways that parents can support us and collaborate with us without the collaboration taking place at school. Here is a list of ideas generated by teachers as to what parents can do at home. Use these when parents ask "How can I help?"

## Ways That Parents Can Collaborate with Teachers from Home

- ☐ Asking for and acknowledging report cards
- ☐ Calling and listening to teacher's view of situation before reacting
- ☐ Checking daily for notes or papers from school
- ☐ Emphasizing relationships through sorting, classifying, counting, and measuring
- ☐ Encouraging your children about homework
- ☐ Encouraging your children to feel that schoolwork is their job
- ☐ Encouraging your children to wonder about things, to be curious, and to ask questions
- ☐ Focusing on your children's strengths
- ☐ Following through with agreements to your children and to the teacher
- ☐ Giving your children books and magazines for presents
- ☐ Giving your children parent time

- ☐ Giving your children positive messages about their qualities
- ☐ Helping your children develop a sense of responsibility through having responsibilities at home
- ☐ Helping your children to know their community
- ☐ Helping your children to notice changes
- ☐ Listening to your children
- ☐ Monitoring and limiting television watching
- ☐ Monitoring and limiting video game playing
- ☐ Noticing new words used by your children
- ☐ Parents being a model of reading by reading themselves
- ☐ Providing study space in the house
- ☐ Reading at home to your children
- ☐ Sending your children to school on time
- ☐ Setting bedtime that gives students appropriate rest
- ☐ Signing permission slips in a timely manner

**FROM RESEARCH**
More opportunities for parent input need to be created.

—*Baker (1997)*

**FROM RESEARCH**
On-going clear communication with parents is an important aspect of successful school effectiveness.

—*McCormack-Larkin (1985)*

# Summary

> Patience + Practice = Progress
> For you and your child
> —*Dinkmeyer, McKay, and Dinkmeyer (1997)*

You have numerous options to create positive opportunities with the parents of your students. Establishing the *Crucial C's of Parental Support: Parent/Teacher **C**ommunication, Parent-Teacher **C**onnection,* and *Parent/Teacher **C**ollaboration* leads to parents being the central support or keystone in your *RESPECT supportive arch. Planning* and *preparing* for *Parent/Teacher Conferences* helps to maximize the benefits of Teacher/Parent communication. Use *active listening skills* when parents are upset or angry. Consider the value of *parent education* classes and/or materials. Give suggestions to parents as to how they can *help at home through home collaboration strategies.*

> " If you promise not to believe everything your child says happens at this school, I'll promise not to believe everything he says happens at home. "
> —*Anonymous English Schoolmaster*

> " If the future of society is our children, then the key to that future rests primarily with parents and teachers. "
> —*Popkin (2002)*

# Reflection Questions

1. What strategies will you use for on going communication with parents?
2. Develop a plan for communicating with parents during parent/teacher conferences.
3. Identify indicators that you are connecting with parents.
4. Give examples of how you could collaborate with parents in your classroom.

# References

Baker, A. (1997). Improving parent involvement programs and practice: A qualitative study of parent perceptions. *School Community Journal* 7 (1): 9–35.

Barber, R. J., & Patin, D. (1997). Parent involvement: A two-way street. *Schools in the Middle* 6 (4): 31–33.

Brandt. (1998). Listen first. *Educational Leadership* 55 (80): 25–30.

Dinkmeyer, D., McKay, G., & Dinkmeyer, D. (1997). *Parent's handbook: Systematic training for effective parenting.* Circle Pines, MN: American Guidance Service.

Dinkmeyer, D., McKay, G., McKay, J., & Dinkmeyer, D. (1997). *Parenting teens: Systematic training for effective parenting of teens.* Circle Pines, MN: American Guidance Service.

Dinkmeyer, D., McKay, G., Dinkmeyer, J., Dinkmeyer, D., & McKay, J. (1997). *Parenting young children.* Circle Pines, Minnesota: American Guidance Service.

Gettinger, M., & Guetschow, K. W. (1998). Parental involvement in schools: Parent and teacher perceptions of roles, efficacy, and opportunities. *Journal of Research and Development in Education* 32 (1): 38–52.

Gottfredson, D. (1993). Managing adolescent behavior: A multiyear, multischool study. *American Educational Research Journal* 30 (1): 179–215.

Kirschenbaum, H. (1999). Night and day: Succeeding with parents at school 43. *Principal* 78 (3): 20–23.

McCormack-Larkin, M. (1985). Ingredients of a successful school effectiveness project. *Educational Leadership* 42 (6): 31–37.

Popkin, M. (2002). *Active parenting now: For parents of children ages 5–12.* Atlanta: Active Parenting Publishing, Inc.

——— . (1998). *Active parenting of teens: Parents' guide.* Atlanta: Active Parenting Publishing Co., Inc.

Popkin, M., Youngs, B., & Healy, J. (1995). *Helping your child succeed in school: A guide for parents of 4–14 year olds.* Atlanta: Active Parenting Publishing, Inc.

Riley, A. (1994). Parent empowerment: An idea for the nineties. *Education Canada* 34 (3): 14–20.

Senter, G., & Charles, C. M. (2002). *Elementary classroom management.* Boston: Allyn & Bacon.

Sullivan, P. (1998). Improving parent involvement: The national standards for parent/family involvement programs. *Our Children* 24 (1): 23.

Watkins, T. (1997). Teacher communications, child achievement, and parent trait in parent involvement models. *Journal of Educational Research* 91 (1): 3–14.

# Putting It All Together

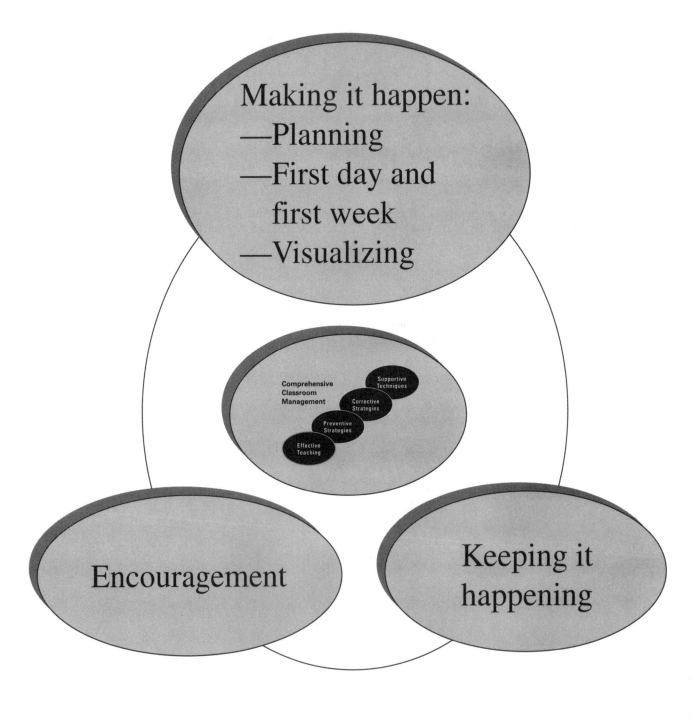

Making it happen:
—Planning
—First day and
first week
—Visualizing

Comprehensive
Classroom
Management

Supportive
Techniques

Corrective
Strategies

Preventive
Strategies

Effective
Teaching

Encouragement

Keeping it
happening

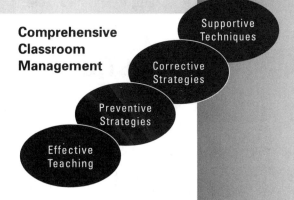

## OBJECTIVES

Learners will be able to:

- Develop their own management plan, including strategies for their first day and first week of teaching.
- Draw from many "options" of effective teaching, proactive preventive strategies, practical corrective strategies, and positive supportive techniques in order to create optimal learning "opportunities" in your classroom.

## CHAPTER SNAPSHOT

- **Making It Happen**
- **First Day and First Week**
- **Class Agreements**
- **Visualizing Success**
- **Keeping It Happening**
- **Encouragement: Go Get 'Em!**

# Making It Happen

The last chapter in this book presents an opportunity for you to plan for the beginning of your teaching experience or for the first day of the rest of your teaching career, if you are an in-service teacher. Planning is critical to your success and to your students' success. Research shows that teachers who start off with direct instruction of rules and procedures and make clear their expectations for behavior and academics in their classroom have fewer behavior problems the rest of the year. The extra bonus is that you will actually make up the time invested in those early days of teaching responsible behaviors in that first week of school (Woolfolk, 2001). Actively involving students in this process adds greatly to its effectiveness. Involvement in creating the initial environment engenders students' ownership of the class resulting in more follow-through and cooperation.

# First Day and First Week

So, just what is it that effective teachers and classroom managers do on the first day of school and during that first week that makes such a difference for the rest of the year? Two things: they set the atmosphere for a learning environment and establish a community of learners. Setting the atmosphere means that you are claiming responsibility to set up and maintain a place where learning is encouraged by everyone in that environment. Establishing a community of learners means that you teach your students their responsibilities as learners and how they can contribute to the positive learning environment. You and your students build an environment together with your expert knowledge of how to learn and how to maintain an environment that will foster learning. You do the effective teaching and coach the students on how to learn. They are responsible for learning, and cooperating with you and the other learners in the classroom.

You will establish some rules and procedures that are non-negotiable, for example, school-wide rules on absences and tardies, fire drill procedures, and other safety issues. You build with the students rules or a code of conduct that outlines the rules and procedures that you are willing to negotiate with the students, and allow them both choices and power in setting up their learning environment. With those choices come consequences—positive consequences for responsible choices, and negative consequences for irresponsible choices. Drawing from the information covered in chapters 8 through 15, you can coach your students toward making reasonable rules and procedures, with logical and appropriate consequences.

# Management Plans

Your plan for establishing this atmosphere needs to be done before the first day of class. What are you willing to negotiate? What issues will you predetermine? Will you establish a written contract or code with your students? Will you post your rules and procedures on a bulletin board or on the wall? Do your rules and procedures follow the principles of effective teaching? Have you considered the annoying little things like lunch counts, late and missing assignments, illness that results in a lot of make-up work, grading policies, extra credit policies, storage spaces, student movement in and out of the classroom, student movement within the classroom, field trip rules, cues for being quiet? The list goes on.

After you have thought about each of the issues above, and any other issues unique to your school, content, and grade level, you will want to come prepared with a management plan on the first day, including the list of negotiables and non-negotiables. You will want to prioritize the list of rules and procedures, and present them in an order that matches the needs of your students and the requirements of the school. For example, kindergarteners need to know where the restrooms are and where to put their new bottles of paste (keeps your floor dry and keeps them from eating their paste). Newcomers to the middle school or junior high will need to know about hall passes, when they can go to their lockers, and how to navigate the school when they go from class to class. High school students will need to know about safety procedures in labs, parking, and excused absences for extracurricular activities. A mnemonic to remember the three big areas for beginning your classroom is **POP:**

**P**lan: Rules, procedures, opening welcome, and first comments
**O**rder of first day events: Priorities, what students need to know first
**P**ractice: Important procedures for safety and to facilitate learning and classroom organization.

# Process for Developing Your Own Management Plan

*Effective teaching component:*
*Section II Chapters 2–7*

> Decide what you will do to have effective communication in your teaching.
> Consider what you will do to know and meet the needs of your learners.
> Plan for effective execution of your lessons.
> Establish the teaching/assessment/learning connection from the beginning of your instruction.
> Commit to reflecting about your teaching.

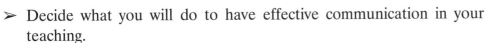
There are no short-cuts to any place worth going. ""

*Preventive component:*
*Section III Chapters 8 and 9*

➤ Make a list of negotiables and non-negotiables that you will use to plan rules and procedures in your classroom.

➤ Write scenarios that you can use to help your students practice your rules and procedures on the first day of class.

➤ Write the non-negotiable procedures (step-by-step, be clear) that you will teach your students on the first day of class. For example, evacuation procedures for fire drill or other emergency.

➤ Put your list of procedures in order by priority, from the most important for your students to know to the least important, but still necessary to know. Write a lesson plan for teaching these procedures. Include the scenarios to role-play as activities to help your students learn the procedures.

➤ Find or make several posters to put up in your classroom that will remind you of your important role in society as a teacher to help you get through the challenging days. Post them before the first day of class.

*Corrective component:*
*Section IV Chapters 10–13*

➤ Decide which corrective strategies you will use when misbehavior occurs for various levels of seriousness.
  • "A" Options for Distracting Misbehaviors
  • "B" Options for Controlling Misbehaviors
  • "C" Options for Anger/Violent Misbehaviors

➤ Think about what strategies you will use to help you follow the keys of using as few words as possible and controlling your reaction.

➤ Determine what consequences you would be comfortable implementing. Remember that you must be willing to follow through with your consequences or the consequences will not help to teach your students responsible behavior.

*Supportive component:*
*Section V Chapters 14–15*

➤ Decide how you will teach responsible behavior to your students.

➤ Discern what strategies you will use to establish harmony in your classroom.

➤ List all of the ways that you will actively involve students in the discipline process.

➤ Determine which activities involving parents you will undertake in your class. How will you communicate, connect, and collaborate with the parents of your students?

➤ Spend a lot of time thinking of ways to encourage your students and to give notice to their accomplishments.

➤ Establish what strategies you will use to help all of your students to feel capable of performing academic tasks.

➤ Choose what you will do to create a class foundation built on positive teacher-student relationships.

# Implementing Your Plan the First Day and First Week

Remember, as a teacher, you have contractual responsibilities for both your students' safety and learning. You are in the place of their parents (in loco parentis is the legal term) as long as the students are in your classroom. That means you need to act like you are in charge. Your body language and the first words out of your mouth on that first day of class need to send that message loudly and clearly. "In charge" is not mean, rather it is firm, business-like, enthusiastic about learning, and demonstrates genuine caring for your students' learning. The first 30 seconds of your first-day presentation will send the message of how business-like you are regarding your classroom management, discipline, and your concern for your students' learning. Make those first words count! You might start with a short speech like:

> "Welcome to ( ____fill in your class____ , e.g., 3rd grade; 10th grade biology; Art class). This year (semester) you can expect me to be responsible for good teaching, and I expect you to be responsible for learning and responsible behavior. Let's talk about how our classroom will run this year. . . . Let's work together to create a class where all of us can enjoy the teaching and learning process. . . ."

At this point you can introduce the rules, procedures, or school issues according to the list of priorities you created when you were planning for this first day. Be sure to actively involve students as a whole group, and ask and answer questions to help establish the classroom as a community of learners. You may want to emphasize both academic goals and character building goals during this first day, but definitely during the first week of classes.

In some situations where students have very low readiness skills for responsible behavior, you may need to start off on the first day or week more towards the authoritarian end of the discipline continuum and teach your pre-established rules rather than create your rules with the students. In that case, the students at least have involvement through generating examples and non-examples of the rules. The goal would then be to use strategies from each of the four components—effective teaching, preventive, corrective, and supportive—to gradually teach your students to participate responsibly in class decision-making.

## First Day and First Week Strategies

➤ Set the atmosphere for a learning environment.
➤ Explain your discipline program and strategies that you will be using and their rationale.
➤ Establish a community of learners.
➤ Create rules or a code of conduct together.
➤ Collaboratively design activity procedures.
➤ Implement accountability procedures.
➤ Jointly devise consequences.
➤ Initiate class building activities.
➤ Incorporate team building activities (if using groups).
➤ Communicate your academic and character building goals.
➤ Conduct initial class meeting.
➤ Teach about chill out time—how it will be used and its purpose.

# Class Agreements

You may want to formalize your initial presentations and your students' involvement during the first week of classes by putting the rules, procedures, and consequences in writing in the form of a contract or code of ethics or class agreements, and have each student sign the form. You should include a signature line for your name, the date, and possibly a line for a parent or guardian to sign, indicating that the form was taken home for parents or guardians to review. This may come in handy for a future parent/teacher conference in which you may need to solicit help from the home front to deal with a persistent behavior problem at school. Some sample forms are included in the appendix for immediate use or for modification to fit your exact needs.

Visual reminders of class agreements add to their effectiveness. "No Dice" was used in a senior high school. "Respect" was used in a multi-grade classroom, both upper elementary and junior high levels. Both were very effective visual reminders when taught to students in conjunction with responsible choices, logical consequences, and student involvement in setting up the logical consequences. The themes of "Respect," "Powerful Learning," and the mnemonic "No Dice" helped students remember the desired behaviors for their classroom.

| POWERFUL LEARNING |
| --- |
| Polite |
| Prompt |
| Prepared |
| Put-Ups Only |
| Personal Best Schoolwork |

| CLASS RULES | |
| --- | --- |
| N | Negligent |
| O | Off task |
| | |
| D | Disruptive |
| I | Insubordinate |
| C | Cheating, lying, stealing |
| E | Eating, drinking |

| RESPECT |
| --- |
| Yourself |
| Other People |
| Property |

# Visualizing Success

Annual Gallup polls indicate that issues about classroom management and solving discipline problems consistently rank at the top of all teachers', counselors', school psychologists', administrators', and parents' concerns. The intent of this book is to give you a way to implement effective teaching strategies to prevent unproductive and irresponsible student behaviors. Then the book offers you *options* for dealing with misbehavior that turn the irresponsible choice into a teachable moment and an *opportunity* for you to teach all the students in your classroom how to make responsible choices, and concurrently maintain the focus on learning. Visualizing yourself teaching effective lessons, engaging students in learning, preventing discipline problems, and successfully implementing the ABC's of effective discipline strategies can help your confidence grow. Working through the chapter reflection questions, and developing solutions to the management scenarios at the end of the corrective chapters can also build confidence in your ability to manage your classroom.

> " Courage does not always roar. Sometimes, it is the quiet voice at the end of the day saying, 'I will try again tomorrow.' "

# Keeping It Happening

Teaching is an emotionally and physically demanding occupation. You will need all of your emotional, mental, and physical strength to maintain daily presentations, prevention, and monitoring of student learning and behavior. Invest in your future—take the time to keep yourself physically healthy and fit. Take time for yourself for recreation, to keep your mental edge. Take time for relaxation to keep rebuilding your emotional energy. Model healthy living for your students. Incorporate stress management techniques into your life on a regular basis.

## Teacher Stress Management Techniques

| DURING SCHOOL | |
| --- | --- |
| Journaling and writing | Talk to another educator |
| Count to ten | Static exercises |
| Deep breathing | Draw |
| Read own book during silent reading | Go play with kids |
| Read a funny poem | Take a break |
| Listen to music | Squeeze a ball |

| OUTSIDE OF SCHOOL | |
| --- | --- |
| Go for a drive | Garden |
| Journaling and writing | Take a walk in nature |
| Take a shower or bubble bath | Watch favorite comedy |
| Read a favorite book | Exercise |
| Paint | Make a gift for someone special |
| Meditate | |

It is much easier to stay on top of management when you are feeling well, and you are less likely to ignore situations that may have the potential to escalate into a discipline situation. You will also be more likely to be able to control your reaction. When your teaching is consistently well planned and effective for your learners, and when your classroom management is consistent (your students know you are with-it!), teaching and management are both easier.

# Encouragement: Go Get 'Em!

You, as teachers, have the opportunity to touch the future. You have one of the most complex, least understood, most demanding, least appreciated jobs in the world today. Your compensation is predominantly your students. Looking back **TOP** teachers have three characteristics:

> **Thinking:** Always thinking about teaching, students, content.
> **Observant:** Always observing their students, their environment.
> **Passionate:** They love kids, teaching, and learning.

> ❝ Those who educate children well are more to be honored than even their parents, for these only give them life; those the art of living. ❞
> —*Aristotle*

It is the last characteristic that keeps many teachers teaching year after year. They are passionate about kids, teaching, and learning. If you have this passion for kids, teaching, and learning, you will find, as Jaime Escalanté observed, that:

> ❝ Teaching is fun! ❞

Now, go make difference in your world—teach!

> ❝ I beg of you to stop apologizing for being a member of the most important profession in the world. ❞
> —*William G. Carr*

> ❝ A teacher affects eternity; he can never tell where his influence stops. ❞
> —*Henry Adams*

> ❝ I touch the future—I teach. ❞
> —*Christa McAuliffe*

# References

Woolfolk, A. (2001). *Educational psychology*, Eighth edition. Boston: Allyn & Bacon.

# *Appendix*

## Comprehensive Classroom Management

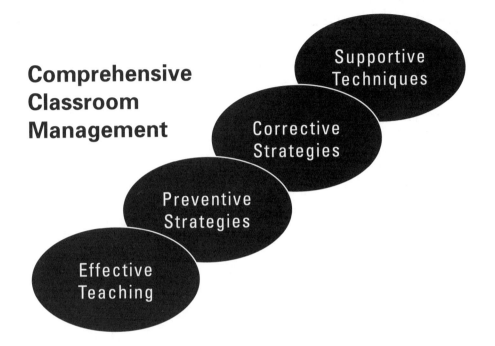

The following pages include classroom management plans, codes of conduct, lists of classroom rules, chill out refocus forms, behavior incident reports, contracts, parent conference forms, and other forms that you may find useful in your classrooms. You are free to copy and use or modify any of these forms.

# Responsible Person Contract
## (Rules negotiated with students during first week of class)

Responsible people:

➢ work to the best of their ability
➢ clean up after themselves
➢ take care of things around them
➢ fix things they break
➢ replace things they lose
➢ care for people
➢ keep belongings in good shape

A responsible person is:

➢ careful
➢ helpful
➢ obedient
➢ careful about personal health
➢ careful to practice good manners

Responsible people treat others like they want to be treated.

I promise to be a responsible person coming to and going home from school, while I am at school, and on field trips.

Student signature _____ Date _____

Parent/guardian signature _____

# Code of Conduct

1.  We will treat others as we want them to treat us.

2.  We will be honest.

3.  We will be careful.

4.  We will make things right that we do wrong.

5.  We will be careful not to distract others.

6.  We will use good language.

7.  We will do our work efficiently.

8.  We will follow directions carefully.

9.  We will keep ourselves and our things neat and clean.

10. We will be helpful.

11. We will always practice good manners.

12. We will act like responsible people.

I will act like a responsible person and will encourage others to do the same.

_____  _____
Date                                Student's signature

_____  _____
Date                                Teacher's signature

_____  _____
Date                                Parent's or Guardian's signature

# Code of Respect

In our quest to help students learn that they are connected to everything in this universe, that through developing strong self-esteem and a respect for oneself and others, they have a greater chance of living in a peaceful world, we have developed a Code of Respect.

**GOAL:** To increase the level of respect among students and adults at our school.

Three principles govern all rules at our school:

1. Students will respect the rights of others to learn. Students will:
   - Be in class on time
   - Be prepared to learn
   - Follow classroom rules

2. Students will respect the rights and properties of others. Students will:
   - Use self-control
   - Be courteous to others
   - Respect others' property
   - Keep school and its grounds clean

3. Students will respect the rules that govern behavior on our campus and on our school buses:
   - Exit the building by outside classroom doors only
   - Keep off berms and fences
   - Line up and play behind yellow line at outside entrances
   - Use quiet voices and feet inside
   - Use hall passes when moving about the building

   Students will NOT:
   - Bring weapons, illegal substances, or their look-alikes to school
   - Chew gum
   - Wear hats in the building
   - Play or congregate at front doors
   - Swear or use rude language or gestures
   - Hang on basketball rims
   - Throw rocks or snowballs

*(coninued)*

# Consequences

**Classroom/School:**

Appropriate staff determine consequence.

Misbehavior may result in a 30-minute detention after school.

**Bus:**   *Rules:* remain seated, hands to self, no loud talking or noises, face forward, courteous behavior, do not distract driver in any way.

*First report:* Warning and phone call or note to parents

*Second report:* Off bus for 2 days

*Third report:* Off bus for 5 days

*Fourth report:* Off bus for remainder of school year

Should student's bus privileges be denied, state law requires the student to continue at school.

While school rules and consequences may vary slightly depending on the individual teacher, all rules will be in accordance with the three principles listed earlier.

If a student is misbehaving, the teacher may notify the parent or guardian. Should the behavior not improve or be of a very serious nature, the principal and teacher may decide the offense is a Major Disciplinary Violation. Parent or Guardian will then be notified as to the violations, and action will be taken.

The following may be considered usual treatment for a Major Disciplinary Violation. However, the principal has the authority to treat each student individually in the most appropriate and most effective manner. Whenever the principal believes a student is involved in a Major Disciplinary Violation, any of the following proceedings may be initiated:

A. In-house suspension / half day.

B. In-house suspension / full day.

C. Informal (including emergency) or formal out-of-school suspension proceedings.

D. Referral to proper law enforcement authority.

E. Expulsion proceedings.

Major Disciplinary Violation may include cases of the following:

➢ fighting

➢ loss of self control

➢ damaging school property

➢ swearing, harassing, name calling

➢ hurting others

➢ drugs, weapons, or look-alikes

➢ gang behavior or dress

➢ habitual rule violations

> The school district has a zero tolerance policy for students who bring weapons, illegal substances, or look-alikes to school. Students doing so risk suspension and possible expulsion from school.

# Chill Out Refocus Form

Name _____ Date _____

Teacher_____ Time _____

1. Problem

   _____

   _____

   _____

2. What did I want?

   _____

   _____

   _____

3. What could I do next time?

   _____

   _____

   _____

4. What could help me make a responsible choice?

   _____

   _____

# Contract

Name _____

Date _____ Date to Meet Again _____

What is the problem behavior?

What is the responsible behavior needed?

What is our plan to lead to responsible behavior?

What incentives will be used?

What consequences will be used?

What support will be given?

We agree to this contract:

Student's Signature _____

Teacher's Signature _____

Parent's Signature _____

# Late Paper Pass
### Third Quarter 2003 / Mr. Jordan
### Unexcused late assignments will NOT be accepted
### without this pass attached.

---

# Hall Pass
## Third Quarter 2003 / Mr. Jordan

# Hall Pass
## Third Quarter 2003 / Mr. Jordan

# Hall Pass
## Third Quarter 2003 / Mr. Jordan

You must receive permission before you can leave the room. Take the pass with you to visit the office, library, or the bathroom. NEVER LEAVE THE CAMPUS! Give your pass to Mr. Jordan when you return to class. Unused passes are each worth one extra credit point each. You will not be allowed to leave class without a pass (either one of these or one from the office). If you have TBS (Tiny Bladder Syndrome) and can't make it through a block period, please bring a note from home.

# Refocus Form (Primary)

Name _____ Date _____

What did you do?

What made you do it?

☐ Sad

☐ Mad

☐ Wanted attention

☐ Other _____

What will you do next time?

Are you ready to join your class?   ☐ Yes   ☐ No

# Refocus Form: Sample 1 (Intermediate)

Name _____ Date _____

Teacher _____ Time _____

| What was your behavior? |
|---|
|  |

| What did you want? |
|---|
|  |

| What will you do next time? |
|---|
|  |

Are you ready to join your class?   ☐ Yes      ☐ No

# Refocus Form: Sample 2 (Intermediate)

Name _____ Date _____

Teacher _____ Time _____

1. What was your behavior? _____

   _____

   _____

   _____

2. What did you want? _____

   _____

   _____

   _____

3. What will you do next time?_____

   _____

   _____

4. Are you ready to join your class?  ☐ Yes      ☐ No

# Refocus Form: Sample 1 (Secondary)

Name _____ Date _____

Teacher _____ Time _____

| What was your behavior? |
| --- |
| |

| What did you want? | |
| --- | --- |
| | Attention from others. |
| | To be in control of the situation. |
| | To challenge the teacher's authority. |
| | To avoid doing my homework. |
| | To be sent home. |
| | To cause problems for others because I don't like myself. |
| | To cause problems for others because they don't like me. |
| | To cause problems for others because I don't know what I should be doing. |
| | I wanted revenge. |
| | I wanted: |

| What will you do next time? |
| --- |
| |

Are you ready to join your class?  ☐ Yes  ☐ No

# Refocus Form: Sample 2 (Secondary)

Name _____ Date _____

Teacher _____ Time _____

1. What was your behavior? _____

   _____

   _____

   _____

2. What did you want?

   ☐ I wanted attention from others.
   ☐ I wanted to be in control of the situation.
   ☐ I wanted to challenge the teacher's authority.
   ☐ I wanted to avoid doing my homework.
   ☐ I wanted to be sent home.
   ☐ I wanted to cause problems for others because I don't like myself.
   ☐ I wanted to cause problems for others because they don't like me.
   ☐ I wanted to cause problems for others because I don't know what I should be doing.
   ☐ I wanted revenge.
   ☐ I wanted _____ .

3. What should you do next time? _____

4. Are you ready to join your class?   ☐ Yes        ☐ No

# Action Plan
## A Plan to Get My Behavior Back on Target

Name _____

Date _____

Problem:

Ideas for a solution:

    1.
    2.
    3.
    4.
    5.
    6.

Consequences for not improving behavior:

    1.
    2.
    3.
    4.

Outcomes for improving behavior:

    1.
    2.
    3.
    4.

Student signature: _____

Parent or guardian signature: _____

Teacher's signature: _____

# Problem Solving Worksheet 1

Name _____

Date _____

What did you do? _____

_____

Does what you did help you? _____

Did it help others? _____

What can you do differently? What is your plan? _____

_____

_____

What do you need me to do? _____

_____

_____

_____

Are you going to be able to follow this plan? _____

_____          _____
Student signature                                          Teacher signature

# Problem Solving Worksheet 2

Name:

Date:

| What did you do? |
|---|
| |

Does this help you? _____ Did it help others? _____

| What can you do differently? What is your plan? |
|---|
| |

| What do you need me to do? |
|---|
| |

_____          _____
Student signature                                           Teacher signature

# Theraputic Learning Center
# Behavior Form

Name _____ Date _____

Time of day _____ Subject _____

1. What were you doing when you got sent to the Time Out Room? _____

_____

_____

2. Which statement best tells about your behavior?

☐ I fought someone (pushed, shoved, tripped, kicked, scratched, hit).
☐ I would not follow directions.
☐ I was rude when talking to the teacher or students.
☐ I argued with the adult in charge.
☐ I made so much noise that others couldn't think about their work.
☐ Other _____

_____

3. Circle the picture that describes your mood:

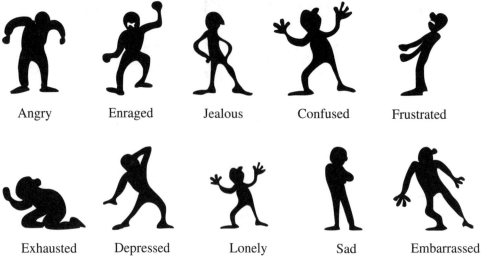

Angry     Enraged     Jealous     Confused     Frustrated

Exhausted     Depressed     Lonely     Sad     Embarrassed

4. I wanted:

- ☐ attention from students
- ☐ attention from my teacher
- ☐ to be the boss
- ☐ to not do my work
- ☐ to be sent home
- ☐ to get even
- ☐ other _____

_____

5. Did you get what you wanted? ☐ Yes ☐ No

Why? _____

_____

6. Next time, I will _____

_____

Sign:

_____     _____
(Student)                   (Teacher)

# Behavior Agreement Sample

Offenses _____

Date of offense _____ Date of agreement _____ Termination date _____

In the interest of _____ Birthdate _____ Age _____

## Voluntary Agreement

We, the undersigned, understand this contract is voluntary. It is an agreement of behavioral change in lieu of punishment when the terms of this agreement are fulfilled.

_____ admits that he/she is responsible for the above offense, which occurred on this date: _____

## Stipulation

1. Length of agreement: The length of this agreement shall be _____

2. Plan for change: The above behavior shall be changed in the following manner:

    a. _____

    b. _____

    c. _____

    d. _____

3. Completion: After successfully completing this agreement, the above mentioned offense(s) shall be dropped.

4. Other stipulations:

I, the undersigned, understand my rights and agree on the above terms.

Student _____ Date _____

Parents/Guardian _____ Date _____

Assistant Principal _____ Date _____

Counselor _____ Date _____

# Parent Conference Record

Student _____ Date _____

Grade _____ School _____

| | |
|---|---|
| *Specific Positive Comment* | *Student Strengths* |
| *Areas for Growth* | *Social Skills* |
| *Study Habits* | *Help Needed from Parents* |
| *Parent Concerns* | *Follow-up Plan* |

# Discipline Documentation
## Science Department/Mountain View High School

| Student's Name | | Date |
|---|---|---|
| Grade (10)  (11)  (12) | Class: (AP Bio) (Env. Sci.) (Com. Bio.) | Time |

**Misbehavior:** (Disruptive Talking/Horseplay/Other _____ )
Additional details of the incident:

Explain on the backside why this type of behavior negatively affects the learning process for yourself and other students, and why it will *not* happen again.

_____               _____
Student's signature                                              Parent's signature

THIS COMPLETED FORM IS DUE BY THE NEXT SCHEDULED CLASS. FOR MORE INFORMATION, CONTACT MR. JORDAN AT 555.2222 EXTENSION 222.

- - - - - - - - - - - - - - - - - - - - - - - - - - - - - - - - - - - - - - - - -

# Discipline Documentation
## Science Department/Mountain View High School

| Student's Name | | Date |
|---|---|---|
| Grade (10)  (11)  (12) | Class: (AP Bio) (Env. Sci.) (Com. Bio.) | Time |

**Misbehavior:** (Disruptive Talking/Horseplay/Other _____ )
Additional details of the incident:

Explain on the backside why this type of behavior negatively affects the learning process for yourself and other students, and why it will *not* happen again.

_____               _____
Student's signature                                              Parent's signature

THIS COMPLETED FORM IS DUE BY THE NEXT SCHEDULED CLASS. FOR MORE INFORMATION, CONTACT MR. JORDAN AT 555.2222 EXTENSION 222.

# Classroom Management Plan Handout Sample

My name is Ms. Kyle and I will be your student's American Government teacher. I am looking forward to working with you and your student.

In American Government students will be introduced to and taught the following: citizenship, history, geography, global connections, diversity, and environment. American Government is a year-long course required for seniors.

Text: *Magruder's, American Government* by William McClenaghan

## Goals

This class is designed to give your students an overview of the American political system. They will need this as they leave high school and become productive members of society. Following are specific goals and learning objectives.

1. Know how to contact and how to voice your opinion to local, state, and federal government officials.
2. Study the Constitution of the United States; know its contents, and how it affects the law making process.
3. Learn the American governing process and how we as citizens can take part.
4. Become aware that every citizen can have an impact when they understand the government and how it works.

## Classroom Rules

As we will learn in this class on government, rules and laws are a part of being in a "society." Our society for the school year is the classroom, and we will set up rules and procedures to enable us to provide the best atmosphere for learning and teaching. The public has a voice in any society and you are also encouraged to discuss concerns and suggestions with me. Improvements to procedures and beneficial alterations to the procedures are always welcome.

We are all adults, so the classroom rules are minimal.

1. The Golden Rule
   ➢ Respect others and their property
   ➢ Honesty
   ➢ Come to class on time and ready to learn
   ➢ No food or drink in the classroom
   ➢ One person speaks at a time

2. Obey all high school rules as posted in your student handbook

# Procedures

1. No late assignments accepted except in the case of an excused absence.
   > Missed assignments will be due next class period attended by the student.
2. In the event a student has trouble with a particular assignment, arrangements may be made with the teacher for a new due date. This will be done on a case-by-case basis.
3. Student may request grade status at any time. Status of grade will be given to the student by the next day at the latest.
4. Make-up tests will only be scheduled in the event of an excused absence.

# Discipline

1. *First Offense:* Warning during class
2. *Second Offense:* Student and teacher will meet to discuss solutions to situation
3. *Third Offense:* Parent or guardian will be contacted and a meeting will be arranged to discuss solutions to situation
4. *Fourth Offense:* Referral to the office and follow the guidelines in the student handbook

Any major offense or violation of school policy will be directly referred to the office and guidelines set by the high school will be followed.

# Grading

American Government is a year-long course. Grades will be earned by a point system. All assignments, tests, projects, participation will be given a point value and all points awarded will be added up at the end of the term or semester. The grade will be determined by the students' percentage of the total points earned for the term or semester.

*Example:* 1000 total points possible for the semester.
Student earns 850 points.
That would be an 85%.

*Grades:*  90 to 100    A
80 to 89    B
70 to 79    C
60 to 69    D
59 and below  F

# Top 10 Lab Rules

1.  No food or drink is permitted in the laboratory at any time.

2.  Closed-toe shoes are required during the labs.

3.  Long hair must be secured behind the head.

4.  Behavior that is dangerous to self or others is not allowed and will result in immediate removal from the activity. Continued inappropriate behavior will result in a loss of lab privileges and other disciplinary actions.

5.  If you are injured, notify Mr. Jordan immediately so First Aid can be administered.

6.  Spills must be cleaned up immediately to prevent slips and falls. Towels are located at each sink.

7.  Backpacks and books must be stacked on top of or underneath your desk. They should not be taken to the lab tables or left in the aisles.

8.  Clean up of the lab stations and supply table is expected after each activity.

9.  No personal experimenting without permission from Mr. Jordan. Follow the instructions given *precisely,* unless Mr. Jordan indicates otherwise.

10. Care must be exercised with glassware, open flames, chemicals, and any organisms.

I have read the lab safety guidelines above and agree to follow them. If I choose not to follow these guidelines I understand that there will be appropriate consequences for my actions. I also understand that I may be responsible for the cost to repair damaged equipment if I am being negligent.

_____          _____
             Student signature                                                        Date

Don't hesitate to contact me at school: email@schooladdress.org
School phone: 555.2222

Or at home: homemail@home.net
Home phone: 555.2223

# Glossary

**A-Options for Distracting Behaviors** Choices of corrective strategies to use with the first level of seriousness of misbehavior: **A**ctive Body Language and **A**ttention Focusing Strategies

**Accountability** When arranging your room, consider whether your room arrangement allows you access to all the students to hold them accountable for their schoolwork. You need to be able to easily monitor all of the students' schoolwork.

**Accountability Options** Options you choose from to hold students responsible for their learning tasks.

**Accountability Procedures** The specific options you choose for your class to hold students responsible for their schoolwork, and thereby their learning, in order to prevent problems.

**Acknowledge the Student's Power** A Button Pusher Escape used when you are working with students choosing controlling behaviors that say, "You can't make me." Designed to sidestep a power struggle about whether or not you can "make" students do something. You agree that you can't make them do it, but then focus on what their choices are if they do not.

**Active Body Language** Options to give a firm nonverbal message, so there is minimal disruption to the lesson; it communicates to the students who choose distracting behaviors to stop and to move on to responsible behavior. Firm, business-like, and supportive, but not attacking or mean.

**Affirmations** A type of encouragement that highlights students' positive qualities, strengths, and character virtues. Includes hardworking, honest, helpful, lively, involved, determined, open-minded, sharing, cooperative, persevering, perceptive, creative, detailed, responsible, trustworthy, loyal, dependable, courageous, sincere, candid, principled, reliable, supportive, accepting, diligent, self-disciplined, kind, or considerate.

**Albert et al.'s Approach** A discipline approach that espouses that behavior is based on choice. Students misbehave to fill their unmet need to belong. You can influence students to make responsible behavior choices using encouragement, intervention, and collaboration. Encouragement is your most powerful tool. Students need to feel "capable" of performing tasks, "connected" to the teacher and other students, and that they can make a "contribution" to class.

**Allow and Encourage Learner Questions** An aspect of **A**ssessment, the fourth category of the CLEAR Model. Establish a question-friendly atmosphere in your classroom about the topic in the lesson, so students will want to ask questions. The nature of the questions they ask offers insight into the level of understanding of the concepts with which they are working. You can use Bloom's taxonomy or the hierarchy of Socratic questions to judge the sophistication of your learners' questions.

**Ample Feedback** An aspect of **A**ssessment, the fourth category of the CLEAR Model, emphasizing providing enough information to students—specific comments and explaining why—so that the learners know how to improve on the next similar task. Teachers need to be specific as to strengths and weaknesses of the performance, why their answers or work products were wrong (if their work was not up to criteria), and specific suggestions on how to improve, including examples.

**Anger Management** A responsible behavior skill that focuses on students recognizing their anger and its sources, identifying its triggers, developing

305

strategies to get it under control, and using those strategies to deal with anger in a constructive manner.

**Angry and Violent Misbehaviors—The "C" Level**  The highest level of seriousness of misbehaviors that some students exhibit. These students don't know how to deal with their angry feelings in an appropriate way and their misdirected anger spills out into the classroom. Angry and violent behaviors include one or more of the following: hurting others physically or emotionally, destroying things, intimidation of others and other bullying behaviors, violent actions (intense physical harm).

**Appropriate Touch**  A non-verbal Active Body Language choice using physical touch in a suitable way. A light pat on the back communicates "stop" to a student choosing distracting behavior. A hand gently touching the shoulder gives a desist message.

**Ask Questions to Assess Understanding**  An aspect of Assessment, the fourth category of the CLEAR Model, emphasizing using questions (Bloom's cognitive taxonomy and Socratic questioning) to check whether learners are getting the lesson. Ask questions that will help lead learners to make connections with personal experiences and previously learned concepts (personal and academic linking).

**Assess Learners' Understanding**  An aspect of Assessment, the fourth category of the CLEAR Model, emphasizing reading body language to determine student learning and effectiveness of the teaching. Constantly monitor and observe your learners.

**Assessment—Fourth category of the CLEAR Model: All "A's"**  Assess learners' understanding; Ask questions to assess understanding; Allow and encourage learner questions; Assign a variety of assessment activities; and Ample feedback.

**Assign a Variety of Assessment Activities**  An aspect of Assessment, the fourth category of the CLEAR Model, emphasizing making traditional assessments worthwhile and authentic assessments (real world demonstrations and performances). Assessments include quizzes, work sheets, tests, laboratory procedures, demonstrations, performances, role-playing, writing papers or reports, and creating a video or audiotape. Your methods of assessment should match your learners, your content and objectives, teaching models, and the activities you choose to use for the learning experiences.

**Attention Focusing Strategies**  Options (some verbal, some non-verbal) for directing or redirecting students to concentrate on the learning tasks, rather than enacting distracting behaviors. When verbal, they also focus your verbal interaction, so you only say what needs to be said at the moment of misbehavior.

**Authentic Assessments**  Real world applications of learned knowledge and skills. Examples include: piano recitals, speeches, sporting events, science fairs, building a model, mentorship, internships, school-to-work jobs, school newspaper, school annual, closed circuit TV, art, or photography.

**Authoritarian Management Style**  "My way or the highway," teacher-in-charge approach. Teacher makes sure that the students obey with little student involvement or choice. In the extreme form the teacher rules by fear using threats and intimidation.

**B-Options for Controlling Behaviors**  Choices of corrective strategies to use with the second level of seriousness of misbehavior: Button Pusher Exits, Brief Choices, and Business-like Consequences.

**Bloom's Cognitive Taxonomy**  Different levels of thinking that can be focused on in lessons or in questioning strategies: Knowing (lowest level of difficulty), Understanding, Applying, Analyzing, Evaluating, and Creating (highest level of difficulty).

**Body Carriage**  The way you carry yourself when you are dealing with a discipline situation. You stand tall and project an "I mean business" demeanor that says you are committed to bringing about responsible behavior choices.

**Brief Choice Language**  A Button Pusher Escape in which brief interaction is combined with choices, which give students a sense of control over their lives. First you explicitly state the appropriate responsible behavior. Then you use the word "or" followed by what the consequence will be if the student continues to choose an inappropriate behavior.

**Business-like Consequences**  A corrective strategy used with controlling angry and violent behaviors that holds students responsible for poor behavior choices by having a consequence for their actions. The Five R's of Consequences are: Related, Reasonable, Respectful, Reliably Enforced, Real Participation.

**Button Pusher Escapes** Strategies to sidestep a power struggle when a student makes a provoking comment. Options are: Acknowledge the Student's Power, Table the Matter, Let's Chat, "To You To Me" Statements, Humor, Redirect the Student, and Responsible Thinking Questions.

**C-Options for Anger and/or Violent Behaviors: Keeping above "C" Level** Choices of corrective strategies to use with the third level of seriousness of misbehavior: Consequences, Chat Time with Students, Contracts, and Curbing Violence.

**Capable Strategies** The sixth supportive option in the RESPECT mnemonic focuses on building up students' sense of "I can do it."

**Character Development and Education** A responsible behavior skill that focuses on instilling character virtues that are basic to the development of good character. Include: caring, citizenship, compassion, courage, courtesy, fairness, good judgment, impulse control, helpfulness, honesty, integrity, kindness, leadership, perseverance, trustworthiness, reliability, responsibility, and understanding.

**Charles' Synergetic Approach** Discipline approach that espouses students have basic needs that are met when teachers create a classroom community. Teaching and learning need to be pleasurable and satisfying and compatible with the students' basic needs of dignity, enjoyment, power, security, hope, competence, and acceptance.

**Chat Time with Students** One of your options for working on long-term solutions with angry and/or violent students. Involves getting together with the student and having a chat about the problem to actively involve the student in the discipline process. Can be pulling a student to the side or scheduling a time to have a more in-depth chat.

**Check for Learning Differences** An aspect of Communication, the first category of the CLEAR Model, emphasizing varying instructional communication for various differences in learning style, for example, auditory, visual, kinesthetic or tactile, and global versus detailed.

**Chill Out Time** A corrective strategy for dealing with the initial situation with a volatile student. Dealing with their angry feelings is their main need, so chill out time helps them recognize their anger and calm down when it is starting to build up. You have a definite place and process pre-arranged with your students for them to calm down when they are losing control and to process their misbehaviors.

**Choice Levels** A corrective strategy used with angry and/or violent students who are uncooperative. Respond in a controlled, business-like manner using Brief Choice Language to keep narrowing the choices available to the student who is refusing to cooperate.

**Choice Time** A supportive option in which you set aside time that the students can use in any way they choose as an incentive for responsible choices. Can actually save you time in the long run in terms of fewer problem situations that need to be dealt with. Motivates students to make responsible choices so they can participate in choice time.

**Choices** Options to involve your students in appropriate curriculum decisions and how they can do their assignments or which assignments they may choose.

**Class Building Activities** A supportive strategy to create a learning community in which everyone gets to know each other on a human-to-human level, so they can figure out how to work together and get along. Get all students in the class up, moving around, interacting with one another, getting to know one another better, and working together in an energizing manner.

**Class Bulletin Board** A class building activity in which the class works together on a bulletin board that represents the class.

**Class Contracts** A class supportive option in which you put the rules, procedures, and consequences in writing and have each student sign the form. It can be taken home for parents or guardians to review and sign.

**Class Goals** A class building activity in which the class establishes aims together to foster the students working together toward common aims.

**Class Meetings**   Class building activities designed to involve students in problem-solving and class decision-making. Empower students and act as a laboratory for the democratic process. Incorporate the following: forming a circle, beginning with compliments or appreciations, creating an agenda, seeking win-win solutions, planning classroom activities, and closure.

**Class Projects**   A class building activity in which the class decides on a class project to work on collaboratively.

**Class Themes**   A class building activity in which students choose a class motto, a class banner, or a class flag that represents the spirit of the class.

**Classroom Climate**   The environment, the atmosphere in your class. You want to create a warm, inviting, supportive climate.

**Classroom Responsibilities**   Give students a positive sense of power, and free you up so you have more time to help students by assigning tasks in the class to students. Examples include: materials monitor, lunch count monitor, role taking monitor, class messengers, line monitor, equipment monitor, computer monitor, librarian, visitor monitor, classroom meeting facilitator, class newsletter editor, class news reporters, and substitute monitor.

**CLEAR Model by Rogien**   New way to view all teaching strategies, not a new teaching strategy in and of itself, that helps teachers to make good decisions about implementation of a wide variety of teaching strategies in an effective manner. CLEAR teaching includes: **C**lear communication, accommodation of **L**earner differences, effective lesson **E**xecutions, as well as accurate **A**ssessments, and careful **R**eflection for improvement of teaching.

**Cognitive Behavior Model**   A teaching approach that emphasizes using first overt self-guidance, then faded self-guidance, and then covert self-guidance: "I do it, we do it, you do it."

**Collaboration**   One of the Crucial C's of Parental Support that emphasizes a variety of options to actively involve parents in their children's education and classroom functions, so they feel a part of the classroom. Creates alliances with parents as partners.

**Collaborative Management Style**   Teacher and students working together toward self-discipline and responsible behavior choices. Active involvement of students in the discipline process. "Voice and choice" so students feel ownership of the classroom and cooperate in creating a positive learning environment.

**Coloroso's Approach**   A discipline approach that emphasizes it is important to treat students with respect and to give them the power and the responsibility to make decisions. Teachers need to provide guidance and support, so the students can learn inner discipline and to manage themselves.

**Communicability**   When arranging your room, consider whether your room arrangement allows for good communication between teacher and students, and among students, when working in groups.

**Communication**   One of the Crucial C's of Parental Support that emphasizes many options for on-going communication with parents.

**Communication**   The first category of the **CLEAR Model,** which contains six principles of effective teaching embodied in the mnemonic "SPEECH": **S**peak fluently, **P**oint out key ideas, **E**xplain clearly, **E**xamples relevant to the students, **C**heck for modalities (audio, visual, kinesthetic), and **H**ighlight: repeat, review, summarize.

**Communication Skills**   Responsible behavior skills that encompass listening skills, paraphrasing another's ideas, clarifying information, and summarizing.

**Community Circle**   A class building activity in which students communicate with one another about topics designed to bring the class together as a community of learners.

**Concept Attainment**   A teaching approach that emphasizes "Yes" and "No" examples. Have learners look for similarities and differences and propose hypotheses, then test each hypothesis with more teacher-supplied examples. The object is to discover the rule (concept). When the hypothesis seems correct, students generate examples for the teacher to check.

**Conflict Resolution**   A responsible behavior skill that includes knowing what the steps are for resolving conflicts, getting to practice those steps, and having opportunities to put them to use when conflicts arise.

**Connection between Parents and Teachers**   One of the Crucial C's of Parental Support that emphasizes options that create positive relationships between you and the parents of your students to further the goal of establishing parent/teacher partnerships.

**Contracts**   An option particularly used with students choosing angry or violent misbehaviors, but can be used with others as well. Write down agreed upon solutions and sign so follow-through will be more likely. Can use a more formalized contract, which builds in consequences and incentives.

**Controlling Misbehaviors—The "B" Level**   Second level of seriousness of misbehaviors in which students resort to inappropriate behavior to meet their legitimate need for a sense of control over their lives. They lack a responsible way to feel in control, pull power plays, and try to manipulate things to be the way they want them to be both overtly and passively, and defy adults through words or actions or both.

**Cooperative Learning Principles—Johnson and Johnson**   A teaching approach that focuses on incorporating positive interdependence, face-to-face interaction, individual accountability, social skills, and group processing. Emphasizes both academic and social objectives.

**Corners**   A class building activity in which there is a different topic to be discussed in each corner of the room. Students choose the topic they want to explore and practice communication skills while discussing.

**Corrective Component**   One of four integral aspects of management and discipline that focuses on being prepared with practical strategies to deal with the moment of misbehavior. Recognize the type of misbehavior to use an intervention strategy that fits the situation. Options for dealing with different levels of misbehaviors: **A** Options for Distracting behaviors, **B** Options for Controlling behaviors, and **C** Options for Angry or Violent behaviors.

**Coupon Approach**   An attention focusing strategy used to reduce a particular behavior, but not eliminate it altogether. When a student asks an inordinate number of questions as an attention-getting device, you do not want to stop that student from asking questions completely, but merely learn how to manage the multitude of questions and to develop the skill to think before asking the question or to seek the answer on his own.

**Crucial C's of Parental Support**   Options for creating positive home and school relationships: Parent/teacher Communication, Parent/Teacher Connection, and Parent/Teacher Collaboration.

**Curbing Violent Behaviors**   Options for dealing with angry or violent students during a volatile episode: control your reaction, use Button Pusher Escapes, send for help, back-up, and support, use slow, deliberate, authoritative language (STOP NOW!), schedule follow-up chat time to develop a contract, and choose supportive strategies.

**Curwin and Mendler's Approach**   A discipline approach that emphasizes discipline based on dignity and hope. Chronic misbehavers usually lose all hope for anything worthwhile at school and teachers must work at reclaiming students who are currently destined to fail and are behaviorally at-risk. It is possible to find long-term solutions, even to angry or violent behaviors. Short-term solutions are usually not effective.

**Decision-Making Skills**   Responsible behavior skills that extend to students having opportunities to make decisions within structured choices, so they can learn effective decision-making and can learn from poor decisions they make.

**Demonstrations**   An aspect of Execution, the third category of the CLEAR Model, emphasizing appropriate demonstrations to help students learn the concept: working examples, modeling skills, modeling cognitive processes, and pointing out similarities and differences.

**Denied or Delayed Access Consequence**   One type of logical consequence in which the students experience denied or delayed access to areas of the classroom or areas of the school. When they use class or school equipment inappropriately, then losing access to the equipment for a period of time is related. An example would be a student banging on the computer keys and then not being able to use the computer for the rest of the period.

**Denied or Delayed Interactions Consequence**   One type of logical consequence used when students have abused the situation in their interactions with peers. An example would be a student who was putting others down and then could not interact with those students for the remainder of the class period.

**Direct Instruction—Hunter Model** A teaching approach that emphasizes getting students set to learn (gaining student attention, creating anticipation), stating the lesson objectives, presenting information effectively, checking for understanding, giving guided practice, and allowing for independent practice.

**Discovery Learning** A teaching approach that emphasizes questioning, inductive reasoning, and intuitive thinking. Can be guided or unguided. Begin with examples. Ask questions to lead students to discover the big idea.

**Distract the Distractor** An attention focusing option in which you divert the student by asking a question without embarrassing the student, or ask the student to perform a task for you.

**Distracting Misbehaviors—The "A" Level** First level of seriousness of misbehaviors students exhibit that sidetrack you from the lesson or divert the attention of the other students and delay or interrupt the flow of the lesson. These are low-level, annoying behaviors that don't cause strong reactions in us, but do irritate us. Common distracting behaviors are: pencil tapping, calling out, sharpening pencils, roaming the room, playing with objects, and making weird noises.

**Down Time** Time in which the students are not actively engaged in learning activities. Comes from a variety of sources: not having materials ready, inefficiently passing out materials, non-instructional tasks, like attendance, lunch count or book money, and interruptions.

**Dreikur's Approach** A discipline approach that teaches students they can choose their behavior. Teachers need to help the students develop social interest, so they will be motivated to choose socially useful behavior that contributes to the class. Encouragement is essential. Need to have a democratic, or collaborative, discipline style for discipline to flourish, as effective discipline does not work in an autocratic or permissive classroom.

**Effective Praise** Part of the fifth supportive option in the RESPECT mnemonic, focuses on giving feedback to students about accomplishments. Needs to be: apprecia-

tive rather than controlling, informative feedback rather than evaluative, genuine, specific, non-verbal communication congruent with the praise message, and using a variety of phrases.

**Effective Teaching Component** One of four integral aspects of management and discipline that focuses on instructional opportunities and options. Have a rich, relevant curriculum implemented through a wide variety of teaching strategies that actively involve students in their own learning. The CLEAR Teaching Model highlighted in this component emphasizes learning and the decisions you make to facilitate learning.

**Emmer, Evertson, and Worsham's Approach** A discipline approach that emphasizes effective classroom management to prevent problems. "Good management is based on students' understanding of what is expected of them." Classroom managers who are effective organize and design the class ahead of time and in the first week of school, so expectations are clear.

**Emotional Intelligence Development** A responsible behavior skill that emphasizes the emotional development of students—their awareness and control of their own emotions, their empathy and relationships with others.

**Encouragement** Part of fifth supportive option in the RESPECT mnemonic, focuses on responsible behavior choices and any student growth toward that. Do not have to wait for a finished product, as with praise, can encourage positive steps, movement, improvement, progress of the student and students' efforts and strengths. Focuses on getting students to look within for validation and examine their own reactions to their accomplishments and their strengths.

**Engaging Learners** An aspect of **L**earners, the second category of the CLEAR Model, emphasizing that you involve students in learning that they perceive is worthwhile. Learning activities need to engage students, challenge them, and demonstrate that you have high expectations for their success.

**Enthusiasm** An aspect of **E**xecution, the third category of the CLEAR Model, emphasizing the vivacity with which something is done. Genuine enthusiasm means showing a natural passion for your learners, your subject, and teaching, and your enthusiasm keeps you on track, business-like, and focused.

**Environmental Options**   Options to create a classroom climate conducive to learning. Need to be predetermined, taught to the students and jointly constructed, adopted, and maintained. Establishing the environment options includes: Rules and Code of Conduct, Procedures, Arranging the Room, and Working the Room.

**Establishing Class Harmony**   The second supportive option in the RESPECT mnemonic focuses on establishing a warm, supportive environment that has everyone feeling they are an important part of the class. The feeling of "our class" and the "learning community" is created through: Class Building Activities, Team Building Activities, and Class Meetings.

**Examples**   An aspect of Communication, the first category of the CLEAR Model, emphasizing that examples used by you need to have relevance, be clear to the learners, and be specific.

**Execution of the Lesson—"MODELS"**   is the organizing mnemonic for this third category of the CLEAR Model: Matching the model of teaching to the lesson, Objectives, Demonstrations, Enthusiasm, Linking, and Stay with the topic. Choose the best models of teaching to match your learners, your content, and your own teaching strengths.

**Expectations**   An aspect of Learners, the second category of the CLEAR Model, emphasizing setting appropriate expectations for your learners including behavior expectations, academic expectations, and rules, procedures, and standards. Students will rise (or sink) to the level of expectation set by you and you will tend to get what you expect from your students. Having positive expectations and high expectations gets you better quality and quantity of results.

**Explaining Clearly**   An aspect of Communication, the first category of the CLEAR Model, emphasizing that your explanations need to be step by step, contain logical connections, and be clear from the learners' perspective.

**Expressing Appreciation**   A particular type of praise in which you thank them for their efforts academically and behaviorally, emphasizing the positive impact that student's actions have on others.

**Expository Teaching: David Ausubel Model**   A teaching approach that begins by using advance organizers. Concepts are presented with examples and non-examples to clarify the concept. Refer back to advanced organizer to link the organizer with the concept in the lesson. Emphasizes deductive reasoning.

**Fred Jones's Approach**   A discipline approach that teaches effective body language is one of your most valuable discipline tools. Effective teaching strategies reduce misbehaviors. An incentive system motivates students to choose responsible behavior.

**Glasser's Approach**   Glasser emphasizes the importance of providing quality instruction, so you can meet the needs of your students. Class meetings are an integral tool to accomplishing quality instruction.

**Grandma's Rule**   A verbal attention focusing option that you use when utilizing incentives. Delivered as "When . . . Then . . ." statements.

**Group Alerting**   Options to gain and focus students' attention. Keeps students involved and attentive by calling on them regularly.

**Highlights of the Lesson**   An aspect of Communication, the first category of the CLEAR Model, emphasizing the highlights of lessons by one or more of the following behaviors: repeat, review, synthesize, summarize, and closure.

**Homework Buddy**   Student involvement option in which everyone has a homework buddy to help keep on track with what the homework assignments are and letting an absent homework buddy know what she missed.

**Humor**   A Button Pusher Escape used to seize the moment and deflect when a student is provoking a power struggle. Does *not* include sarcasm, harsh or bitter language, or intentionally cutting remarks. Make fun of yourself or the situation; but not the student.

**Incentives**   A supportive option that encourages and motivates students to action. Through giving students something desired after responsible behavior, they are motivated to accomplish academic tasks and responsible behavior commitments.

**Inquiry and Problem-Based Learning**   A teaching approach that begins with a puzzling event, learners formulate hypotheses, collect and analyze data, draw conclusions, reflect on original problem, and reflect on the thinking process.

**Invite Learner Input**  An aspect of **R**eflection, the fifth category of the CLEAR Model, emphasizing inviting your learners to give their input (for example, on a brief student survey) about your teaching in order to improve your teaching.

**I-Statements**  An effective way to communicate about negative behavior. Have the following three parts: I feel _____ (Feeling Word) _____ when you _____ (Specific Behavior) _____ because _____ (The Effect of the Behavior) _____. A fourth optional part adds, "I would prefer that you . . ." or "I would appreciate if you would . . ." and then you fill in what the specific responsible behavior would be.

**Keys of Effective Delivery**  Critical keys to implementing the corrective strategies are "Use as Few Words as Possible" and "Control Your Reaction."

**Kinesthetic Symbols**  Hand gestures and other body movements that translate a concept into a movement in order to facilitate memory of the learning.

**Kohn's Approach**  A discipline approach that emphasizes classrooms' need to focus on critical thinking, decision-making, and caring about others to create a classroom community. Involving students in the decision-making process teaches them to make effective decisions. Kohn believes students cannot learn to make good decisions unless they have opportunities to practice making decisions.

**Kounin's Approach**  A discipline approach in which prevention is more important than handling misbehavior. Effective teaching influences discipline more than discipline strategies. Lesson management, variety, and keeping students actively involved are key.

**Kyle, Kagan, and Scott's Approach**  Win-Win Discipline is built on Three Pillars: Teacher and students are on the same side working together as allies, not as adversaries. Shared responsibility with the teacher and students co-creating solutions is needed for sustained results. The goal of discipline is long-term learned responsible behavior.

**Learners—"PEOPLE"**  is the organizing mnemonic for this second category of the CLEAR Model, which focuses on accommodating learner needs and differences: **P**acing, **E**xpectations, **O**ne-on-One scaffolding, **P**ause for reflection and connection, **L**inking lessons to learners, and **E**ngaging learners.

**Lecture**  A teaching approach that emphasizes presenting information verbally. Typical format is introduction, body of the presentation, and closure. Visuals often used to illustrate points. Examples are often included to clarify points.

**Let's Chat**  A Button Pusher Escape that helps you to change the dynamics from having a heated discussion while class is going on. What you do is acknowledge the student's frustration and offer him or her a definite meeting time that occurs later.

**Levels of Seriousness of Misbehaviors—"ABC" Options**  Most misbehaviors categorize into three levels of impact on the teacher and other students: "A" Distracting Behaviors, "B" Controlling Behaviors, and "C" Angry and Violent Behaviors. There are different corrective strategies that are effective at each level.

**Linking**  An aspect of **L**earners, the second category of the CLEAR Model. The emphasis is on connecting lessons to learners' personal experiences, learner interests.

**Linking**  An aspect of **E**xecution, the third category of the CLEAR Model, emphasizing the connections between the current lesson and previous learning. This type of linking is academic in nature—linking with other academic concepts the students have been learning in this class, or in other classes. This type of linking contrasts with the linking under **L**earners in the CLEAR Model. The linking under **E**xecution is academic linking. The linking under **L**earners is linking to the students' personal interests.

**Loss or Delay of Activity Consequence**  One type of consequence in which the students experience a loss or a delay of an activity in school. An example of this would be students being delayed by the teacher in going to a learning center, when their assignment was not completed because they were misusing the class time available to do the assignment.

**Making Mistakes a Learning Opportunity**   A supportive option in which you emphasize that when you learn new information, making mistakes is a natural part of the process. Mistakes are a feedback system letting students know what they know and still need to learn. Whenever you (student or teacher) put out an effort to learn, you will make some mistakes; so instead of fearing or dreading mistakes, learn from your mistakes.

**Management Plan**   Choices you make for your class about options from each of the four components of management and discipline: Effective Teaching, Preventive, Corrective, and Supportive.

**Management Styles**   A continuum of management styles with collaborative or democratic in the middle and authoritarian and permissive on each extreme end.

**Matching the Model of Teaching to the Lesson**   An aspect of Execution, the third category of the CLEAR Model, emphasizing selecting appropriate models of teaching for the content being taught.

**Metacognition**   Thinking about your thinking. Thinking about your teaching, while you are teaching.

**Modeling Self-Management**   You exhibit and demonstrate respectful, business-like interaction with students as part of teaching responsible behavior to your students, in spite of how you may be feeling inside.

**Movability**   When arranging your room, you need to consider whether it is possible to move about the room easily. You need to walk near all of the desks. Students need to move around and get to one another. They need to be able to work in groups or individually, if needed. If there is an emergency that requires evacuation, your room set-up also needs to facilitate a quick and safe exit.

**Multi-Disciplinary Team (MDT)**   Most common venue for interaction among various members of a staff in order to help students. A team of educators meets on a regular basis to make recommendations about students' needs. May have different names in different locales.

**Multiple Intelligences**   Gardner theorized that we have eight areas of ability: Verbal and Linguistic, Math and Logical, Visual and Spatial, Musical and Rhythmic, Bodily and Kinesthetic, Interpersonal, Intrapersonal, and Naturalistic Intelligence.

**My Time: Self-Evaluation**   An aspect of Reflection, the fifth category of the CLEAR Model, emphasizing daily review and planning that occurs after each day is done, during breaks, or you can use a pause during a lesson to do a quick self-evaluation.

**Name Dropping**   Name Dropping is an Attention Focusing strategy in which you merely slip the student's name into what you are saying a time or two. It alerts the student to the need to make a change in his behavior with minimal disruption of the lesson.

**Nelsen, Lott, and Glenn's Approach**   A discipline approach that emphasizes looking for solutions rather than punishment. Creating an encouraging learning environment, so you have a climate of acceptance, respect, and encouragement, helps decrease discipline problems.

**NO DICE**   A mnemonic that is a visual reminder of elements of a management plan: These behaviors are off limits: Negligent, Off task, Disruptive, Insubordinate, Cheating (lying, stealing), and Eating (drinking).

**Objectives**   An aspect of Execution, the third category of the CLEAR Model, emphasizing making objectives of the lesson obvious and clear statements of what you intend your learners to learn by the end of the lesson. Knowing what intended outcome(s) you have in mind helps learners to focus on the key points of the lesson and helps you in preparing, presenting, and assessing the effectiveness of your lesson.

**One-on-One Scaffolding**   An aspect of Learners, the second category of the CLEAR Model, emphasizing offering individual assistance and attention to your students: one-on-one help at their desks following a presentation, in working groups during an activity, or before or after class when a student comes to you for extra input.

**Other Teachers: Peer Reviews**   An aspect of Reflection, the fifth category of the CLEAR Model, emphasizing seeking out a teacher in a similar content area or grade level who you know to be an effective teacher, and asking for a peer evaluation to give you insights to stimulate your reflection process.

**Overlapping**   A skill of being able to do more than one thing at a time in the classroom that helps to manage the lesson. You are able to work with a small group, but still be aware of what behaviors other students in the class are choosing.

**PACE**   A mnemonic that captures the essence of your prevention options. You choose <u>P</u>roactive Options, <u>A</u>ccountability Options, <u>C</u>hoices, and <u>E</u>nvironment Options in order to prevent problems in your class before they start.

**<u>P</u>acing**   An aspect of <u>L</u>earners, the second category of the CLEAR Model, emphasizing that people learn at different rates. You need to match the timing and tempo of your lessons with the abilities and learning styles of the learners.

**<u>P</u>arent/Teacher Conferences**   One of the Parent/Teacher <u>C</u>ommunication options that emphasizes: plan ahead; be prepared with examples and samples; start positive; use active listening; establish a partnership; consult parents as resources; emphasize student's strengths as well as challenges; tell the truth; plan a follow-up; and end positive.

**<u>P</u>arents and Staff Involvement**   The fourth supportive option in the RESPECT mnemonic focuses on active involvement of parents and other staff in the discipline process.

**<u>P</u>ause for Reflection and Connection**   An aspect of <u>L</u>earners, the second category of the CLEAR Model. Teachers should use strategic pauses during the lesson to allow learners time to mentally process what they are learning, to understand the incoming information, and make links to previously learned concepts.

**<u>P</u>eer Counselors**   Student involvement option in which students with training and guidance counsel one another. Peers are able to relate on the same level.

**<u>P</u>eer Mediators**   Student involvement option involving students as mediators to solve problems. Gives a legitimate sense of power and control in the school. Can turn a student heading for trouble into being part of the solution. Conducting training with the students and adult supervision is integral.

**<u>P</u>eer Recognition**   Student involvement option in which students give acknowledgment to one another for their accomplishments and contributions to the class to foster a sense of a learning community.

**Peer Tutors**   Student involvement option in which students who finish their work quickly and need extra stimulation are utilized as tutors on a choice basis. Beneficial for both the tutor and the student being tutored.

**People Search**   A class building activity in which the students search to find others with certain experiences or qualities. "Find a person who has _____ ."

**Permissive Management Style**   "Whatever happens" students-in-charge approach that usually creates permissive classrooms in which there are too many choices, a lack of boundaries, and a chaotic, unpredictable atmosphere.

**<u>P</u>ointing Out Key Ideas and Difficult Points**   An aspect of <u>C</u>ommunication, the first category of the CLEAR Model, emphasizing drawing attention to the key points you want students to learn and what might be difficult for the students.

**POP**   A mnemonic that is a visual reminder of elements of a management plan: **P**lan: rules, procedures, opening welcome and first comments; **O**rder of first day events: priorities, what students need to know first, and **P**ractice: important procedures for safety, and to facilitate learning and classroom organization.

**Prevention Component**   One of four integral aspects of management and discipline options emphasizing organizing and designing the classroom to avoid discipline problems developing in the first place. Setting the **PACE** is the focus: <u>P</u>roactive options, <u>A</u>ccountability options, <u>C</u>hoices, and <u>E</u>nvironmental options.

**<u>P</u>roactive Options**   The process of organizing and designing the class at the beginning, utilizing effective lesson management, and clarifying expectations to students, so that you prevent management problems.

**Procedures**   Options you choose that delineate activities in the classroom—how to do everyday tasks. Typical procedures spell out activities like, "This is how we come into the room and leave . . . get a drink . . . sharpen pencils . . . pass out papers, etc."

**Proximity**   Proximity is both a deterrent (prevention strategy) when you are "working the room" and a valuable tool to deal with misbehavior while it is happening (corrective strategy). When a student is choosing a distracting behavior, often the best thing to do is to walk over and continue teaching while standing right next to this student.

**Quality Schools**  A movement started by Glasser which espouses meeting students' basic needs in schools by delivering an engaging and relevant curriculum.

**Read Supervisor Comments**  An aspect of **R**eflection, the fifth category of the CLEAR Model, emphasizing reading comments from supervisors carefully, and comparing them to the CLEAR Model. Build suggestions into your next lesson plans to implement the next time you teach.

**Real Participation**  For students to have ownership and learn from consequences, their involvement in the process of designing them and knowing them ahead of time is essential. Students involved in the decision-making process know the implications of the choices they are making.

**Reasonable**  Logical consequences need to fit the level of the disruptive behavior. Consequences need to be reasonable with regard to intensity and frequency of the disruptive behavior and reasonable to you, so that you will follow through with them.

**Redirect the Student**  A Button Pushing Escape to refocus the student from misbehavior to responsible behavior. The student says, "All the other kids are doing it. Why don't you talk to them?" Your answer would be something like, "We are talking about the choices you are making, not those of other students. I will talk to other students at other times. Please focus on your choices."

**Reflection—"MIRROR"**  is the organizing mnemonic for this last category of the CLEAR Model, which focuses on psychologically looking in a mirror for the purpose of improving your teaching and your learners' learning before you teach, while you are teaching, and after you have taught a lesson. **M**y time: self-evaluation; **I**nvite learner input; **R**ead supervisor comments; **Re**frame your teaching; **O**ther teachers: peer reviews; **Re**solve problems toward improved learning.

**Refocus Notes**  A non-verbal option to deal with distracting behaviors. Instead of interrupting your teaching, you write what you want the student to cease doing on a note or post-it and quietly put it in front of the student who is distracting.

**Reframe Your Teaching**  An aspect of **R**eflection, the fifth category of the CLEAR Model, emphasizing restructuring your perspectives and problems and reflective resolutions. Looking from your learners' perspectives and a supervisor's perspective and your perspective to give you new insights for improving your instruction.

**Related**  Logical consequences need to have a clear connection between the behavior and the result. Clear to the student that "I chose to do this and this is happening to me because of what I chose to do," so they see the connection between the consequences and their behaviors.

**Resolve Problems Toward Improved Learning**  An aspect of **R**eflection, the fifth category of the CLEAR Model, emphasizing using the information gathered to actually improve teaching and learning in your classroom to have continuous improvement.

**RESPECT**  A mnemonic that epitomizes the options in the Supportive Component: **R**esponsible behaviors intentionally taught; **E**stablishing school-wide harmony; **S**tudent involvement; **P**arents and staff involvement; **E**ncouragement and effective praise; **C**apable strategies; and **T**eacher-student relationships.

**Respectful**  Logical consequences need to be planned and implemented in a way that maintains the dignity of the student. Consequences need to be delivered in a respectful manner if you want students to pay attention to them and to think about their own behavior choices.

**Responsibility for One's Actions**  A responsible behavior skill that emphasizes students developing the ability to admit mistakes and accept consequences of their choices. Learning from their mistakes is key.

**Responsible Behaviors Intentionally Taught**  The first supportive option in the RESPECT mnemonic focuses on the importance of actually teaching students positive behavior choices: character development, communication skills, social skills, anger management, conflict resolution, responsibility for one's actions, self-control, decision-making skills, and emotional intelligence development.

**Responsible Thinking Questions** A Button Pusher Escape in which you ask the student questions to refocus when a problem situation is developing. The questions are directed at getting the student to think about what she is choosing to do and processing her own behavior. The goal is to redirect the student to choosing responsible behavior, with questions like, "What are you doing?" "What should you be doing?" "What could you be doing?"

**Restitution Consequences** An option used when students are choosing angry and violent behaviors, focused on repairing the damage that was done. Students should make reparations for hurtful, destructive behaviors. If a student messes something up, the student cleans up the mess. If a student breaks something, then the student fixes or replaces the broken item.

**Ripple Effect** Behaviors are contagious. Realizing this helps you to be timely in dealing with misbehavior before it has a chance to be "catching" and to encourage responsible behavior so it will spread.

**Room Arrangement** The way you organize your classroom furniture, materials, etc. A workable room arrangement helps prevent classroom problems.

**Rules and Code of Conduct** Options for creating what are acceptable and unacceptable behaviors in your class. They are the Do's and Don't's for your classroom.

**Self-Control Skills** Responsible behavior skills that involve students learning to recognize when they are losing control of their emotional reactions and having coping strategies that allow them to calm themselves down and choose appropriate behavior.

**Self-Fulfilling Prophecy** Students are greatly impacted by the expectations you have of them. They often end up acting a certain way because that was what was expected of them.

**Signals** Prompts to get students focused for whole group instruction or discussion. You can have a hand signal, an auditory signal, or a light signal.

**Similarity Groups** A class building activity in which groups are formed based on similarities of various students. Discussions and paraphrasing take place about the topics that are generated to form the groups.

**Simultaneous Response Modes** Options to involve all students in giving responses to questions at the same time in order to continually check their understanding of concepts and to keep them focused on the lesson. Students can give signals or simultaneously write down and show their answers.

**Smooth Transitions** The skill of moving smoothly from one lesson to another or one aspect of a lesson to another aspect. You have materials ready and preplan what you are going to do next. You plan what the students need to know and have in order to work on the lesson. The opposite of smooth transitions is jerkiness, vagueness, or forgetting key points that you will have to reteach later.

**Social Skills** Responsible behavior skills that incorporate what students need to be able to interact effectively with one another like: greeting each other, taking turns, disagreeing without fighting, considering other viewpoints and sharing materials.

**Socratic Questioning** Teacher does not present material, but uses questioning techniques to lead students to analyze, critique, evaluate their own thinking and beliefs to foster high-level learning. Socratic questions: ask learners for clarification of a statement or response to a teacher-initiated question, ask for examples, request evidence to support a point, and question assumptions.

**Speaking Fluently** An aspect of **C**ommunication, the first category of the CLEAR Model, emphasizing avoiding vagueness in spoken and written communication and adjusting for learners' level, being precise and using language that the learners understand.

**Standards** Criteria, expectations of quality and quantity, cut-off scores, required performances, etc., to let students know how well things need to be done. You need to establish the parameters as to how you want their assignments done.

**Stay with the Topic** An aspect of **E**xecution, the third category of the CLEAR Model, emphasizing keeping with one topic long enough so learners really learn the concepts.

**Structured Choices** You give choices in the modalities in which the assignments can be completed in order to engage students and accommodate different learning styles.

**Student Involvement**   The third supportive option in the RESPECT mnemonic focuses on empowering students to help them to feel ownership of the class through active involvement in the discipline process. Helps them be part of the solution rather than part of the problem: classroom responsibilities, study buddies, homework buddy, peer tutors, peer mediators, peer counselors, peer recognition, and student led conferences.

**Student Led Conferences**   Student involvement option in which students are in charge of conducting the conference between the students, their parents, and the teachers with the teacher guiding the process and holding students accountable for accuracy in the conference. Puts the responsibility for the choices made, both behaviorally and academically, on the student's shoulders.

**Study Buddies**   Student involvement option in which everyone in class is assigned a study buddy, who can help with assuming responsibility for their own assignments. Helps with developing study skills, like recording assignments, note taking, and outlining. Students support each other in following through with assignments.

**Supportive Component**   One of four integral aspects of management and discipline that focuses on helping students to learn RESPECT for themselves, other people, and for property. Giving students the support they need to choose appropriate behavior through **R**esponsible behaviors intentionally taught, **E**stablishing classroom harmony, **S**tudent involvement, **P**arent and staff involvement, **E**ncouragement and effective praise, **C**apable strategies, and **T**eacher-student relationship.

**Sustaining Expectation Effect**   Once you form a negative expectation of a student, it is possible that the students could make some positive changes and you might not notice them. You do not want your negative expectations to be sustained.

**Table the Matter**   A Button Pusher Escape used with students choosing controlling behaviors to indicate the need to close things down for now. You leave the door open to discuss the problem at a later time, but you indicate that now during the lesson is not the appropriate time.

**Target Stop Do**   An Attention Focusing option to focus your verbal interaction and to redirect the student from misbehavior to responsible behavior. The Target is the student who is enacting distracting behaviors. The Stop is the behavior that needs to be stopped. The Do is the responsible behavior that needs to replace the misbehavior.

**Teacher Stress Management Techniques**   Supportive options focused on your taking the time to keep yourself physically healthy and fit, taking time for yourself for recreation, to keep your mental edge, and to keep rebuilding your emotional energy. Model healthy living for your students.

**Teacher-Student Relationship**   The last of the RESPECT Supportive strategies in which the focus is on options to create positive relationships between teachers and students. One of the primary motivators towards responsible behavior choices.

**Teaching Pause**   An Active Body Language option in which you pause in your teaching for a few seconds when the whole class is exhibiting distracting behaviors. Stop teaching and scan the room getting eye contact, giving a non-verbal message that "What I have to say is important enough that I am not going to say it until everyone is listening."

**Team Building Activities**   Activities designed to get students to know each other in small groups, to work more effectively together, to create a positive climate in the class and to build positive relationships in the class. Involve interviewing members of the team, taking turns discussing a topic, working on a team project together, developing a team statement, or engaging in lively brainstorming together.

**The Look**   An Active Body Language option in which you get eye contact with a student who is distracting, and maintain that eye contact for a few seconds to communicate the need to cease the misbehavior, without resorting to words. Use a firm look with a business-like demeanor, but not an angry or hostile one.

**TOP Teachers**   A mnemonic to illustrate characteristics of effective teachers: **T**hinking, **O**bservant, and **P**assionate.

**"To You To Me" Statements**   A Button Pusher Escape in which you recognize the student's perspective in the problem situation, but then offer your perspective on the matter. Gives you an opportunity to deal with the student's challenging remark without taking it personally or fighting with the student.

**Understandability**   Your room arrangement gives a message to others about what your class is like—about your teaching style and your classroom climate. That message needs to be consistent with what you want it to say about what it is like to learn in your class.

**Usability**   When arranging your room, you need to consider if areas and supplies that the students will need to use are accessible to them and to you. They need to get to the supply shelves, the pencil sharpener, and the drinking fountain.

**VACUUM: The 6 "Abilities" of Room Arrangement**   A mnemonic to help you use your space effectively, so it will enhance your instruction and not detract from it. The 6 "Abilities" of Room Arrangement are Visibility, Accountability, Communicability, Understandability, Usability, and Movability.

**Variety and Interest**   Implementing lessons that are enjoyable, varied, actively involve the students, and tap into students' interests is essential to avoiding problems. Teacher enthusiasm is also a key to the interest level.

**VIABLE**   A mnemonic that represents the goals of Establishing Classroom Harmony. Everyone in the class needs to feel Valued, Included, Accepted, Belonging, Listened to, and Encouraged in order to create a class capable of cooperation and growth.

**Visibility**   When arranging your room, you need to consider if visibility is facilitated for all students, so they are able to see the board and the overhead. You need to have all students visible to you so you can visually scan what they are doing.

**Voice Change**   An option in which you can change your voice to refocus student attention using an accent or a voice from a celebrity, a computer voice, or a whisper.

**Withitness**   A teacher characteristic that projects that you are on top of the situation in the classroom and are aware of what is going on and deal with situations in a timely manner.

**Working the Room**   A prevention strategy in which you put proximity to good use in your classroom on an ongoing basis by moving around, interacting with students, and monitoring what they are doing.

# References

Abrams, B., & Segal, A. (1998). How to prevent aggressive behavior. *Teaching Exceptional Children* 30 (4): 10–15.

Adler, A. (1957). *Understanding human nature.* New York: Premier Books.

Akin, T., Dunne, G., Palomares, S., & Schilling, D. (1995). *Character education in America's schools.* Spring Valley, CA: Innerchoice Publishing.

Albert, L., DeSisto, P., Kyle, P., LePage, A., McGuire, M., Roy, W., Smith, F., Soriano, A., & Zygonc, Y. (1996). *Cooperative discipline.* Circle Pines, MN: American Guidance Service.

Apple, M. W., & Beane, J. A. (1995). *Democratic schools.* Alexandria, VA: Association for Supervision and Curriculum Development.

Armstrong, S. B., McNeil, M. E., & Houten, R. V. (1988). A principal's in-service training package for increasing teacher praise. *Teachers Education and Special Education* 11 (3): 79–94.

Armstrong, T. (1994). *Multiple intelligences in the classroom.* Alexandria, VA: Association for Supervision and Curriculum Development.

Armstrong, T. (1999). *ADD/ADHD alternatives in the classroom.* Alexandria, VA: Association for Supervision and Curriculum Development.

Atherley, C. (1990). The implementation of a positive behaviour management programme in a primary classroom: A case study. *School Organization* 10 (2&3): 213–228.

Baker, A. (1997). Improving parent involvement programs and practice: A qualitative study of parent perceptions. *School Community Journal* 7 (1): 9–35.

Barber, R. J., & Patin, D. (1997). Parent involvement: A two-way street. *Schools in the Middle* 6 (4): 31–33.

Baringer, D. K., & McCroskey, J. C. (2000). Immediacy in the classroom: Student immediacy. *Communication Education* 49 (2): 178–186.

Barrett, E. R., & Davis, S. (1995). Perceptions of beginning teachers' in-service needs in classroom management. *Teacher Education and Practice* 11 (1): 22–27.

Bender, W., & Golden, L. (1989). Prediction of adaptive behavior of learning disabled students in self-contained and resource classes. *Learning Disabilities Research* 5 (1): 45–50.

Berliner, D. C. (1987). Ways of thinking about students and classrooms by more and less experienced teachers. In J. Calderhead (Ed.), *Exploring teachers' thinking.* London: Cassell Educational Limited.

Black, S. (1996). The character conundrum. *American School Board Journal* 183 (12): 29–31.

Boostrom, R. (1991). The nature and functions of classroom rules. *Curriculum Inquiry* 21 (2): 193–216.

Brandt (1998). Listen first. *Educational Leadership* 55 (80): 25–30.

Brandt, R. (1995). Punished by rewards? A conversation with Alfie Kohn. *Educational Leadership* 53 (1): 13–16.

Brooks, B., & Kann, M. (1993). What makes character education programs work? *Educational Leadership* 51 (3): 19–21.

Brophy, J. (1987). Classroom management as instruction: Socializing self-guidance in students. *Theory into Practice* 24 (4): 233–240.

Brophy, J. (1998). *Motivating students to learn.* Boston: McGraw-Hill.

Burden, P. (1995). *Classroom management and discipline.* New York: Longman.

Bush, A. J., & Cruickshank, D. R. (1977). An empirical investigation of teacher clarity. *Journal of Teacher Education* 28 (2): 53–58.

Castle, K., & Rogers, K. (1994). Rule-creating in a constructivist classroom community. *Childhood Education* 70 (2): 77–80.

Charles, C., & Senter, G. (2002). *Elementary classroom management.* Boston: Allyn & Bacon.

Charles, C. M. (2002). *Building classroom discipline.* Boston: Allyn & Bacon.

Coloroso, B. (1994). *Kids are worth it!: Giving your child the gift of inner discipline.* New York: Avon Books.

Crowley, E. P. (1993). A qualitative analysis of mainstreamed behaviorally disordered aggressive adolescents' perceptions of helpful and unhelpful teacher attitudes and behaviors. *Exceptionality: A Research Journal* 4 (3): 131–151.

Cruickshank, D. (1987). *Reflective teaching: The preparation of students of teaching.* Reston, VA: The Association of Teacher Educators.

Cruickshank, D. R., & Others (1979). Clear teaching: What is it? *British Journal of Teacher Education* 5 (1): 27–33.

Curwin, R., & Mendler, A. (1997). *As tough as necessary.* Alexandria, VA. Association for Supervision and Curriculum Development.

Curwin, R., & Mendler, A. (1997). *As tough as necessary.* Alexandria, VA. Association for Supervision and Curriculum Development.

Curwin, R., & Mendler, A. N. (1988). *Discipline with dignity.* Alexandria, VA: Association for Supervision and Curriculum Development.

Derry, S. (1989). Putting learning strategies to work. *Educational Leadership* 47 (5): 4–10.

Dewey, J. (1933). *How we think.* Chicago: Henry Regnery.

Dinkmeyer, D., & Dreikurs, R. (2000). *Encouraging children to learn.* Philadelphia, PA: Brunner-Routledge.

Dinkmeyer, D., McKay, G., McKay, J., & Dinkmeyer, D. (1977). *Parenting teens: Systematic training for effective parenting of teens.* Circle Pines, MN: American Guidance Service.

Dinkmeyer, D., McKay, G., Dinkmeyer, J., Dinkmeyer, D., & McKay, J. (1997). *Parenting young children.* Circle Pines, MN: American Guidance Service.

Dollard, N. (1996). Constructive classroom management. *Focus on Exceptional Students* 29 (2): 1–12.

Dowd, J. (1997). Refusing to play the blame game. *Educational Leadership* 5 (8): 67–69.

Doyle, W. (1985). Recent research on classroom management: Implications for teacher preparation. *Teacher Education* 36 (3): 31–35.

Dreikurs, R. (1968). *Psychology in the classroom.* New York: Harper & Row.

Dreikurs, R., Grunwald, B. B., & Pepper, F. C. (1982). *Maintaining sanity in the classroom: Classroom management techniques.* New York: Harper & Row, Publishers.

Dunn, K., & Dunn, R. (1978). *Teaching students through their individual learning styles.* Reston, VA: National Council of Principals.

Dunn, R., & Griggs, S. A. (1988). *Learning styles: Quiet revolution in American secondary schools.* Reston, VA: National Association of Secondary School Principals.

Dunn, R., Gemake, J., Jalali, F., & Zenhausern, R. (1990). Cross-cultural differences in learning styles of elementary age students from four ethnic backgrounds. *Journal of Multicultural Counseling and Development* 18: 68–93.

Egeland, P. (1996/1997). Pulleys, planes, and student performance. *Educational Leadership* 54 (4): 41–45.

Emmer, E. (1994). Towards an understanding of the primacy of classroom management and discipline. *Teaching Education* 6 (1): 65–69.

Emmer, E. T., Evertson, C. M., Clements, B. S., & Worsham, M. E. (1994). *Classroom management for secondary teachers.* Boston: Allyn & Bacon.

Evertson, C. M., & Emmer, E. T. (1990). *Preventive classroom management.* Boston: Allyn & Bacon.

Evertson, C. M., Emmer, E. T., Clements, B. S., & Worsham, M. E. (1997). *Classroom management for elementary teachers.* Boston: Allyn & Bacon.

Fertman, C. I., & van Linden, J. A. (1999). Character education: An essential ingredient for youth leadership development. *NASSP Bulletin* 83 (609): 9–15.

Fifer, F., Jr. (1986). Effective classroom management. *Academic Therapy* 21: 401–410.

Flanders, N. (1970). *Analyzing teaching behavior.* New York: Addison-Wesley.

Fleming, D. (1996). Preamble to a more perfect classroom. *Educational Leadership* 54 (1): 73–76.

Floden, R. E., & Klinzing, H. G. (1990). What can research on teacher thinking contribute to teacher preparation? A second opinion. *Educational Researcher* 19 (4): 15–20.

Ford, E. E. (1996). *Discipline for home and school.* Scottsdale, AZ: Brandt Publishing.

Freiburg, H. (1996). From tourist to citizens in the classroom. *Educational Leadership* 54 (1): 32–36.

Fry, P. (1983). Process measures of problem and non-problem children's classroom behavior: The influence of teacher behavior variables. *British Journal of Educational Psychology* 53 (1): 79–88.

Furlong, M., Morrison, G., & Pavelski, R. (2000). Trends in school psychology for the 21st century: Influences of school violence on professional change. *Psychology in the Schools* 37 (1): 81–90.

Gardner, H. (1983). *Frames of mind: The theory of multiple intelligences.* New York: Basic Books.

Gardner, H. (1989). Multiple intelligences go to school. *Educational Researcher* 18 (8): 4–10.

Gardner, H. (1993). *Multiple intelligences: The theory into practice.* New York: Basic Books.

Geocaris, C. (1996/1997). Increasing student engagement: A mystery solved. *Educational Leadership* 54 (4): 72–75.

Gerzon, M. (1997). Teaching democracy by doing it! *Educational Leadership* 54 (5): 6–11.

Gettinger, M., & Guetschow, K. W. (1998). Parental involvement in schools: Parent and teacher perceptions of roles, efficacy, and opportunities. *Journal of Research and Development in Education* 32 (1): 38–52.

Ginott, H. (1971). *Teacher and child.* New York: Macmillan.

Glasser, W., & Dotson, K. (1998). *Choice theory in the classroom.* New York: HarperCollins.

Glasser, W. (1986). *Control theory in the classroom.* New York: Harper & Row.

Glasser, W. (1992). *The quality school.* New York: HarperPerennial.

Glasser, W. (1993). *The quality school teacher.* New York: HarperPerennial.

Gliessman, D. (1987). Changing complex teaching skills. *Journal of Education for Teaching* 13 (3): 267–275.

Gliessman, D., & Pugh, R. (1984). Conceptual variables in teacher training. *Journal of Education for Teaching* 10 (3): 196–208.

Gliessman, D. H., Pugh, R. C., Brown, L. D., Archer, A. C., & Snyder, S. S. (1989). Applying a research-based model to teacher skill training. *Journal of Educational Research* 83 (2): 69–81.

Goleman, Daniel. (1997) *Emotional intelligence*. New York: Bantam Books.

Gottfredson, D. (1993). Managing adolescent behavior: A multiyear, multischool study. *American Educational Research Journal* 30 (1): 179–215.

Greenberg, P. (1992). Ideas that work with young children: How to institute some simple democratic practices pertaining to respect, rights, responsibilities, and roots in any classroom (without losing your leadership position). *Young Children* 47 (5): 10–17.

Greenblatt, R., Cooper, B., & Muth, R. (1984). Managing for effective teaching. *Educational Leadership* 41 (5): 57–59.

Gregorc, A. F. (1982). *Gregorc style delineator: Development, technical, and administrative manual*. Maynard, MA: Gabriel Systems.

Grolnick, W., & Ryan, R. (1990). Self-perceptions, motivation, and adjustment in children with learning disabilities: A multiple group comparison study. *Journal of Learning Disabilities* 23 (3): 177–184.

Hatton, N., & Smith, D. (1994). *Facilitating reflection: Issues and research*. Paper presented at the Conference of Australian Teacher Education Association (24th, Brisbane, Queensland, Australia, July 3–6, 1994).

Hawkins, D., Doueck, H., & Lishner, D. (1988). Changing teaching practices in mainstream classrooms to improve bonding and behavior of low achievers. *American Educational Research Journal* 25 (1): 31–50.

Hines, C. V. (1981). *A further investigation of teacher clarity: The observation of teacher clarity and the relationship between clarity and student achievement and satisfaction*. Unpublished doctoral dissertation, the Ohio State University.

Hines, C. V., Cruickshank, D. R., & Kennedy, J. J. (1985). Teacher clarity and its relationship to student achievement and satisfaction. *American Educational Research Journal* 22 (1): 87–99.

Holland, D. (1979). *An investigation of the generality of teacher clarity*. Unpublished doctoral dissertation, Memphis State University.

Jensen, E. (1998). *Teaching with the brain in mind*. Alexandria, VA: Association for Supervision and Curriculum Development.

Johnson, D., & Johnson, R. (1991). *Teaching students to be peacemakers*. Edina, MN.: Interaction Book Company.

Johnson, D., & Johnson, R. (1996). Peacemakers: Teaching students to resolve their own and schoolmates' conflicts. *Focus on Exceptional Children* 28 (6): 1–11.

Johnson, D. W., & Johnson, R. T. (1995). *Reducing school violence through conflict resolution*. Alexandria, VA: Association for Supervision and Curriculum Development.

Jones, F. H. (1987). *Positive classroom discipline*. New York: McGraw-Hill Book Company.

Jones, J. T., & Jones, F. H. (1994). *Positive classroom discipline*. Santa Cruz, CA: Fredric H. Jones & Associates, Inc.

Joyce, B., Weil, M., & Calhoun, E. (2000). *Models of teaching*. Sixth edition. Boston: Allyn & Bacon.

Kagan, L., Kagan, M., & Kagan, S. (1998). *Classbuilding*. San Clemente, CA: Kagan Publishing.

Kagan, L., Kagan, M., & Kagan, S. (1998). *Teambuilding*. San Clemente, CA: Kagan Publishing.

Kagan, S., & Kagan, M. (1998). *Multiple intelligences*. San Clemente, CA: Kagan Publishing.

Kagan, S. (1994). *Cooperative learning*. San Clemente, CA: Kagan Cooperative Learning.

Kagan, S. (1999). Cooperative learning and character development video. National Video Resources.

Kennedy, J. J., Cruickshank, D. R., Bush, A. J., & Myers, B. (1978). Additional investigations into the nature of teacher clarity, *Journal of Educational Research* 72: 3–10.

Kirschenbaum, H. (1999). Night and day: Succeeding with parents at school 43. *Principal* 78 (3): 20–23.

Kohn, A. (1996a). What to look for in a classroom. *Educational Leadership* 54 (1): 54–55.

Kohn, A. (1996b). *Beyond discipline: From compliance to community*. Alexandria, VA: Association for Supervision and Curriculum Development.

Kounin, J. (1977). *Discipline and group management in classrooms*. Revised edition. New York: Holt, Rinehart, & Winston.

Kyle, P. (1991a). Developing cooperative interaction in schools for teachers and administrators. *Journal of Individual Psychology* 47 (2).

Kyle, P. (1991b). *The effects of positive discipline strategies and active student involvement in the discipline process upon selected elements of classroom climate*. Doctoral dissertation, University of Idaho.

Kyle, P. (1999). Cooperative discipline and violence prevention. In W. Bender, G. Clinton, R. Bender (Eds.), *Violence prevention and reduction in schools*. Austin, TX: Pro-Ed.

Kyle, P., Scott, S., & Kagan, S. (2001). *Win-win discipline course workbook*. San Clemente, CA: Kagan Publishing.

Land, M. L. (1987). Vagueness and clarity. In M. Dunkin (Ed.), *The international encyclopedia of teaching and teacher education* (pp. 392–397). New York: Pergamon.

Land, M. L. (1980). Teacher clarity and cognitive level of questioning: Effects on learning. *Journal of Experimental Education* 49 (1): 48–51.

Land, M. L., & Smith, L. R. (1979). The effect of low inference teacher clarity inhibitors on student achievement. *Journal of Teacher Education* 30 (3): 55–57.

Leinhardt, G. (1988). Situated knowledge and expertise in teaching. In J. Calderhead (Ed.), *Teachers' professional learning* (pp. 146–168). London: Farmer Press.

Lew, A., & Bettner, B. L. (1995). *Responsibility in the classroom: A teacher's guide to understanding and motivating students.* Boston: Connexions Press.

Lewis, C., Schaps, E., & Watson, M. (1996). The caring classroom's academic edge. *Educational Leadership* 54 (1): 16–21.

Lutz, J. (1983). Attitudes key to school success. *Executive Educator* 5 (11): 26, 30.

Markman, E. M. (1981). Comprehension monitoring. In W. P. Dickson (Ed.), *Children's oral communication skills* (pp. 61–84). New York: Academic Press.

Mazza, J., & Overstreet, S. (2000). Children and adolescents exposed to school violence: A mental health perspective for school psychologists. *School Psychology Review* 29 (1): 86–101.

McCormack-Larkin, M. (1985). Ingredients of a successful school effectiveness project. *Educational Leadership* 42 (6): 31–37.

Mendler, A. N. (1992). *What do I do when . . . ?* Bloomington, Indiana: National Educational Service.

Metcalf, K. K., & Cruickshank, D. R. (1991). Can teachers be trained to make clear presentations? *Journal of Educational Research* 85 (2): 107–116.

Murphy, C. (1995). Managing students: Building positive attitudes in the classroom. *Schools in the Middle* 4 (4): 31–33.

Nelsen, J. (1987). *Positive discipline.* New York: Ballantine Books.

Nelsen, J., Lott, L., & Glenn, S. H. (1993). *Positive discipline in the classroom.* Rocklin, CA: Pima Publishing.

Nicholson, G., Stephens, R., Elder, R., & Leavitt, V. (1985). Safe schools: You can't do it alone. *Phi Delta Kappan* 66 (7): 491–496.

Nisbett, R. E., & Wilson, T. D. (1977). Telling more than we can know: Verbal reports on mental processes. *Psychological Review* 84 (3): 231–259.

Perkins, D. N., & Solomon, G. (1989). Are cognitive skills context-bound? *Educational Researcher* 18: 16–25.

Peterson, T. (1996). Discipline for discipleship. *Thresholds in Education* 22 (4): 28–32.

Popkin, M. (2002). *Active parenting now: For parents of children ages 5–12.* Atlanta, GA: Active Parenting Publishing, Inc.

Popkin, M. (1998). *Active parenting of teens: Parents' guide.* Atlanta, GA: Active Parenting Publishing, Inc.

Popkin, M., Youngs, B., & Healy, J. (1995). *Helping your child succeed in school: A guide for parents of 4–14 year olds.* Atlanta, GA: Active Parenting Publishing, Inc.

Pressley, M., Burkell, J., Cariglia-Bull, T., Lysynchuk, L, McGoldrick, J. A., Schnieder, B., Snyder, B. L., Symons, S., & Woloshyn, V. E. (1990). *Cognitive strategy instruction that really improves children's academic performance.* Cambridge, MA: Brookline Books.

Proctor. (1984). Teacher expectations: A model for school improvement. *The Elementary School Journal* 84 (4): 469–481.

Pugach, M. C. (1990). *Self-study: The genesis of reflection in novice teachers?* Paper presented at the Annual Meeting of the American Educational Research Association (Boston, MA, April 17–20, 1990).

Purkey, W., & Stanley, P. (1991). *Invitational teaching, learning, and living.* Washington, DC: DEA Professional Library, National Education Association.

Riley, A. (1994). Parent empowerment: An idea for the nineties. *Education Canada* 34 (3): 14–20.

Rockwell, S. (1993). *Tough to reach, tough to teach: Students with behavior problems.* Reston, VA: Council for Exceptional Students.

Rogien, L., & Anderson, H. (2001). *Gifted and aberrant behavior.* Paper presented at the Northern Rocky Mountain Educational Research Association Regional Conference, Jackson Hole, WY.

Rogien, L. (1995). *Effect of training in cognitive awareness of student knowledge on lesson planning and micro teaching for secondary preservice teachers.* Unpublished manuscript, Indiana University, Bloomington, IN.

Rogien, L. (1998) *The effects of cognitive strategy training in clarity of instruction on lesson planning and instruction for pre-service teachers.* Doctoral dissertation. Ann Arbor, MI: UMI Dissertation Services (Microfilm).

Rogien, L. (1999). Socratic questioning. *A guide for starting and improving gifted and talented high school programs.* Idaho State Department of Education, Boise, ID.

Rogien, L. R. (1995a). *The effect of interactive video training in types of explanation on preservice teachers lesson planning and peer teaching.* Unpublished manuscript, Indiana University, Bloomington, IN.

Rosenshine, B., & Meister, C. (1992). The use of scaffolds for teaching higher-level cognitive strategies. *Educational Leadership* 49 (7): 26–33.

Rosenshine, B., & Furst, N. (1971). Research on teacher performance criteria. In B. Smith (Ed.), *Research in teacher education* (pp. 37–72). Englewood Cliffs, NJ: Prentice Hall.

Rosenthal, R. (1995). Critiquing Pygmalion: A 25-year perspective. *Current Directions in Psychological Science* 4: 171–172.

Rosenthal, R., & Jacobson, L. (1968). *Pygmalion in the classroom.* New York: Holt, Rinehart, & Winston.

Scherer, M. (1992). Solving conflicts—Not just for students. *Educational Leadership* 50 (1): 14–17.

Shandler, S. (1996). Just rewards: Positive discipline can teach students self-respect and empathy. *Teaching Tolerance* 5 (1): 37–41.

Shockley, R., & Sevier, L. (1991). Behavior management in the classroom: Guidelines for maintaining control. *Schools in the Middle* 1 (12): 14–18.

Short, P., & Short, R. (1988). Perceived classroom environment and student behavior in secondary schools. *Research Quarterly* 12 (3): 35–39.

Smith, L. R. (1982). *Training teachers to teach clearly: Theory into practice.* Paper presented at the annual meeting of the American Educational Research Association (New York, NY, March 19–23, 1982).

Smith, L. R. (1984). Effect of teacher vagueness and use of lecture notes on student performance. *Journal of Educational Research* 78 (2): 69–74.

Smith, L. R. (1985). A low-inference indicator of lesson organization. *Journal of Classroom Interaction* 21 (1): 25–30.

Smith, L. R., & Cotten, M. L. (1980). Effect of vagueness and discontinuity on student achievement and attitudes. *Journal of Educational Psychology* 72 (5): 670–675.

Smith, L. R., & Land, M. L. (1981). Low-inference verbal behaviors related to teacher clarity. *Journal of Classroom Interaction* 17: 37–42.

Smith, S. (1978). The identification of teaching behaviors descriptive of the construct: Clarity of presentation. *Dissertation Abstracts International* 39 (06): 3529A. (University Microfilms No. 78-23,593).

Snyder, S. J., & Others. (1993). *Instructional clarity: The role of linking and focusing moves on student achievement, motivation, and satisfaction.* Paper presented at the Annual Meeting of the American Educational Research Association (Atlanta, GA, April 12–16, 1993).

Sorsdahl, S., & Sanche, R. (1985). The effects of classroom meetings on self-concept and behavior. *Elementary School Guidance and Counseling* 20 (1): 49–56.

Sparks-Langer, G. M., & Colton, A. B. (1993). Synthesis of research on teachers' reflective thinking. In A. Woolfolk (Ed.), *Readings & Cases in Educational Psychology.* Boston: Allyn & Bacon.

Spielberger, C. D. (1962). The role of awareness in verbal conditioning. In W. Eriksen (Ed.), *Behavior and awareness.* Durham, NC: Duke University Press.

Stallings, J. (1977). *Learning to look.* Belmont, CA: Wadsworth.

Sternberg, R. J., & Horvath, J. A. (1995). A prototype view of expert teaching. *Educational Researcher* 24 (6): 9–17.

Sternberg, R., Okagaki, L., & Jackson, A. (1990). Practical intelligence for success in school. *Educational Leadership* 48 (1): 35–39.

Stone, S. (1993). Issues in education: taking time to teach social skills. *Childhood Education* 69 (4): 194–195.

Sudzina, M. R. (1997). From tourists to citizens in the classroom: An interview with H. Jerome Freiberg. *Mid-Western Educational Researcher* 10 (2): 35–38.

Sullivan, P. (1998). Improving parent involvement: The national standards for parent/family involvement programs. *Our Children* 24 (1): 23.

Sweeney, J. (1992). School climate: The key to excellence. *NASSP Bulletin* 76 (547): 69–73.

Taylor, J. (2001a). *Form defiance to cooperation: Real solutions for transforming the angry, defiant, discouraged child.* Roseville, CA: Prima Publishing.

Taylor, J. (2001b). *Helping your ADD child.* Roseville, CA: Prima Publishing

Trindale, A. L. (1972). Structures in teaching and learning outcomes. *Journal of Research in Science Teaching* 9 (1): 65–74.

Trotter, T., & Walker, W. R. (2001, January). *Violence and at-risk youth.* Workshop conducted at the Idaho Counseling Association Annual Conference, Coeur d' Alene, ID.

Trotter, T., & Walker, W. R. (2002, January). *Violence and at-risk youth.* Workshop conducted at the Idaho Counseling Association Annual Conference, Idaho Falls, ID.

Tulving, E. (1968). Organized retention and cued recall. In Klausmeier, H. J., & O'Hearn, G. T. (Eds.), *Research and development toward the improvement of education.* Madison, WI: Dember Educational Research Services.

Valli, L. (1990). Teaching as moral reflection: Thoughts on the liberal preparation of teachers. In *Proceedings of the National Forum of the Association of Independent Liberal Arts Colleges for Teacher Education,* 4th edition. Milwaukee, WI: November 9–11, 1990.

Vasconcelllos, J., & and Murphy, M. (1987). Education in the experience of being citizens. *Educational Leadership* 45 (2): 70–73.

Wade, R. (1997). Lifting a school's spirit. *Educational Leadership* 54 (8): 34–36.

Wagner, A. C. (1987). Knots in teachers' thinking. In J. Calderhead (Ed.), *Exploring teachers' thinking.* London: Cassell Educational Limited.

Wang, M., Haertel, D., & Walberg, L. (1994). What makes children learn? *Educational Leadership* 51 (4): 74–79.

White, J. (1979). Clarity and student opportunity to learn: An investigation of two components of instructional communication as assessed by situational testing of pre-service teachers (Doctoral dissertation, University of Maryland). Dissertation Abstracts International, 40, 5319A.

Williams, J. (1983). *The stability of teacher clarity in relation to student achievement and satisfaction.* Unpublished doctoral dissertation, The Ohio State University.

Witkin, H. A., Moore, C. A., Goodenough, D. R., & Cox, R. W. (1977). Field-dependent and field-independent cognitive styles and their educational implications. *Review of Educational Research* 47: 1–64.

Woolfolk, A. (2001). *Educational psychology,* Eighth edition. Boston: Allyn & Bacon.

Zeichner, K. M. (1987a). Teaching student teachers to reflect. *Harvard Educational Review* 57 (1): 23–48.

Zeichner, K. M. (1987b). Action research and teacher thinking: The first phase of the Action Research Project at the University of Wisconsin—Madison. Paper presented at the Annual Meeting of the American Educational Research Association (Washington, DC, April 20–24, 1987).

# Index

*Note:* The bold, underlined letters in the index entries reflect terms and letters used throughout the text as mnemonic devices.